AN UNEXPECTED MP

AN UNEXPECTED MP
CONFESSIONS OF A POLITICAL GOSSIP

JERRY HAYES

Biteback Publishing

First published in Great Britain in 2014 by
Biteback Publishing Ltd
Westminster Tower
3 Albert Embankment
London SE1 7SP
Copyright © Jerry Hayes 2014

ISBN 978-1-84954-645-4

10 9 8 7 6 5 4 3 2 1

A CIP catalogue record for this book is available from the British Library.

Set in Caslon

Printed and bound in Great Britain by
CPI Group (UK) Ltd, Croydon CR0 4YY

To Doggie, Puppy and Lolly

CONTENTS

CHAPTER 1

IN THE BEGINNING

Some people enter politics for the noblest of ideals. They want to change the world into a better, kinder and gentler place. They want to save the environment, eradicate child poverty and improve the lot of everyday folk.

For them, politics is all about serving the community.

And then there are those with well-deserved inferiority complexes who want status, power and position. Those who would sell their grannies for a red box and a medium-range family saloon, and who make dreary speeches that no one else wants to make and sign letters that nobody else wants to sign.

Few believe me, but I entered the House of Commons purely by accident. I was in my twenties, doing well at the Bar, and although I'd risen through the ranks of the Young Conservatives I had no desire to be an MP. I have always had a deep suspicion of those who have had an overwhelming desire to get elected since an early age. They tend to have strong views about Europe and gay marriage and harbour an unhealthy interest in the death penalty. They are the ones at Tory Party conferences who spend all their waking hours at fringe meetings with other odd, wild-eyed teenagers with spots and bow ties. And they are the ones who at the end of it all go home to their mothers' basements and play Call of Duty until the early hours; that is, when they are not pretending to be thirteen-year-old girls on the internet. They also collect Thatcher memorabilia and regard her every word and deed with the zeal of a creationist preacher.

I was never one of those.

I joined the Young Conservatives for the noblest of reasons and the sort of ideals the Buddha, Gandhi and Mother Teresa would have applauded. It is the motivating force that has made Britain the Mother of all Parliaments and the Empire the envy of the world: a shag.

So I was surprised to be sounded out by one of the party grandees, asking if I would like to stand for selection in Harlow, which was just down the road. I told him he was mad. But he just told me that even if I became the candidate I had no hope of winning. And they were desperate. I wasn't even on the candidates list.

So that's why on 9 June 1983 there were two very stunned people in the Harlow leisure centre. I had just defeated the longstanding Labour MP Stan Newens and had a majority of a little over 3,000. And I hadn't a clue what to do. I had just turned thirty.

In those days there was no induction into Parliament. No little booklet of helpful hints. No mentoring. I just sat at home and waited for the post. Sure enough, after a day, an envelope with the Crowned Portcullis logo appeared on paper that would have made the Andrex puppy proud. It was headed 'The Whip' and telling me to roll up to Committee Room 14 and not to be late.

The next day I proudly introduced myself to the policeman

at Carriage Gates and encountered the first of many Westminster Catch-22s that were to dominate my life.

'And how can I help you, young man?'

'Actually, I'm an MP.'

'That's what they all say. Where's your pass? I thought not. Now bugger off.'

After twenty minutes of intellectual discussion he eventually understood that before I could get a pass I had to be allowed access to the pass office.

Well, at least I didn't call him a pleb.

So, with all the other newbies of '83 I entered the cavern that is Committee Room 14. Here I would see the full majesty of power and my sticky little fingers would be tantalisingly close to the controls.

In my dreams. The Chief Whip gave cursory congratulations, then reminded us that our job was to support the government and that our area whips would tell us how to vote. If you had views, get rid of them now. We were now part of Maggie's barmy army. At ease.

I looked around the room. Most seemed fairly normal, but there were a few who looked as if they had just escaped from the *Star Wars* bar. This was going to be an interesting five years.

And who was going to give me my opinions? A delightful man who in those days always dressed in grey suits. I was told that he was the most popular man in the Commons, without any enemy on the radar screen. His name was John Major. How things would change.

My first task was to collect my adulatory mail. When I look back I realise how unspeakably bumptious I must have been. The truth is that I was desk-less, secretary-less and utterly clueless. I entered the Commons post office with a cross between a swagger and a pimp's roll. I'll never forget my first letter: it was a congratulatory note and cheque from the Cooperative Society.

> Dear Mr Hayes,
> What wonderful news. We look forward to working with you in promoting the Socialist cause. Please accept £100 towards your campaign.

Was it my beard? My youth? Was it something I had said?

But it was going to get worse. Making a beeline for me were two middle-aged gentlemen. Hands were extended.

'Congratulations,' they chirped, 'welcome to the House; may you have many happy years. By the way, have you found yourself a pair?'

I hadn't a clue what they were talking about until they explained that it meant teaming up with a member of the opposite party on unimportant votes to cancel each other out. Having a pair would excuse attendance.

Now I was becoming a little confused.

'But aren't you guys Conservatives?'

'Of course we are, that's why you can choose which of us to pair with!'

'But I'm a Tory too!' I exclaimed, puffing out my pathetically self-important chest.

This news was about as welcome as a rat sandwich to Nick Budgen and Douglas Hogg, who then turned on their heels in search of a real Labour MP.

Then I recognised a familiar face. David Mellor. He was a junior minister. I introduced myself.

David isn't always as nice as he looks. In those days he gave the impression of being the school swot who had just shagged the headmaster's daughter. And his suits always looked as if he had left the coat hanger in. He looked at me as though he had discovered a new species of bug. And when it comes to sneering he can teach George Osborne a thing or two and make Ed Balls seem a man of charm and sensitivity.

'Mmm,' he hissed, 'don't suppose you are a new Tory MP, are you?'

Thank God. Recognition at last!

'Yes,' I smiled excitedly.

'Good,' he grunted, as he punched me playfully in the stomach, and swaggered off like Flashman on crack, muttering, 'It's always good to hit a new Tory MP on the first day.'

Years later when Mellor was outed for having an affair with some actress we nicknamed Olive Oil, a knight of the shires showed me a newspaper cutting with a photo of the bedroom where the trysts had taken place. The scene was not one from *Romeo and Juliet*, but a grimy mattress and an empty bottle of sherry. The old boy was not at all happy, his red face quivering with rage. 'What a bloody disgrace. He's let the party down. The man's a bounder!'

'Well, it's only a shag!' I exclaimed.

'Silly boy,' boomed my knight. 'I don't care about her or that foul pit. Just look at that bloody bottle. Cyprus sherry. And he calls himself a Tory. He's got to go.'

But despite Mellor's inability to pass a belt without kicking below it, I grew to rather like him. In the dying days of

Thatcher, when the massed graves of her enemies were being danced on by her peculiars, I asked Mellor what it was like being a minister in such turbulent times. 'God!' he exploded. 'It's like being in the OK Corral. The woman is shooting at everything that moves.'

The time had come for me to share my great political insights with my new colleagues, so I marched into the Smoking Room – in those days, a Tory watering hole. There, Julian Amery, a fellow with such a plummy voice and impressive war record it was said that he was born with a silver hand grenade in his mouth, was holding court. I went to introduce myself, with no doubt that he had been awaiting my arrival with a keen interest.

'Dear boy, please don't bother. I haven't bothered to learn a Tory MP's name since 1964' was perhaps not the warm response I had expected. He then threw up on the carpet, called for a waiter to clear up and ordered another large brandy.

It was the first of many put-downs which sensibly planted my feet back on the ground. The simple truth dawned on me that I may be an MP, but I knew next to nothing. And did the government want me for my great policy ideas? Of course not. I was just meant to troop through the right lobby at the right time. What I find so depressing is that so many of the 2010 intake take themselves far too seriously and give a very good impression of being firm believers in an Onan Nation Society.

The Smoking Room is a place where a young Member can learn a lot from the old stagers. To sit at the feet of Harolds Wilson and Macmillan and listen to their war stories was a privilege. And there was never a queue, as those in their second parliament had heard them all before.

One evening I joined a jolly group, one of whom was a lovely man called Richard Holt. Poor old Richard was not blessed with matinee idol looks: he was a large man with snaggle teeth and a red face which looked as if it had been carved out of a lump of Spam. As a director of William Hill, he always had a wad of £50 notes the size of a baby's head in his back pocket. To be honest, I can't remember who else was there, but we were all enjoying a good laugh when George Brown, former deputy leader of the Labour Party, swayed in our direction. He was rather drunk. Nothing new, then.

'May I join you wicked Tories?' he slurred. And down he slumped.

He eyed us all one by one. And then his gaze fell upon Holt.

'Who's that ugly bugger?' he enquired.

We explained and then enjoyed a rather surreal conversation with a political legend. Brown staggered to his feet to leave us and paused to impart what we were expecting to be words of great wisdom which we would remember for the rest of our lives. Brown swayed towards Holt, pointing a pudgy finger. The moment had come.

'And as for you, Holt, you're the ugliest cunt I've ever met.' At that, he left us: turned, waved, smiled and bumped into the door.

But this was only the beginning of fourteen years of delightful, bizarre and improbable experiences in the Commons and, later, the press. And that is what this book is really about. The people, the gossip and the sheer insanity of it all. In politics, what doesn't kill you makes you stranger.

One story, from a few years later, should set the scene for what is to follow. In the late 1980s, Colin Moynihan, an Olympic gold medallist cox, thought up a wheeze to raise money for charity. We were to have a parliamentary regatta. In theory this was a fine idea, but in reality putting elderly, infirm, unfit and mostly drunk MPs into rowing boats for a race in the most dangerous part of the Thames is a potential disaster. Health and safety would never allow it today. Insurance companies would roll their eyes in horror. To make matters more interesting, the event was sponsored by Beefeater Gin, who provided a free gin tent on the terrace. It was staffed by very pretty girls dressed as beefeaters in miniskirts. Very mini skirts. Free gin, MPs and pretty young girls in short skirts are a dangerous mix. Particularly when it was discovered that one of the lovelies was, in the interests of keeping up morale, administering blowjobs round the back of the tent. This had the makings of a perfect day, but Nature and Margaret Thatcher, for once, joined forces.

There was a very strong tide, which made it very difficult to row up to the starting point. Even more difficult if you have never been in a racing rowing boat before and damn near impossible if you have spent all afternoon being served free gin by the Beefeater lovelies. Things were not made any easier when Thatcher decided to muscle in. The water was choppy, the tides dangerous and one policewoman had fallen in and been sucked under Westminster Bridge. But Thatcher's publicity boys came up with a brilliant idea. Enthrone her on a steam boat renamed *No Turning Back* and let her make royal progress among the boats. This would have worked rather well if she wasn't always in such a bloody hurry. Thatcher appeared Boudicca-like on her yacht, which was going so fast that the wake sank Jim Callaghan's boat, raising all sorts of nightmare scenarios. Quite how nobody was killed or seriously injured on this day is a total mystery.

But for me, things got worse.

I can't remember who won my race, as my only goal was to stay alive. In celebration of survival I thought it would be rather a good idea to prop up the gin tent bar some more. After a few more noggins I encountered a panic-stricken whip. There was a debate on South Africa and everyone was either at the regatta or in the gin tent and incapable of speech let alone making one. As I could at least walk mostly unaided and was moderately coherent I was ordered into the chamber to say a few helpful words as I had recently returned from South Africa. Mercifully, in those days there were no television cameras in the chamber. But what made my bowels turn to water was the sight of Thatcher steaming onto the front bench to listen.

I have never had the nerve to read what on earth I said. But by the scowl on her face it appeared that my comments about the 'evil regime' did not go down a treat.

Mind you, Michael Howard would probably be of the view that Nelson Mandela was proof that prison works.

CHAPTER 2

THE TEA ROOM

The Tea Room sounds like a cosy, quaint little establishment run by a couple of old ducks in pinnies serving cream teas and piping-hot crumpets dripping in thick, yellow butter. The one in the House of Commons is rather different. It serves all the usual comestibles and is staffed by some delightful old and some quite young ducks. But that is as quaint as it gets. It is in reality a cesspit of intrigue, plots, dark humour, character assassination and occasional fisticuffs. If the chamber is the cockpit of the nation, the Tea Room is a theatre of the absurd, feeding the cravings of the terminally cynical and providing endless free entertainment for the rest of us.

Breakfast time was always the most fun and was like walking onto the set of a long-running soap. It was joyous to watch Terry Dicks survey the room in search of the poor whip tasked with collecting intelligence for the Chief. Terry would plonk himself down next to his victim, take a slurp from his tea and begin his charm offensive, usually along the following lines:

'So, what fuck-ups have you wankers planned for us today then?'

This would always whet the appetites of the bored and those

in search of a bit of red meat, who would slink over and catch what was usually going to be a first-class row.

Terry, although to the right of Genghis Khan, is a thoroughly entertaining bloke, though perhaps not always the most sensitive and politically correct of people, as Norman Fowler as Secretary of State for Health and Social Security found out. Norman was introducing a hard-hitting campaign to fight the spread of HIV when Dicks limped (he had suffered from cerebral palsy since childhood) over, looking for some sport. We all knew that his words of wisdom would be interesting.

'Well, Norman, how's your campaign coming on, then?'

Fowler then gave us a detailed analysis of what his department was doing to educate gay men about the importance of wearing condoms. He then made the mistake of asking Terry what message he thought should be central to the campaign.

'Easy,' says Dicks. 'Just tell 'em that if you shove your willy up someone's bum you're going to catch more than a cold.' Norman made his excuses and left while Terry went in search of another victim.

He once fought Jim Callaghan's Chief Whip Michael Cocks in his Bristol seat. Mike, a delightful old bruiser who locked himself in the Whips' Office until he had a written assurance of a peerage, used to dine out on his remarks about when Terry stood against him.

'Cocks or Dicks, whoever you vote for, you will elect a prick,' he would grin.

But the AIDS campaign revealed just how naive a lot of MPs were about sex. Norman Fowler is meant to have remarked 'Crikey' when a Cabinet colleague explained what oral sex was. And, to the amusement of fellow drinkers in

Annie's Bar, I did my best to fill in Eric Heffer on the subject. He was rather bemused. 'Good God! I was in the RAF and I've never heard of such a thing. I wouldn't ask Doris to do that.' I am sure that she was greatly relieved.

But my favourite story about Fowler's very brave and effective campaign was seeing Willie Whitelaw, then Deputy Prime Minister, looking ashen-faced and forlorn, nursing a bucket of whisky in the Smoking Room. I asked him what the matter was. His rheumy old oyster eyes looked up at me as he slowly shook his head as if ridding himself of a terrible memory.

'I've just spent an hour with Margaret,' he groaned.

'Well,' I said cheerily, 'grim, but not the end of the world.'

'Really? Not the end of the world? I was explaining to her what anal sex was.' I thought it best to leave him to his whisky. Nowadays he would probably be given counselling.

Someone who would have thought that counselling was a left-wing aberration was the cheeringly acrimonious Nick Budgen, the Member for Enoch Powell's old seat, Wolverhampton. To hear him chortling over some acid piece he had written in a broadsheet was a joy. He once gave me some interesting advice about writing.

'I only take the cover off my typewriter for reasons of either money or malice. Preferably both.' Dear Nick only had one fault: he was notoriously mean – not in spirit but in cash. I'm sure that I grew my beard while waiting for him to buy a round. It never happened.

Douglas Hogg was another Tea Room regular. Dougie is a lovely guy but could get rather irritable with those who annoyed him. And there were quite a few of them. One such fellow was an old right-winger called Ivor Stanbrook.

At the time, Dougie was in the Whips' Office, a job which needed tact, discretion and sensitivity – not, perhaps, qualities he possessed in abundance. I can't remember what offence Ivor had committed but I do recall Hogg being dragged off the poor fellow as he had him by the lapels shouting, 'Bounder, cad, bastard.' He was sensibly moved from the Whips' Office to a ministry.

But Ivor was a funny old stick. He used to be chairman of the backbench Constitutional Affairs Committee, and for some bizarre and inexplicable reason I was secretary. He always insisted we met in Committee Room 14, the largest in the House. Yet usually it was just me, him and the vice-chairman, Robert Cranborne. Once, I made the mistake of calling him by his first name at a meeting. 'Order, order, all questions should be addressed through the chair!' he barked.

'But Ivor, there are only you and me here!'

It didn't make a difference.

Sometimes it was very difficult to keep a straight face and not dissolve into fits of giggles, as when the very, very strait-laced Peter Viggers (he of duck house fame) slumped into a chair, deeply upset. The poor fellow was close to tears. I asked what the matter was.

'Last night I did something that I was deeply ashamed of. I really can't bear thinking about it,' he lachrymosed. As you can imagine, a small crowd of unwell wishers assembled. A moment of madness on Clapham Common? A shake too far at a urinal in the Victoria railway station lavatories? Oh God, not the most unforgivable of sins, shagging a royal corgi? Our imaginations ran wild until finally he confessed.

In a voice quaking with emotion he told of his wickedness and shame.

'Last night I voted against the government.'

'For fuck's sake,' leered Budgen, 'I did that three times last week.' And off he stormed to cadge a drink in Annie's Bar.

But the Tea Room could be a place where great personal dramas were played out. There was the time when some old boy was caught in bed by a tabloid with someone who wasn't his wife. He was in such a state that his long-suffering wife was allowed into the Tea Room to escort him home. As this very tweedy matron led him to the car park, all we could hear was his wailing: 'Daddy's been a very bad boy.' After a week of educative waterboarding at home, he returned a new man.

Poor old Geoffrey Dickens got himself into a spot of bother too. Despite being a rather large man he had a penchant for escorting girls to tea dances and then whisking them back to his flat. At last his conscience could bear the weight of guilt no more. So Geoffrey decided to confess all at a press conference. After his *mea culpa* had run its course, he answered questions from the hacks. As proceedings were drawing to a close, one asked him how his wife had taken the news.

Geoffrey went as white as a sheet, began to goldfish, and fled the room. He'd forgotten to tell her and was off to catch her before she caught the six o'clock news.

Dickens was a good sort in a hearty, beefy, not too cerebrally gifted, right-wing sort of way. Unbeknown to him he became involved in a famous Tea Room plot. This was at a time when the papers were doing their usual trick of taking soundings on who could replace Thatcher if the number 39 bus curse finally struck. One tabloid was doing a telephone survey. So we decided to rig it. To the shock of No. 10 and the confusion of the press, the man most likely to succeed Thatcher was not Heseltine, Lawson or even Major, but one G. Dickens. It was a good day's work.

The same malarkey was indulged in by Labour MPs furious that they had to vote for a woman on the shadow Cabinet. They rigged the vote and a rather eccentric (but rather nice) elderly MP called Mildred Gordon was duly elected. She was never allowed to a meeting. I saw Mildred the other week, still going strong at ninety.

Not too many grandees were regular Tea Roomers, but Ted Heath would sometimes grace us with an appearance. When in a good mood he was great value, but when he was in a sulk, he was best avoided. When Peter Walker was his minder he warned Ted that he really ought to press the flesh a bit more and mingle with the backbenchers. So Peter took him to the Tea Room and pointed out a knight of the shires who had just made a speech. This was a great opportunity for Ted to show charm and empathy.

'Prime Minister, Sir George made a speech today.' Sir George (or whatever his name was) eagerly awaited the prime ministerial pat on the back.

'I know,' grumbled Ted, 'I heard it was bloody awful.' Peter never took him to the Tea Room again.

One day, Ted had heard it was my birthday and asked me if I'd care to join him for dinner in the Members' dining room. How could I refuse? If he was on form it would be fun. Sadly, he was at his grumpiest, made worse when we were joined by Douglas Hurd, who was then Home Secretary, and Nigel Lawson, the Chancellor. Both used to work for him when he was Prime Minister. There was lots of talk about 'that woman' and, quite remarkably, he treated Hurd and Lawson as if they were a couple of unruly sixth formers. Being gentlemen and knowing that this was an off day, they took their punishment with a smile. And he still owes me a pound from when he was queuing up for a cup of tea and discovered that he had no money, so I obliged. My heartfelt thanks was a grunt.

But Ted could be enormous fun. His fortieth-year-in-the-House celebration at the Savoy was one such occasion. The guests were glittering, the food and wine magnificent and a string orchestra played discreetly in the background. The only person not enjoying herself was Thatcher. When it was time to leave I went to thank Ted for a wonderful time. I commented to him that she seemed to be having rather an uncomfortable lunch. I pointed out that she had been stuck in between two people she loathed, Sonny Ramphal, Secretary-General of the Commonwealth, and Bob Runcie, the Archbishop of Canterbury. Ted's smile grew to a grin, his grin to a belly laugh and then those famous shoulders started to gyrate.

'That was rather the point.' Bless.

But the Thatcher-ten-years-of-fun party at the Savoy was a pretty dismal affair. I remember appearing in a newspaper diary saying that I was pathetically grateful that there wasn't a terrorist attack as there were people there I wouldn't want to appear dead with. For some reason Ted didn't attend.

But my favourite Tea Room story is when one of the well-known womanisers peered up from his *Telegraph* crossword when asked what plans he had for the day.

'Well,' he said languidly, 'I think I will go and fuck a Member's wife.'

'Whom?' we enquired. This rather nonplussed him.

'Actually, I haven't decided yet.'

Not so long ago I was dining at the Ivy with a friend when a well-known Labour politician strolled in. My friend's face turned ashen. 'God, I can't stand that bloody man.'

'Why?'

'I'll tell you later.' And after we staggered into the sunlight, he uttered words used many times about this particular politician.

'He fucked my wife.'

This seems to be a bit of a recurring theme in Parliament.

CHAPTER 3

THE CHAMBER

N othing on earth can prepare you for making your maiden speech in the chamber. Luckily, my area whip was John Major. He gave me some very good advice: don't be in too much of a rush, just spend a few weeks sitting, watching and learning. And then, when you think you've got the feel of the place, come to me and we'll go through your speech.

The chamber has its own political ecosystem. Like the weather, it can be very unpredictable and change in a flash. It is also a great leveller. It doesn't matter who you are or what you have achieved, you stand there alone and utterly defenceless.

Imagine making a speech in front of three hundred bored, cynical old pros who are not there to listen but to make their own point. Start being pompous or clever with that lot and they will shout, heckle, bawl and do just about anything to put you off your stride. Or they might just do it anyway out of devilment.

Dennis Skinner is a past master of this. Along with the *Spitting Image* puppet of David Steel sitting in David Owen's top pocket, Skinner's merciless heckling was Steel's nemesis. He should have just laughed it off.

Humour is the key. When they are baying for your blood, a

little self-deprecatory joke doesn't go amiss. That is why Hague and Cameron are so good at the despatch box and the likes of Iain Duncan Smith and Philip Hammond get a rough time. The only modern exception to this rule is Theresa May, not exactly the Frankie Howerd of the Commons. She can reduce an opponent to a quivering wreck just by one laser-beam stare.

But the master of the despatch box was Tony Blair. A genuinely nice guy and a mesmerising performer in the chamber, it is desperately sad that this supremely gifted politician will be viewed in history through the prism of the Iraq War and a tragedy that Labour's most successful leader should be vilified by his own party. Worse, in a nod to North Korea, Ed Miliband's hounds are gradually airbrushing Blair out of history. Soon all that will be left of him will be the Cheshire Cat grin slowly fading above the shadow Cabinet table.

Thatcher, like May, was an exception to the humour rule. She had none at all. But her sheer strength of will cowed everything in her wake. In the chamber she was a force of nature. I was sitting ten feet away from her when she made her famous 'No! No! No!' speech and pulverised Neil Kinnock.

I was also sitting in the same place years later, for her final appearance as Prime Minister, when she holed Skinner below the waterline with her 'I'm rather enjoying this'. It brought a tear to my eye. And I had voted against her.

One of the golden rules in politics is that those who appear to be rather nice often aren't and those who seem ferocious are rather engaging.

Two names come to mind: Dennis Skinner and Norman Tebbit.

Skinner is regarded by those who don't know him as a

national treasure. In reality he is a ghastly, bigoted, self-obsessed shit. I will qualify that. Even shits would regard him as a shit. He is probably the most unpopular man in the Commons and his own party despise him. But reading his press you would think that he is an institution. Although, in a bizarre unpleasant sort of way, I suppose he is. The sort of institution that requires its guests to wear jackets with buckles round the back.

What confirmed his copper-bottomed shittery for me was an incident after the Brighton bombing. John Wakeham, the Chief Whip, had lost his wife and was horribly injured. It took weeks for him to return to Parliament. One afternoon, the chamber was packed for an important debate. Suddenly, the main doors swung open and there, standing on crutches, was a very frail Wakeham. Painfully, he hobbled to his place on the front bench. The debate came to a halt. In one movement the House rose in respectful silence for the courage of a man who had suffered so much at the hands of the enemies of this country.

Well, all of us stood save for Skinner, who sat scowling in his place. What a revolting little man.

On the other side of the coin is Norman Tebbit. Another man who suffered terrible personal loss at the bombing, he was a Rottweiler in the chamber and was nicknamed the Chingford Skinhead by Kinnock. But actually he is a really nice guy with a twinkle in his eye. And a great sense of humour.

Although we did have a little falling-out. Just after the 1987 election I'd had a night out with a newly elected mate, Steve Day. I'd spent a night at his flat and we walked to the House the next morning. It was a beautiful day, the sun was shining and we had a spring in our step. As we entered the Members' cloakroom an enormous bulletproof limo glided to a halt. A gothic gloom descended and party chairman Norman Tebbit, with a smile like the brass plate on a coffin, marched in.

'Morning, Norman. Lovely day, mate,' I smiled.

But rather than the cheery grin I expected I received a curt 'What's so lovely?'

'What's the matter?'

'You, you cunt. I saw you on the *News at Ten* last night. Asking for more money for pensioners and the health service.'

'But I was only being reasonable.'

At that, Norman came up close and started prodding me in the chest, and gave me the full hairdryer.

'It's not your job to be reasonable. Your job is to unquestioningly support your leader and your party, in that order.'

And, with a snarl, off he strode. Norman was not having a good day. And now neither was I.

A few years later I was making a film for *Newsnight*. John Major was Prime Minister and the Amish wing of the party was causing him grief over Europe. Tebbit made a speech of such disloyalty towards Major that it would have led to summary execution in Zimbabwe. Afterwards he was surrounded by the usual dandruff-flecked ghastlies, who were in a state of damp-gusseted ecstasy over his words. I sauntered up with a mischievous glint in my eye.

'Unquestioning loyalty to your leader, eh? Who's the cunt now?'

It didn't go down well.

One little ritual that all Cabinet ministers perform is to invite new MPs in for a drink. I suspect the idea is that if ever they had pretensions of becoming Prime Minister (you'd be amazed how many do, which shows they are masters not of mass- but of self-delusion) they at least got a brownie point for giving you a couple of glasses of warm white wine. These first ministerial encounters could be tremendously revealing.

Keith Joseph (nicknamed the Mad Monk) was delightful, but tortured. He would sit there as Education Secretary, a vein throbbing rhythmically on his temple, raging that his civil servants wouldn't let him actually do anything.

Transport Secretary Nick Ridley (grandson of Lutyens and a gifted artist himself) was a wily old fox with a great sense of humour. But he did have the unnerving habit of sitting on top of his desk, chain-smoking and scratching his crotch.

Michael Heseltine, the classiest of class acts, of whom I'm a great fan, was far too grand to bring us in in small groups. He got the whole ghastly experience (for him, not us) over in one go by inviting all the new intake en masse. Then, in his great room at Defence and standing by a portrait of Lloyd George (Hezza is Welsh too), he made a cracking, rousing and inspirational speech. It was a not-terribly-subtle hint that one day he wanted to be leader. But we loved it.

After his resignation over the Westland affair I bumped into him at a party conference and he offered to give me a lift back to my hotel. As we were walking towards the exit he was accosted by a pack of journos. 'What's it like not being in the Cabinet, Mr Heseltine?' was the deeply insightful question.

'Well, I do miss my ministerial car,' he said with sadness as he led me to a magnificent limo, bristling like a porcupine with aerials and far, far grander than anything the government could provide. He also had the same driver.

Hezza was kind enough to campaign for me in Harlow in

1992. He was then Deputy Prime Minister and I was on the IRA death list so we both had armed security at the time. He is the master of the walkabout and I was very excited about leading him through the main shopping centre. However, our security guys sounded a word of warning. They were worried that there could be trouble. That there were some left-wing agitators and a lot of press and television. 'Best avoid,' was their advice, 'but it's up to you guys.' 'Press' and 'trouble' are two words which have the same effect as 'dog' and 'doorbell' to Hezza and me. Our eyes sparkled, and in unison we shouted, 'We'll do it!' And what an experience. No hand was unshaken. No baby unkissed. Young mothers and pensioners alike melted to his charm. I remember some poor old dear being backed into a corner by the crowd. Hezza, eyes ablaze and hand extended, came to the rescue.

Many years before, when he was at war with Thatcher, my favourite *Mirror* front page was a cartoon of him swinging through the jungle in a loin cloth with Margaret dressed as Jane. The caption was 'Me Tarzan, you pain'. It will be a long time before we see his like again.

Always at the end of first ministerial drinks we would be treated to the parting words 'Feel free to knock on my door; you will always be welcome.'

There was one exception to this: Tebbit, whose parting words were, 'Always feel free to knock on my door. I will, of course, tell you to fuck off.'

He was joking. I think. Actually, I'm rather fond of the old devil.

The chamber can be a cruel and heartless place, where reputations can be shredded in a single debate and hopes dashed by a crass question or an incompetent answer. But it can be capable of great compassion, forgiveness and humanity. The sad and unexpected death of Labour leader John Smith is a case in point. One morning I was in the gym and I saw his secretary receive a phone call. She went as white as a sheet and burst into tears. She had been told that John had just died of a heart attack. I quickly showered and dressed and saw on the annunciator that the Leader of the House would shortly be making a statement. An hour later, the chamber was crowded. Everyone had heard. And when Tony Newton, the Leader of the House, made his speech, most of us were in tears, as John was loved by us all. Yet despite our distress, in the back of our minds we knew that politics was going to change forever. Tony Blair was the hot favourite to win the leadership and he would be lethal.

John Smith was seriously good news, but was a little overweight and treated white wine as a soft drink. Once, he was on a train up to Glasgow and found himself sitting next to Gordon Brown and a very rough-and-ready Glaswegian MP called Tommy Graham. Tommy was a nice bloke but perhaps not a candidate for *Brain of Britain*. You weren't likely to drown in his gene pool. The journey was coming to an end and, as Tommy was not involved in the high-octane conversation between Brown and Smith, he felt he needed to make an impression. As the train was pulling in to Glasgow, he made an announcement.

'See tha fence over theeer?' he said in his impenetrable Glaswegian accent. 'Thass weer I shagged the missus for the feer taame.' And who said that the age of romance is dead?

There were some speakers who could pull the crowds. As soon as their names appeared on the annunciator the chamber would fill. Michael Foot, Tony Benn and Enoch Powell were firm favourites. Footy was at his best without a note and Powell presented beautifully crafted works of intellectual art. I shared a desk in the library with Enoch for a few months. A tiny, trim little man, with piercing blue eyes and a strong Black Country accent. Macmillan refused to have him sit opposite him in Cabinet as he was of the view that 'he had the eyes of a fakir'. Enoch was always studiously polite, but didn't like to be disturbed. He had a way of dealing with snorers. He would creep up behind them and bang two large books together. It always worked.

He also was rather irritated by the then Commons barber. He was more lethal with a cut-throat razor than Sweeney Todd and made me look as if I had been hurled through a car windscreen the one and only time I used his services. He also never stopped talking. This used to annoy Enoch, as he wished to be immersed in his own thoughts. So on one occasion the barber asked him what sort of haircut he would like. The grim reply was, 'A silent one.'

Enoch, although sometimes a little quirky and remote, had a dry sense of humour. Back in the mists of time I was travelling on the train to Oxford to stand in for Ken Clarke (then Secretary of State for Health) at an Oxford Union debate, and found that Enoch was sitting in the seat next to me. We had a delightful chat and as we were walking in the direction of the Union a chanting mob could be heard. Poor Enoch had to put up with a lot of abuse after his Rivers of Blood speech. On one occasion we appeared on *Any Questions* together. Protesters water-bombed us and the programme came off air for about ten minutes. So I thought that a few words of encouragement were needed during our Oxford walk.

'I'm sorry you have to put up with so much abuse, it must be dreadful.'

He smiled and simply said, in that lilting Black Country accent, 'If you listen carefully you will hear that the abuse is aimed at you, not me. I'm off to dinner with some friends.' And with that he raised his trademark homburg hat and disappeared into the night. He, of course, was quite right. It was my blood the mob was baying for.

The chamber is the ideal killing field for the assassin. Winston Churchill famously put the boot into Neville Chamberlain with 'England has been offered a choice between war and shame. She has chosen shame and will get war.' But weeks later the *coup de grâce* was given by Leo Amery (Julian's father), who invoked the words of Oliver Cromwell when he dissolved the Long Parliament: 'You have sat here too long for any good you are doing. Depart, I say, and let us have done with you. In the name of God, go!'

The most devastating and lethal speech I ever heard was Geoffrey Howe's resignation statement. It was said that it took him ten years to make it and ten minutes for his wife Elspeth (a formidable lady) to write it. In those days, if you attacked the leadership it was done through coded language. If ever there was any likelihood of trouble, rather than sit on the benches I'd pop up to the overspill gallery, whereby I was facing colleagues and could see their expressions and gauge the mood of the party. For those not old enough to remember, Thatcher's star was not just on the wane, it was about to explode. Neil Kinnock was twenty-nine points ahead in the polls. Ministers were being ignored and humiliated by her and none more so than the quiet, gentle and academic Howe. We thought that he would be mildly critical and did not expect the detonation of a political grade-A weapon whose shock waves still resonate throughout the party. It is well worth looking at the film clip. Sitting just behind Howe was my old chum the ginger-haired David Sumberg. When the knife is finally plunged you can see Sumberg's look of shock and watch him mouth the words 'fucking hell'. That really summed it up. We knew that now the Lady's days were numbered.

A golden rule is that whenever you expect trouble in the chamber it rarely happens. The debate on the Westland debacle, in which Heseltine resigned from Cabinet as secret papers on the ownership of that helicopter company had been leaked to the press, was expected to be a cliffhanger, perhaps the end of the government. To paraphrase, it was all about whether Westland should be owned by the Americans or the Europeans. Hezza thought it was a No. 10 plot to undermine him, which it probably was. In fact, the Attorney General, Sir Michael Havers, treated this extremely seriously and bravely threatened to send Scotland Yard into No. 10 unless there was full cooperation. Thatcher never forgave him and eventually sacked him as Lord Chancellor some years later.

The time came for the big debate. Although this was essentially a beltway story, the whips were very jittery about the outcome. We were told that the Lady had a letter of resignation in her handbag. Although I never believed a word of it.

This was Neil Kinnock's big chance for a knock-out blow. We watched with trepidation as he rose to speak. We shouldn't have bothered: he bombed. Too wordy, too shouty, and missing his target.

But Westland claimed the scalp of Trade Secretary Leon Brittan, whose department was accused of leaking the document. I like Leon. Kind, decent, honourable and intelligent. His problem was that he was very tall, a QC, and had the look of an armed robber with a stocking stretched over his head. People thought that he was talking down to them when nothing could be further from the truth. What deeply disturbed me was the whiff of anti-Semitism that began to pollute certain sections of the party. A number of colleagues whispered that the trouble with this Cabinet was that there were too many Estonians and not enough Etonians. I felt ashamed of them.

But I do like Neil Kinnock. He is brave, good-hearted and great company. He was just unlucky and had a propensity to bang on a bit. He once helped end any hope of a ministerial job for me under the Lady, although I was doing rather well on that score myself. At Prime Minister's Questions he shouted at her to give the Hon. Member for Harlow a job. Well, that was it.

I was once at a do where he and Hezza were speaking. We were on a three-line whip, which means that the only excuse for non-attendance is death. I looked at my watch. Five minutes to go. Damn, I was stuffed. When we eventually headed for the door I was looking a bit forlorn. I was due a serious bollocking from the whips. Neil sidled over.

'Don't worry, boyo, I'll give you a lift back.'

So there I was in the back of the Leader of the Opposition's car with the man himself, sweeping through Carriage Gates.

Heaven knows what people would have thought. Neil read my mind.

'Leave it to me, boyo. Look those whip bastards in the eye and tell them you were with me. I'll ring the Chief and explain.' To his credit, he did. And my genitalia remained intact. For the time being.

It is hard to believe that cameras were only introduced into the chamber in the late 1980s – and then only after a row. But the absence of television hid a number of sins, notably of extreme drunkenness and bad behaviour. Viewers would have missed the swaying and the final collapse onto the benches of Nicky Fairburn after slurring a question. They would have also missed a rather drunken Ron Brown throwing the mace to the ground and a senior Labour whip marching in to punch him in the stomach, throw him over his shoulder and give him a good kicking, within earshot of us all.

Dear old Ron was affable but quite bonkers. His face was horribly scarred after he had received 5,000 volts in an industrial accident. The word was that this had scrambled his brain. I remember coming back from a run and having a shower in the Members' changing room, then a rather Victorian affair with a tanning lamp that was built in the '20s and looked as if it was on loan from Dr Frankenstein's laboratory. A very dangerous machine indeed. Anyhow, as I was sluicing myself down, I heard gruntings and groans and then squeals of ecstasy. I looked in the end cubicle and there was Ron indulging in Ugandan discussions.

We eventually had a rather pompous debate about what to do with Ron, who, although as mad as a box of frogs on speed, was quite a pleasant guy. One Tory, it may have been Peter Bottomley, rose to support him. Dear old Peter, although well-meaning, inadvertently had us rocking in the aisles and crying with laughter. 'Does the House not think', he said portentously, 'that we are using a sledgehammer to crack a—' but before the word 'nut' could be uttered the House was too paralysed with mirth to do anything but whoop for the joy of it all.

Viewers would also have missed out on Dr Alan Glyn, the Member for Windsor. Poor old Alan was very elderly and very infirm and, according to the wonderful Steve Norris, had 'more dandruff than a dead badger'. He was a small man with a limp and a Hitler moustache. The limp, he claimed, was as a result of him being a British spy monitoring the Soviet invasion of Prague. The truth is that he fell asleep by the road and a Land Rover ran over his leg.

The old boy had pretty well lost the plot in the 1980s and could barely walk or talk. He would just raise a paw in welcome and wobble off into the distance. Although he did keep repeating, when occasionally speech was restored, that he was both a doctor and a barrister and 'fucking useless' at both. The joke was that people wore medical alert bracelets with 'not to be treated by Dr Glyn' on them.

Alan always used to stay at the same hotel in Windsor on election night, with his wife, the delightfully dopey Lady Rosola. In the middle of the night he was desperate for a pee and wandered into what he thought was the bathroom. In fact it was the wardrobe, which fell on top of him. The old boy, after a bit of a struggle, fell asleep. The next morning Lady Rosola noticed that he wasn't there and assumed he'd gone off to a meeting. So she went home. Of course, Alan was still asleep in the upturned wardrobe, only to be found by a startled chambermaid several hours later.

Another little oddity viewers would have been interested in were the hairy grey suits worn by Toby Jessel, the Member for Twickenham. I once asked him what they were made of.

'Why, poodle hair, of course,' he replied, in a way that suggested that anyone who didn't have a suit made of the stuff must be very eccentric. Evidently some relative used to breed poodles and gave him a bolt of their hair once a year. Perfectly normal.

The chamber can also show empathy and love. This was evidenced in one of the last days before Geoffrey Dickens tragically died. He was an enormous man, as broad as he was tall. In another incarnation he had been a nightclub bouncer. Sadly, he was struck with cancer, and he wanted to see his old friends for the last time. It was a pitiful sight. There was not an ounce of flesh on him. He hardly had a voice and was connected to a chemo drip. It is on these occasions that the House is at its best. People from all parties rallied round, patted him on the back, gave him a hug, shook him by the hand and wished him well. We all knew that this was the last time he would be with us. It was.

Geoffrey, in his heyday, was an old right-winger with a foghorn voice. Everyone flooded into the chamber to hear his speech in favour of Clause 28, which prohibited the promotion of homosexuality in schools. Dickens wasn't blessed with the keenest of intellects and he couldn't understand why the House was cracking up with laughter at his attempts to be statesmanlike. Lines such as 'I'm not against homosexuals, many would bend over backwards to help their fellow man' and 'I don't object to homosexuality, it's just that my constituents don't want it rammed down their throats' were delivered with total innocence. He really wasn't being deliberately homophobic, just a bit dim.

Some Members are naturally funny. One of my favourite speeches was by Rhodri Morgan (who eventually became a splendid First Minister of Wales). It was at about 5 a.m. and everyone was fairly worse for wear. He was making a speech about the role of Richard Branson, who had been appointed Litter Czar. He reminded us all of the time Branson and Thatcher did a photo shoot picking up litter in St James's Park. He came out with this cracker:

'Who does she think she is, John F. Kennedy?' This rather confused us and one drunken voice shouted for an explanation.

'Ich bin ein bin liner,' he grinned.

We had been brilliantly set up for that one.

Sometimes a good lunch would generate serious mischief. My famous question to the Chancellor Nigel Lawson comes to mind. As soon as I got to my feet, two well-refreshed grandees picked me up and suspended me over the benches, just to alleviate the boredom of what was to come. This is probably the only time a parliamentary question has been asked in mid-air. Nigel just couldn't understand why my supplementary caused so much hilarity. He was, of course, facing the opposite direction.

Mind you, Nigel was a genius at the despatch box. One night we heard that some official in the Treasury had cocked up a major privatisation. Lawson was due to make a statement at ten. We all trooped in expecting humiliation and disaster. In he marched with a statement scribbled on the back of an envelope. Heaven knows what he said, it was all horribly technical. But it solved the problem and we cheered him to the rafters. He had saved the day. It was a tragedy when he was forced to resign.

One strange ritual which has now been abolished was the little bit of theatre when an MP wanted to raise a point of order during a debate. To be called by the Speaker, the MP would have to reach under the Serjeant-at-Arms' chair and remove a collapsible top hat, sit down, put it on and make his point of order. When finished, he would toss it across the chamber like a Frisbee to anyone else who wanted to raise a point of order. Some of the old boys used to get very excited when the lovely Clare Short sat there in the top hat. They thought that she looked very burlesque. In those days they were a pretty sexist lot. And it could become very uncomfortable when some of the post-erectionists wanted to wax lyrical about the sexual charms of Margaret Thatcher.

Sometimes, Hansard writers (the people who take a shorthand note of proceedings) get it horribly wrong. It's rare, but it happens. The classic was when John Butterfill gave a perfectly straightforward supplementary question to some minister. When he checked the record the next day to admire his words of wisdom, they had been traduced to 'this is total bollocks'. How that ever appeared is still one of the great unsolved parliamentary mysteries. The chamber is a funny old place.

CHAPTER 4

ANNIE'S BAR

One of the most fascinating institutions on the parliamentary estate was Annie's Bar. I say 'was' simply because this jewel in the crown of Westminster watering holes is no more. It is deceased. And it had beautiful plumage. Yet it was pushed off its perch by hair-shirted Blairites who didn't approve of the drinking culture that had dominated the place for so many years and despised by the new breed of well-scrubbed Follettised Labour women who convinced themselves that anyone who was over the age of forty, liked a drink and possessed a penis (whether in working order or not) was the enemy. Quite why women are known as the gentler sex is a total mystery to me. Covering their antics for Her Majesty's press for a few years showed many of them to be the most ruthless, hard-nosed bunch it has ever been my misfortune to encounter, making Lucretia Borgia look like Shirley Temple. You may recall that Barbara Follett was a Labour MP evangelical about getting more women into Parliament and gave hopefuls lessons in what to wear to make an impact with selection committees. We once did a television interview about women.

'And what have the Tories ever done for women?' she snarled.

'Well, we made Margaret Thatcher Prime Minister,' I offered.

'But she was not really a woman, was she?' This caused me sleepless nights. But there is an uncomfortable truth that there are still not enough women in Parliament. Harriet Harman has been fearless and determined, as has David Cameron. But all parties still have a very long way to go. What is an even worse national disgrace is the inequality of pay between the sexes, which still persists.

I was blessed with the extraordinarily high calibre of the women MPs I encountered when I was first elected. The likes of Dame Elaine Kellett Bowman, Dame Janet Fookes, Dame Marion Roe, Dame Jill Knight and Edwina Currie were all highly intelligent, opinionated and incredibly brave. If any mere man tried to patronise them you would find out who the superior sex really was. And on the Labour side you had Audrey Wise, Gwyneth Dunwoody, Harriet Harman, Tessa Jowell, Clare Short and Margaret Hodge; none would take any nonsense. There were many more. All of these women were formidable but kept their femininity. If someone had told them to 'calm down, dear' in the chamber they would have either regarded it as a bad attempt at humour or just defenestrated the poor sod.

I was particularly fond of Gwyneth Dunwoody. She was delightful, but terrified the life out of most of her colleagues. One day I was being playful with her in the chamber. Afterwards I sidled up to her cheerily, saying words to the effect of 'that was fun'. She just smiled at me, said, 'Just like this,' and kneed me in the groin. I had learned my lesson.

Dame Elaine Kellett Bowman, the feisty MP for Lancaster, didn't take any prisoners either. She used to call me Bubbles, after the famous Pears soap painting of a little boy with blond curly hair blowing bubbles. She was well known for treating Budget Day as a very special event. So much so that rather than queue up outside the chamber before it was unlocked to guarantee a seat, she used to sleep wedged against the door on the cold stone floor in a sleeping bag.

One morning I passed her recumbent form only to spot the wonderfully outrageous Nicky Fairbairn standing over her, having a swig from the phial of vodka he used to keep in the top of his silver-topped walking cane. It was, after all, quite late at 8 a.m. 'You know, Jerry, this is how I love to see her. Comatose.' And off he staggered to refill his morning's supply. He wouldn't have had the nerve to say that if she had been awake.

But back to Annie's. It was steeped in history. The one which operated in my day had changed its location several times over the years; it used to be the office of Charles Parnell, who used to smuggle in his mistress, Kitty O'Shea, through the stone-mullioned windows. She was the go-between over Home Rule with Gladstone. It all ended in tears.

Annie's was the preserve of the press and MPs. A place of relative safety (whips were eyed with suspicion) where gossip and stories could be exchanged on lobby terms, which meant that the source would never be disclosed. So when you read a story beginning 'Friends close to...' it very often meant that the guy had planted the story himself.

In the days when he drank, the legendary Chris Moncrieff would down half a dozen pints of Guinness in about twenty minutes before filing another brilliant scoop for the Press Association. Chris is the finest reporter that I have ever come across because he is meticulous and fair. But, more importantly, he is totally honest. People trust him. And in Westminster that's a valuable commodity. A good example of this was when Denzil Davies was shadow Secretary of State for Defence. He was always at odds with Neil Kinnock's policy of unilateral nuclear disarmament. It came to a head one night when he rang up Chris and told him that he was going to resign. Being a true gent, Moncrieff, realising that Denzil was rather worse for wear in drink, said he would ring him back when he had sobered up and if he wanted to change his mind the first conversation would be forgotten. Eventually the call was made and a sober Denzil stuck to his guns. And Chris, through old-fashioned journalism, had secured the story of the year.

Denzil, in the days of Harold Wilson, used to be a Treasury minister under Denis Healey's chancellorship. Denis was a bit of an old bruiser and didn't like Davies's rather mild Welsh manner. Denzil once told me that he could not bear being told that he was a twat or a wanker or a bastard by Healey, so they agreed not to have face-to-faces, just written memos. But it made no difference, as Healey just used to scrawl twat, wanker or bastard in the margins.

The interesting thing about the lobby is that its patrons forge close personal relationships with politicians. It is symbiotic in that the journalist needs a story and the politician needs publicity. Every dog needs a lamp-post; it's just a bit difficult working out which one is which. Some criticise the lobby system as being too cosy. But you are more likely to get to the truth of a story if all parties realise at the outset that everything that is said is unattributable and off the record. Ministers are far more likely to go off-message in private than in public. There is nothing more off-putting to voters than seeing robotic politicians failing to answer questions and sticking rigidly to dull scripts prepared by spin doctors. Rachel Reeves and Chloe Smith, take note. Well, at least Chloe has. She saw the writing on the wall after her *Newsnight* car crash and resigned a few months later.

Chris Moncrieff formed close relationships with everyone who mattered and an awful lot who didn't. He became close to Margaret Thatcher.

I would love to have been a fly on the wall at No. 10 on the very first Red Nose Day, when Moncrieff asked Thatcher to put on a red nose. And despite their friendship, the room became very chilly. She did not oblige. At the time of writing, Chris, who is well into his eighties, is still filing brilliant copy. And the new press bar bears his name. Deservedly so. Although sadly not a lot of serious drinking goes on in there any more. Many of the baby journos don't understand the importance of lunch or a few reviving drinks with MPs. They prefer to be rooted in front of their screens.

The great thing about Annie's Bar is that we had a fantastic camaraderie. No matter what allegiance we had to party or paper, we always helped each other out. One Christmas our delightful barmaid, May, was in floods of tears. She had spent a lot of time putting up the decorations only to witness a foul-mouthed and drunken Ron Davies (he of the last shoot-out at Gobbler's Gulch on Clapham Common) ripping them all down. Harold Walker, the Deputy Speaker, was so enraged that he made the ghastly Davies apologise and redecorate the place.

And you could always tell where certain journalists were by the placing of their drinks. You knew that Peter Dobbie of the *Mail on Sunday* couldn't be all that far away if there was a half of lager by the telephone.

It is worth remembering that in the early 1980s newspaper articles were actually typed on a typewriter. There were neither computer terminals nor laptops. And if you were away from the office (as all political journalists were), you just dictated your copy down the phone to a copy-taker, usually a middle-aged woman in Manchester. The capacity for totally inebriated journos to sober up just enough to be able to dictate a front-page splash from off the top of their heads never ceased to amaze me. I look back in wonderment on how I used to hold up some of the old boys with one hand while pressing the phone to their ear with the other while they dictated staggeringly good copy. One such gifted old friend was Adrian Lithgow of the *Mail on Sunday*. We became really good mates. A great journo and a delightful man. But sometimes a menace after a drink. One night he staggered into Annie's in a terrible rage.

'Which one of you wankers has nicked my contacts book?' he screamed at nobody in particular. At that, a rather starry-eyed kid from the BBC, who had never met a real Fleet Street hack before, nervously smiled. Not a good move. Lithgow grabbed him by the lapels, raised him from his bar stool and threw him against the wall, with the parting words 'you smug bastard' before heading off to the committee room corridor.

One of the most unpleasant experiences both MPs and journalists have to endure is the sheer drudgery and mind-numbing boredom of party conferences. But there was an upside. For three weeks of the party conference season, Annie's Bar goes on the road, in those days to dreary seaside resorts. Ever tried to have a good time in Blackpool that doesn't involve slot machines and vomit? No, neither have I.

Once, I was sent by *The Big Breakfast* to find some youngsters, put them in fancy dress and take part in a daft competition. The trouble is that in the early hours the only people I could find were drunks and those just released from prison. I then had to dress as Elvis Presley and interview a Blackpool landlady with a singing dog. Needless to say the dog wouldn't even bark, let alone sing. Not my finest hour.

The tradition is that at party conferences, newspaper editors book a swish suite at the headquarters hotel, dine with the Prime Minister and then swan back to London, leaving the suite in the safe hands of whoever is covering politics. On one occasion it was Lithgow, then at the *Mail on Sunday*. It goes without saying that a whole crowd of us had rather a lot to drink that night. So I staggered into the twin bed next to Adrian and snored the night away until we were woken by the telephone. It was Lithgow's then girlfriend.

'Where are you?'

'In bed.'

'You've got a woman with you.'

'No, I haven't.'

'But I can hear someone in the background.'

'Oh yeah, but it's a guy.'

'Arrrrrrrgh!' Followed by much shouting, swearing and tears.

'Err, I think she's got the wrong end of the stick here, mate,' says Lithgow, 'and she's on her way up…'

So, with the presence of mind that only three bottles of

Merlot can produce, I threw on some clothes and jumped out of the window. To land in a heap in front of his girlfriend.

'Hi there,' I spluttered, 'Adrian's waiting for you. We had a great night together.'

Well, you know what I meant, but it was rather misunderstood.

Betty Boothroyd, before she became one of the finest Speakers the Commons has ever had, used to be a regular at Annie's and could be found swirled in cigarette smoke with a very large gin and tonic on hand. We would always be greeted with a cheery ''allo luveee'. I was one of the Tories who voted for her. And very proud of that, too. Mind you, it was either her or Peter Brooke, to whom humour is not a joke.

Annie's was not without its political dramas. Ken Clarke, even when in Cabinet, would pop in for a few pints and a cigar. One night, when things were particularly fraught with Thatcher (in those days, most of the time), one young journo rushed in and announced that he'd just heard that Michael Heseltine had resigned. Actually he hadn't (yet), but for the first time I saw the normally ebullient Ken turn as white as sheet, mutter 'oh fuck', and leave the room. The telltale sign of just how serious Ken thought the situation was that he had left his pint on the bar.

Unthinkable.

The Annie's Bar crowd were fantastic. We often said that we were the very first coalition in modern times as we pretty well agreed how the country should be run. Remember, this included two journo legends, Nigel Nelson and Ian Hernon, who were firmly of the left, as were Norman Hogg (who lost out as Labour Chief Whip by one vote) and deputy shadow

Leader of the House John McWilliam. Now put them together with Tony Beaumont-Dark (the only man who could fall asleep standing up with a glass in his hand and not spill a drop) and Barry Porter, both of the right, and you had a very interesting mix.

Barry's memorial service was a very grand affair at the MPs' church, St Margaret's. John Major, Michael Heseltine and most of the Cabinet were there. It was a glittering occasion. I think Hezza rolled up because Barry was the first Thatcherite to publicly support him for the leadership. But at the service a beyond-the-grave note was read out. 'Sorry, Michael, but in the end I still voted for the old girl.' I miss the old devil. Barry, that is.

Annie's was also a great link with the past. Lord Bruce of Donington was another regular. An interesting old boy with a dry sense of humour, he was elected in 1945 and was Nyc Bevan's parliamentary private secretary. He knew Churchill, Lloyd George and all the greats of the time. He was a fund of stories. I once asked him how they compared with our modern politicians. He just smiled, took a pull of his pint and uttered words which any politician with pretensions should never forget: 'All politicians have feet of clay. Most are wankers.'

Yet, despite his left-wing pedigree, Donald was to the right of Genghis Khan.

But we did have one silly game we played just to wind up the whips. In those days, when the division bell rang you had eight minutes to get to the lobbies before the doors were locked. Behind Annie's there was a little-known staircase which was an amazing shortcut. So, when the whips were beginning to panic we would saunter in with twenty seconds to go. And wave to each other as we voted in different ways. And then pop back down for another drink.

Another great character was Sir Fergus Montgomery, a former PPS to the Lady. His nickname was Dame Fergus because he was rather gay. I once asked him over a glass of wine how he managed to bring some of the biggest stars in show business, like Shirley Bassey, in for dinner.

'Easy, dear. When I was a young and pretty teacher I once fucked Noël Coward.'

He was a lovely man.

Annie's Bar summed up to me what politics should really be about. That people of goodwill will disagree but can compromise and be pragmatic. That problems are best solved by not looking at them through the prism of party dogma, but with a genuine desire to solve them. And that those who will be seen as your enemies on election day and in the chamber are really some of the finest and most reliable friends you will ever have.

CHAPTER 5

REBELLION

The Conservative Party in Parliament is no different from any other: they all have their factions. In Thatcher's days it was between 'wet' and 'dry'. This was because she would have the habit of writing 'wet' in the margins of papers or memos from ministers that she thoroughly disagreed with. So those of us on the One Nation side of the party were branded the wets. She is alleged to have said that I was so wet that you could shoot snipe off me.

It wasn't long before I was approached to join a group called the Lollards. We were called this because we met in Bill van Straubenzee's Church Commissioners' flat at Lambeth Palace. The idea was that we would do battle for the party committees with the dries, whose grouping in those days was called the 92. This was founded by Sir Patrick Wall at his home in 92 Cheyne Walk. We both had slates. For us it was a bit of a waste of time as there were more of them, they were better organised and we were a delightful shambles. I remember trying to persuade some of our wealthier and more patrician members to vote for these committees which in reality had very little influence. The excuses were wonderfully laid-back. 'So sorry, old boy, country house party … My dear chap, got a bit of fishing laid on.' And that was the problem: we wets coasted by knowing that the Thatcher machine, like Amazon forest loggers, moved on relentlessly, slashing and burning as we indigenous peoples had our way of life gradually destroyed.

But we Lollards weren't into plotting. Well, not very effectively. We moaned and groaned to each other that the wets were gradually being driven out of Cabinet: Sir Ian Gilmour, Mark Carlisle and Norman St John-Stevas for starters.

Norman was a lovely man. Very bright, very arch, delightfully camp, with a razor-sharp wit. No pretty waiter was safe. What did for him was his waspish humour. The Lady began to tire of his little nicknames for her – 'the immaculate misconception' … 'Attila the Hen' … 'She who must be obeyed'. Once, at a meeting, she suggested that they finish early as she and Norman were going to the opera and he needed more time to get ready than she did. He had a wonderful collection of Queen Victoria's stockings, which he kept in his bathroom.

To be honest, the only committee that really mattered was the 1922, the Tory backbench trade union. They would have regular meetings with the Lady and were so stuffed with her supporters that it was no more than a love-in. Sir Edward du Cann (whom I rather liked) was the chairman. He was a serious operator, but unfortunately got rather tied up with Tiny Rowland's business, Lonrho, which Ted Heath described as the 'unacceptable face of capitalism'. I once had lunch with Rowland's biographer Tom Bower, who wrote biographies of the likes of Maxwell and Al Fayed.

'Who did you like least?' I asked.

'Oh, Tiny. He used to have people killed in Africa.'

I am not suggesting for one moment that Edward knew

or condoned any of this. If he had had the slightest suspicion he would have been out of that company faster than a flasher's mac.

Du Cann was beautifully smooth. Listening to one of his speeches was like wiping your arse with silk. He was also very obliging. The joke was that if you asked him the time he would coo, 'And what time would you want it to be, dear boy?' Once, I shocked the grandees by rushing back for an unexpected vote straight from the gym, still in Lycra. Some of the old boys were apoplectic with indignation. Edward just sidled up and said, 'How delightful you look, dear boy.'

He once told me how Harold Macmillan had invited him in to discuss the possibility of his joining the government. Edward expressed concern about needing to earn some money (like me, he was always fairly broke). In times of difficulty, Mac always poured a large sherry. Du Cann joined the government.

Over the years he attracted rather a bad press, somewhat unfairly. But he was always kind and courteous to me and my friends. He was a gentleman rather than a shit. But a serious player, whom I hope history will not overlook. He skilfully papered over the serious cracks within the party. He was the consummate chairman of the '22.

It wasn't long before I made a very serious error of judgement. Sadly, one of many. I was approached by an emissary of Francis Pym, by now a sacked Foreign Secretary and more bitter than the lemon in his gin, asking if I wanted to join a new policy group to discuss ways in which Thatcherism could be given a more human face. It was to be called Centre Forward. I really should have seen what was going to happen next. The members were the usual suspects: Alan Haselhurst,

David Knox, Hugh Dykes, Peter Temple-Morris. The decent, caring wing of the Conservative Party. And those who were rumoured to have considered defecting to the SDP in 1981.

When I look back it was a rather tame affair, but when news leaked out the Downing Street rubbish machine went into overdrive. You have to understand that Downing Street is designed for one purpose only – to protect the Prime Minister. We were not plotting her downfall, just putting together policies that would put the government more in touch with what people really wanted. Yet at that time she didn't need too much protection.

It was all leaked to the *Sunday Times*, where I was pictured as a 'leader' of this dissident group. Half a dozen of our photographs straddled the front page, making us look like the FBI's most wanted. Next Monday, Norman St John-Stevas spotted me in the lobby, doffed his cloth cap (yes, he really wore one, but it was probably from Lockes), grinned 'hail to my leader' and wiggled into the distance.

What really screwed things up was a speech about to be given by Francis Pym. He told us that it would be mildly critical. I wish it had been. It turned into a personal attack on Thatcher as the sort of woman who hoards tinned goods in the larder. It was actually a reference to a photo shoot by the Saatchis showing her as a prudent housewife when Leader of the Opposition. My constituency association were not at all amused. And the press were after my blood. I panicked and resigned from the committee (as did Tony Baldry). That night, in the division lobby, a very angry David Knox pulled me to one side and testily called me a 'silly, silly boy'. He was right. My error of judgement was not joining the group, but failing to have the courage to publicly argue our corner and not run away at the first whiff of cordite. What a pathetic, cowardly little fool I was. I would never make the same mistake again.

On the night of my fall into ignominy I was invited to drinks with Transport Secretary and arch-Thatcherite Nick Ridley. He gave me some very wise advice. 'In politics, always shoot to kill, never to wound. A wounded animal is a danger-ous and unpredictable beast.' How right he was.

But there was one rather touching tale. After the story first broke, Alan Haselhurst and I were caught talking on a landing in hushed tones by the Lady's PPS, Michael Alison. He even saw us exchange a package. Heaven knows what he reported back to No. 10. The truth is that Alan is one of my dearest friends (who should have been Speaker if the Amish wing of the party hadn't blocked him). The *sotto voce* plotting we were doing was merely sorting out the dates for his godson (my son Lawrence)'s first birthday party. And the mysterious package? A handgun with ammunition? A hand grenade? A deadly poison? No, a yellow mechanical teddy bear for his cot. Thank heavens the *Mail* didn't get hold of that one. He would have been branded the Godfather.

❦

One of the duller duties of an MP is to be a silent muppet on a standing committee – a phenomenal waste of time. The idea is that you are meant to scrutinise legislation. The reality was that government backbenchers were drilled not to say a word, allowing the Opposition to drone on, and then the 'improved' Bill would be presented to the Commons for a third-reading debate before being sent to the Lords, who would seriously have a good look at it and hopefully sort out all the problems created by the lower House. I was put on something called the Health and Medicine Bill as I knew absolutely nothing about either health or medicine. The ideal candidate.

In a bored moment I sat down and read the Bill. I was shocked. It was an utter disgrace. The plan was to save the NHS thirty million quid and this was to be done by abolishing the free sight test and the free dental check-up. 'So what?' you might ask. Just remember that diseases of the eye are silent. A sight test can diagnose glaucoma, HIV and many other diseases. As can the dental check-up, which can spot HIV and cancer of the mouth. Here we were saying to the public that we as a government believed in preventative healthcare but condemning thousands of state pensioners to a life of blindness. That we, as a government who believed in curtailing the spread of HIV and cancer, were condemning thousands to an early death. Of course, it was Treasury-led and backed by an utterly hopeless Secretary of State, John Moore, who, on his appointment, told Cabinet that he could deliver a world-class health service for less money. Oh dear.

And yet this was not the first time these dreadful proposals had been attempted. Before the 1983 election the ministerial line was that these proposals would be 'wrong in principle and act as a deterrent to those who should be encouraged to have their eyes and teeth tested'.

Well, I did what was sensible by the rules. I pleaded with the whips and the Secretary of State. A total waste of time.

So, me and the feisty Jill Knight (now Baroness Knight), a close friend of the Lady and an old-fashioned but decent right-winger, joined forces. She was an expert as her husband was an optician. The rebellion was also joined by a new up-and-coming right-winger named David Davis, who once told me that his favourite pastime in politics was 'bayoneting the wounded'. A good guy.

Well, I did not remain silent as required by the whips. And the committee whip was an old friend called David Lightbown. David was the enforcer. He was twenty-five stone and was not a pushover in any sense. He used to run a factory in Birmingham. When the first IRA bomb went off in Brum, he called in his Irish workforce and sacked them all. He was known as the 'caring' whip.

So, in committee I made a speech quoting all the Cabinet in their letters to constituents in 1979 saying that the plans were 'wrong in principle'. I finished up with a letter from a lady saying the very same thing. It was Margaret Thatcher, written on her prime ministerial notepaper. There was uproar. The caring whip bundled me outside. 'You little cunt, you have just destroyed the Cabinet for writing letters that go back to the days of Gladstone.'

I demurred.

'No more overseas trips for you, lad.'

'Actually, I don't want any.'

'Well, I'll make sure you are deselected then.'

'Well, I did call a meeting of my executive last night and they fully support me.'

And this is when things became little more heated.

'You little shit,' as he thumped me in the chest.

'Oh fuck off, you fat twat,' as I kicked him in the balls.

We were so grown-up in those days. The art of intellectual

debate was alive and kicking. Well, at least kicking. The lovely David Hunt, now Lord Hunt of Wirral, then Deputy Chief Whip, commented to the press that he couldn't possibly adjudicate on every fight in the playground. A few weeks later he pulled me aside and said that if I could vote continuously for the government for six months he would make me a minister. Sadly, I failed.

And then came the third-reading debate of the Health and Medicine Bill. David Mellor was the lead minister. The government's majority on this Bill was in serious jeopardy. And he was pretty annoyed that I had appeared simultaneously on every television channel the night before, and particularly miffed that I had written a prominent piece in the *Evening Standard* which had just hit the news-stands. So, being the sort of man who enjoyed a scrap, he launched into me in a rather personal way.

'Well, my Hon. friend the Member for Harlow would have got a larger fee for his piece in the *Evening Standard* than a sight check would cost if this Bill is passed,' he glowered. This was a strategic mistake. MPs can just about stomach voting for unspeakable crap on whips' orders, but they detest having to put up with a bumptious minister slagging off someone they know is on the right side of the argument. My *Standard* piece had been commissioned by the wonderful Sarah Sands (she of the perpetually undone extra blouse button; now editor of the *Standard*) but I had totally forgotten to ask for a fee.

'I did it for free,' I shouted, glowing with accidental righteousness.

Ian Gow, former PPS to the Lady, was outraged with Mellor. He stormed out of the chamber and would have missed the vote had Thatcher not despatched the police to find him. That night, the government's massive majority was reduced to four. Aha, I thought. This could be fun in the Lords. So it was time to hatch a plot.

I knew Rebecca Runcie rather well, the daughter of Bob, who was then Archbishop of Canterbury and who had won the MC for killing a few Germans. That was about the only thing that Thatcher agreed with him on. He thought the proposals were outrageous too. So we thought of a cunning scheme. He couldn't tell his mad right-wing bishops what to do. But he could send them off for trips abroad on the night of the vote. And this is what he did. But we still lost. As I was sitting up in the MPs' gallery when the result was announced, I caught the eye of John Belstead, leader of the Lords, who shrugged his shoulders with sadness. He was against the Health and Medicine Bill too. Government is a very strange business. And I had become a rebel.

Since the Health and Medicine Bill and the ambulance dispute (which is in another chapter), Ken Clarke thought it would be a good idea to use my energy in a positive way. He asked me to travel the country and persuade GPs that their new contract was a good idea. This was a very tricky job. The British Medical Association is the most ruthless trade union in Britain and they fight low and dirty. Anything that does not provide their members with pots of gold and anything that involves a little bit more work and commitment will be portrayed as an attack on patients, particularly the weak and the vulnerable.

Actually, the Clarke proposals were perfectly sensible, but the BMA was causing trouble. In those days people really trusted doctors and when notices appeared in surgeries urging patients to sign petitions, there was a groundswell of opinion against the proposed contract. This had to be negatived.

At the height of the debate, when tensions were high, I managed to get my todger caught in my flies. It was so painful that I went to see my GP. As I put the poor little thing in his hand, he smiled. 'Is this a good time to discuss our new contract?'

'Ha, bloody ha,' I laughed through the tears.

When I look back, I really didn't vote against the government a great deal. I followed the advice of Harold Macmillan to rebel only on one issue at a time. I suspect what gave me the reputation of being more of a nuisance than I actually was is that when I appeared in the media and was asked a direct question I more often than not gave a straight answer, which was sometimes off-message. In those days the right regarded this as bordering on the treasonous. But if the message is rubbish, what's the point of being an MP?

CHAPTER 6

THE CONSTITUENCY

It is fashionable for commentators to argue for politicians to 'speak human'. This really is the most dreadful nonsense. What the electorate want is for politicians to *be* human. They are fed up with evasive answers from ministers and backbenchers with all the warmth of a speaking clock. It is so obviously a 'line to take'. But what does depress me is that too many politicians don't care for people too much. Their votes, yes. But as people? No way. These types are sadly a growing minority. I remember working a room with a new Member who is now a perfectly adequate minister. He pulled me aside and groaned, 'But aren't they all so awful?' I tried to explain to him that some of them were, but most were just decent people who have never met an MP in their lives before. Be polite, be kind and don't look over their shoulder to find someone to speak to who will be more important for your ghastly career. The likes of him just don't understand that most people are rarely, if ever, likely to meet an MP more than once. If it is a pleasant experience, they will tell all their friends. If it is all about more me, me, mes than Pavarotti, they will tell even more friends what an absolute shit you are.

I know this may sound completely irrational as someone

who was elected for fourteen years, but I really despise tribal politics. Of course, come an election, I can get as low-down and dirty as anyone. But I hate looking at issues under the party political microscope. That is why, apart from general elections, Harlow for me was a politics-free zone. The most important job of an MP is not to be a slave to the whims of your postbag, but to do your best to protect and help your constituents, try to solve their problems and just be there for them in times of need.

It is really not all that difficult if you have a bit of common sense, a semblance of education and a strong desire to do what you think is right, even if the party hierarchy disagree. And the headed notepaper helps a lot, too. So the biggest high you can ever get out of politics is sorting out problems which may seem the end of the world to so many but which you personally can actually resolve. That is the job I really loved.

Selection as a candidate was a weird process. As I've told you, I wasn't even on the candidates list, but luckily my opponents were even more eccentric than I was. Eventually I got the nomination and many assumed that as we couldn't possibly win I should just do the respectable minimum and use Harlow as a launching pad for a safe seat. Wrong. I'd got there and as hopeless as it seemed I was going to give it a go.

In those days Harlow Council was very, very left-wing. When I was elected there wasn't a single Tory on the council. So who was going to sort the election out? Well, I had a lovely old lady from Liverpool called Rose Dickson who was my chairman. And that was about it. So I asked a bright young lad of nineteen called Guy Mitchell to be my election agent (I think I paid him £100) and another youngster called Stephen

Rigden (whom I didn't pay a penny) to be my gofer. They both were brilliant, hardworking and loyal. I owe them an awful lot.

My first priority was to canvass the council estates. The old school thought I was wasting my time. But Thatcher had changed the landscape. Firstly by allowing people to take pride in their council homes (Georgian front doors) and secondly by letting them buy them at massive discounts. So, rather than the abuse that everyone had expected on the doorstep, it was, 'Well, I've bought my home so I suppose I must be a Tory.' Too bloody right, matey. Oh, and the Falklands War helped a bit too. I'd love to be part of the delusion that so many MPs have first time round: 'It was my genius wot won it.' No, old son, you got in on the coat tails of your leader, and 'events'.

I won't bore you with the nuts and bolts of the 1983 election, but one story comes to mind. I was in a particularly grand village (yes, we had them) where every Conservative Party branch meeting started with the list of people 'we would consider for membership'. What a joke. They were actually sifting through candidates! For me this was too grim for words, so I found a list of 'unacceptables' and banged on their doors. My favourite was a house with a brass plate engraved 'Mr and Mrs Dave the Deal'. Another joy was going to a mock Palladian mansion with the most amazingly expensive furniture and paintings. Here in the great hall was an enormously obese haulier throwing darts at a board adjacent to a Gainsborough. These guys were loaded, and donated, but the local party was just too snooty to talk to them.

Once, I popped my card through the door of a bed and breakfast. The poor chap had had a little spot of bother with the police over some minor matter regarding guns. He was so delighted to hear from me that he offered to drive voters to the poll on election night. What was so amazing was that he rolled up with chauffeurs in full livery driving Rollers. Can you imagine driving up to a Tory voter on a council estate with a Rolls-Royce and a liveried driver saying, 'This is Mr Hayes's lift to take you to the polling station'?

However, there was one minor hiccup. A couple of Labour pensioners decided to take advantage and let slip to the driver that they were actually going to vote for my opponent. I asked him how he dealt with it. 'Oh, I dropped them in the middle of nowhere and told them to fuck off.' Not my proudest moment. But the damage was done. I dreaded the headlines. Mercifully, they never came.

A few months before the election, I appeared in court for a young couple who were being evicted from their flat because of drunken parties and an infestation of rats. In evidence, it appeared that they were a rather pleasant pair having a bit of fun. I asked the girl about the rat infestation. She smiled sweetly and told the court that they indeed had a pet rat. I enquired if she had a photograph of it. At that she did better and produced the rat from her pocket. I thought that the old judge was going to have a fit. Far from it, by chance he was a rat fancier, picked the horrible little thing up and tickled his tummy. It transpired that the landlords were just trying to get the property back. So I gave the landlord and his wife absolute hell in the witness box and won the case.

During the election I banged on the door of rather an imposing property. To my horror it was opened by the landlord and his wife. This was going to be a nightmare. So I apologised for disturbing them and said I wouldn't dream of asking them to vote for me after giving them such a rough time in court. To my amazement I was offered an outstretched hand, a smile and not just an offer of support but a donation too. Their logic was that, if I could move heaven and hell against them, what could I do *for* them?

Elections are a funny old business.

Although I was delighted to win in 1983, I felt sorry for the guy I beat, the veteran left-winger Stan Newens. I made a particular point of devoting a large part of my acceptance speech to paying tribute to him, as he was an excellent constituency MP and a thoroughly decent man. Politics can be a rough game and no matter how good you are you can't beat a big swing.

At least I didn't make the mistake of my old pupil master, Ernle Money, who totally unexpectedly beat Sir Dingle Foot in Ipswich in 1970. Ernle didn't even bother to roll up for the count; he just went to the White Swan and got very, very drunk. When his agent realised that Ernle was going to win and have to make a speech he scoured the pubs and eventually found him in a heap. The poor chap couldn't even walk, let alone talk. So the agent went back and made the speech for him, along the lines that Mr Money held Sir Dingle in such high esteem he felt it quite inappropriate to say a few words. Deft footwork.

Surgeries (they are now called advice bureaux) were very rewarding and sometimes a little peculiar. My first constituent was a 93-year-old Chinese man who came to pay his respects, bless him. He didn't have a word of intelligible English and after many smiles and much mutual bowing I led him to the lift, which broke down and we had to call the fire brigade.

Although I think that my wife Alison, who was taking the notes, broke down far worse than the lift as she had to leave the room in fits of giggles.

Then there was a flasher who actually arrived in a dirty mac and wondered if the new Public Order Act would curtail his right to publicly expose himself. I explained to him that it didn't but that it was against the law anyway. He went away muttering how dreadfully unfair it was.

And then there was Mr O'Brien. He hadn't paid any rates or rent for years, as he had named his council house The Freehold. He used to complain that he had been disenfranchised as the council refused to put him on the electoral roll. I asked him if he had ever applied. 'Certainly not. It is a breach of my privacy.' Mr O'Brien was an absolute pain to all incumbents. But one day he saved my bacon. Socialist Workers were demonstrating outside my surgery one day and there was a TV crew in attendance. One of the smelly-socks threw an egg at me just as Mr O'Brien was passing by. I grabbed him and the egg exploded onto his jacket. To which I shouted at the camera, 'Look what these wicked people have done to a poor pensioner.' Then I led him away, gave him a tenner for the dry cleaners and suggested he sod off.

Then there was an intriguing old fellow, a very tall, elderly Irishman built like an ox, who had a grievance that Joe Jennings the bookmakers had failed to pay out a winning over twenty years ago. It was complete nonsense as the locals told me that he had collected the cash, spent it all on booze and passed out. But once a month he would appear. On one occasion he rolled up at a public meeting flourishing a piece of paper. 'I have here a letter from Her Majesty the Queen. She has written that Jerry Hayes is both a liar and a wanker.' I had a sneaking suspicion that this may have been a forgery.

The trouble was that he stayed around afterwards and I was rather worried that he was going to thump me. Eventually it was just me and this enormous bear of a man. And he was coming for me. Mercifully, I remembered that he had been a proud soldier during the war. 'Seamus!' I shouted in my best sergeant-major voice. 'Atten-*shun*!' And all that training from all those years ago clicked in. He stood ramrod straight as I slipped out of the back door.

Almost as scary was when a troubled young man bit the ear off a constituent in the waiting room. I thought this was right out of order so I chased after him and had a bit of a scuffle, both of us rolling around on the market square. I soon realised that I was in trouble, as he was a very big lad. Luckily, someone came to my rescue and the police arrived.

Years later I heard that he had been imprisoned for attempted murder. Then I had a phone call from the chief constable to say that the fellow had confessed to a probation officer that he had plans to kill me. I immediately wrote to Angela Rumbold, the Prisons Minister. A month later I received a reply. It was not very cheering. That a prison shrink had been to see him. That the fellow had decided not to kill me after all. And that he had been released two weeks earlier. Thanks a bunch, Angela.

But the majority of the people I saw had serious problems. Three stick in my mind. One, a delightful foster parent who had looked after a young Nigerian girl since she was a toddler. When the child turned fifteen her mother flew over, kidnapped her and took her back to Nigeria. I had an adjournment debate, meetings with the Foreign Secretary, and eventually I had a meeting with the Nigerian High Commissioner. And what a disaster that was. All the secretaries were dressed in very expensive frocks and the High Commissioner was dripping in gold and a well-tailored Armani suit. Yet his office in those days was ramshackle. All he did was give me a lecture on British colonialism, then said there was a cultural problem and that he could do nothing. The complacent little shit.

Years later I received a lovely letter from the foster mother, thanking me for all my help. Ronke had reached the age of majority and returned home.

But the most moving story of all, which makes me well up just writing this, was a lovely couple who brought their seriously ill daughter to see me, a tiny frail child. She had been pronounced fit to fly by their GP and covered by insurance to have one last holiday with her mum, dad and brother. Sadly, the Greeks gave her the wrong drugs and she needed to be rushed home to a British hospital. The insurance company, a well-known and well-respected one, went back on their policy and refused to fly her back by air ambulance. They would only provide a seat on a charter flight for her and her father. The rest of the family was made to stay in Greece until the holiday ended. Can you imagine the flight, with the father with his dying child, administering morphine suppositories to ease her terrible pain? I am happy to say that I savaged the reputation of that ghastly company on the floor of the House and in the media. The family received compensation but a few weeks later their beloved Sally Ann died. This wonderful family queued up for three hours just to thank me. And yet what had I done? Nothing of substance. When they gave me the news I am not ashamed to say that I totally broke down. There was much crying and hugs all round.

The other incident that moved me, in a rather different way, was when the family of a young warrant officer based in Hong Kong came to see me. He was just about to be awarded the British Empire Medal by the Governor, my old mate Chris Patten. They were the only family he had and they wanted to see their son's moment of pride. They were the sort of people you would describe as the salt of the earth. Kind, decent, had worked hard all of their lives, but relied totally on their state pensions. They had as much chance of getting to Hong Kong as flying to the moon. So I wrote to the Secretary of State for Defence. No joy. And to Chris Patten. Nothing. Nobody would help. And then I remembered that the Swire family were a great benefactor to Old Harlow as their old family home had been converted into St Nicholas School. They own Cathay Pacific and are a thoroughly decent bunch. So I wrote to John Swire and explained the problem. Within a couple of days I received a wonderful letter from him. He was a major in the last war. Warrant officers were the backbone of the British Army. The MOD had behaved like tossers. So he flew this lovely old couple out first class and put them up in his finest hotel. What a gentleman.

I know this book is not meant to be terribly serious, but being a Member of Parliament exposes you to the realisation that the British are a kind, generous and tolerant people. It also makes you understand that so many find themselves in dire and tragic circumstances and bear it with great courage. To try to help them is a privilege far more precious than any office of state.

One of the things an MP has to do is keep their finger on the pulse of what is happening in the major public services. This means regular visits to hospitals, the fire service and the police. Policing in Harlow changed round about the 1990s. Before that, a couple of times a year I would have a great lunch with my divisional commander. These guys would be down-to-earth, practical and loved by their men. The meetings were incredibly valuable and I learned a lot about practical policing. Then, in the 1990s, it all changed. Rather than a few sharpeners in the office and then a cracking good lunch I was greeted by young men who were on the accelerated promotion scheme. Clever fellows, with good degrees, who had spent a few months on the beat then quickly got promoted to sergeant, then inspector, and then off to the office of the chief constable to think of wonderful wheezes to arrange his sock drawer and reorganise the paper clips. Ask for a drink and Satan had entered the room. From a few stiff whiskies and a couple of bottles of red to mineral water and sandwiches. Smooth PR guys with plastic smiles and an eye for the main chance. I was not there to be educated nor to bounce ideas off, but to assist in the next stepping stone of their ghastly careers. They didn't want to discuss policing but policy. Ye gods.

However, there was one little ray of sunshine. One senior officer was having an affair with one of the girls in the finance department. They used to have passionate trysts in the glades of Epping Forest – until it hit the red tops. All caught on film and sound. How could this have happened? The officer forgot that he had approved a surveillance operation of some very dodgy people ... in Epping Forest. One sergeant who led the surveillance team said to me after the miscreant had retired over ill health, 'I think the boys need counselling. It was enough to put you off tapioca and cocktail sausages for life.'

Harlow Council was a funny old set-up. It was outrageously left-wing when I was elected. Ken Livingstone would have been regarded as a bit of a Tory. Back in the day, they used to have late-night debates over the Vietnam War.

At first they regarded me as a terrible right-wing aberration (I think the Lady might have disagreed). My first story in the *Harlow Gazette* seriously upset the comrades. The mere fact that I had been mentioned almost favourably led the council to threaten their advertising revenues if I was ever mentioned again. The reporter, the lovely Ailsa Macintyre, whose fearless reporting I am indebted to, has now moved horribly downmarket. She is now Ailsa Anderson, formerly the press secretary to the Queen and now press secretary to the Archbishop of Canterbury. She is very good news.

Eventually, I rather warmed to the council. We eyed each other very suspiciously. They had never engaged with a Tory before. And then they found one who didn't want to grind the faces of the poor into the dirt and who had a social conscience. It made them very, very confused.

The man I had to do business with was their general manager. Many councillors couldn't understand why he had to talk to me at all. Actually, he was a really good guy and was at pains to explain to them that although I was a wicked Tory I would be willing to try and help them. His name was Dermot Byrne and his son is the well-known Labour politician Liam. Both are good blokes.

But I can understand why the local Labour Party viewed me with such suspicion. These people had come from the East End of London. The boss classes had ripped the heart out of them. The unions, and eventually Labour, had given them a voice and dignity. In those days the Tory politicians were a pretty grim bunch. In fact, my grandmother and most of her family were socialists. She was married to the welterweight world boxing champion, Jimmy Hicks. Sadly, he practised on her. As a working-class woman she went to the police many times to tell them about his brutality. They told her that's what happens in marriage. It's what a woman should expect. Bravely, she divorced him in 1905. Strange that so many years later they both ended up with dementia in the same hospital in adjoining beds. Neither had a clue who the other was. It was desperately sad. My grandmother was a very brave woman. To keep her family of seven in food and clothes she scrubbed the floors of an orphanage. It is now the Snaresbrook Crown Court. When I appear there I feel proud that my grandmother once cleaned those floors to keep my mother alive.

But enough of sentimentality, let's get back to Harlow. I was amazingly lucky to have such great ground troops. Mind you, they were getting on a bit. But they were loyal and hardworking. In the run-up to the 1997 election, which I was doomed to lose, I had a phone call from the chairman of a safe seat. Would I like to stand? Of course I bloody would. But how could I look those who had worked so hard to get me elected in the eye again? For me it was a no-brainer. But the chicken run before the 1997 election, where sitting MPs jumped ship for safer berths, was a disgrace.

I know all MPs say this, but I am so grateful for those who worked so hard for me. Most hadn't a penny to rub together.

During one election, I remember being chased down the road by some fellow who had my election address rolled up in his hand. He was threatening to shove it where the sun doesn't shine. 'Not unless I get to you first,' said I, on my charm offensive. A bit of a bundle ensued. Then he took a good look at me. ''Ere, you're that Jerry Hayes.'

'Yes,' I gasped.

'Sorry, mate, got you muddled with that Labour twat. Fifty quid all right?'

And it was. Harlow was a great place to represent.

And so, David and Betty Roberts, my loyal chairman and friends, and my last agent, Marion Little, thank you for your love and forbearance and for realising that I can be a bit of a handful. And for not telling too many people about it.

But how could I forget Rita Whyte? She was a great supporter who was the former deputy head of a primary school. She spent her life on the run from an abusive husband. Yet her son became an assistant chief constable and her daughter a chairman of a county council. So, when my party start having a go at single mothers I always take a deep breath and will never forget this remarkable woman. I was very proud to take her to a Buckingham Palace garden party before she died.

But the image that will stick in my mind more than any other is when Saddam Hussein visited Harlow. Well, sort of. In the middle of the first Iraq War, Harlow Council gave me a wonderful political present. The daft lefties refused to fly the Union flag over the town hall. When our boys were putting their lives at risk? Insane. So I contacted my mates on the super soar-away *Sun*. I was told to meet a pleasant guy called Robert Jobson at the Harlow Moat House at 9 a.m. for breakfast the next day. So up I rolled to find the normally sleepy dining room packed. Must be some bloody convention. How was I supposed to find Robert? So I stood on a chair and asked if anyone was there from *The Sun*. Much hilarity. They *all* were.

The Sun then invaded Harlow with two tanks, three Page Three lovelies and a Saddam Hussein lookalike. This was spread over three pages the next day, topped with a cartoon of Saddam on the balcony of Harlow Town Hall, doing a Nazi salute. Harlow Council was of course flying the Iraqi flag. Sadly, the lefties didn't see the funny side of all this at all.

Being an MP is round after round of opening things. And I loved it. Harlow is infested with little plaques bearing my name. If you want to have look at a rather expensive brass one, pop in to the Beefeater Inn just outside North Weald. I was told there was going to be a parachute display and then a formal opening. So I peered into the sky and noticed a few little black dots. Then parachutes opened. But as they came nearer to earth they didn't get an awful lot bigger. And they were all very round. When they landed I realised that Beefeater had parachuted in five dwarves dressed as Mr Men Beefeaters. They formed a guard of honour for me to open the place. The things one has to do.

Although I have always enjoyed swanning around being pleasant to people, you really need a great team to back you up.

My wife Alison was a top secretary before I poached her, and with her deputy, Jan, they kept the whole show on the road. It meant Ali could work from home and be there for our two very small children. I had a reputation for dealing with problems quickly and efficiently, but the truth is it was really them. These sorts of partnerships are good for democracy, constituents and family life. But since the expenses scandal, employing any relative is regarded as a mortal sin. That is desperately sad.

CHAPTER 7

BIG BEASTS

L ooking back on my days in the Commons is like reflecting on my childhood. All the days seemed to be sunny and the characters larger than life. But I am pretty sure that they were always far more interesting than today's lot. Many of them are pretty vanilla.

Nick Soames is a case in point. Larger than life in every sense. I am not sure how much he weighs, but were he the Aga Khan, who balances himself against a tray of gold and diamonds every year (God knows why), he would be a very wealthy man. Being the grandson of Winston Churchill mercifully hasn't given him airs and graces. It is also surprising that he is not some hang 'em and flog 'em man of the shires. He, like me, is very much a One Nation Tory (not in the ridiculous Miliband sense), which basically means that we are not obsessed with the certainty that the Germans will soon be jackbooting their way down the Mall and big fat sweating Belgians ordering that our railway timetables be translated into Walloon. In other words, we see the world and its problems pragmatically.

But Nick does have his delightful moments of innocence. In the 1980s in a BBC recording studio the sound man always needed to have a 'level', so he would ask what we had had for breakfast and adjust the sound accordingly with our reply. One of Nick's earliest broadcasts went like this.

'For the level, Mr Soames, what did you have for breakfast, sir?'

'Oh, some cold grouse and half a bottle of breakfast claret. What about you, old boy?'

Once, he came into the Smoking Room rather ashen-faced and sank a large gin and tonic.

'I'm afraid I've done something quite unforgivable,' he wailed.

He had just received a delegation of single mothers and had been rather sniffy about feckless women.

'Feckless, Mr Soames? We are all Falklands widows.' The poor fellow was utterly mortified.

He once told me his father's advice on marriage: 'Get your cock in the till, son.'

Not that either did. And, of course, no paragraph on Nick Soames could ever be complete without the words, which I am sure are apocryphal, of his first wife: 'Having Nick make love to you is like having a wardrobe fall on top of you with the key still in.'

But my favourite story was when, as a young man, he went up to his grandfather asking if he was the most famous man in the world.

'Yes. Now sod off.'

I know Nick can be a bit bombastic in the Toad of Toad Hall sense, but I have a soft spot for him because, beneath all the bluster, he is rather a sensitive soul.

Unlike some others. I suspect that John Prescott has a sensitive side to him; it's just that it is not very apparent if you are a Tory, since he thinks we really are lower than vermin. It was probably being a steward on the cruise liners and having to serve Anthony Eden and his ghastly braying entourage that gave Prescott his hatred not just for the policies but for the class. Although he did get his own back on a particularly patronising Eden by 'accidentally' spilling scalding-hot soup onto his crotch.

I often attempted to be jolly with him but never succeeded in breaking through the barrier. Once, we both appeared (in different studios) on the *Today* programme. I was being at my most irritatingly jovial and gave Prezza a few playful metaphorical jabs. I thought nothing of it until I bumped into him in the Members' lobby later that day. With my legendary judgement and timing I thought this was the time to complete my charm offensive. So I bounced up to him with a grin.

'Hi, John, that was a bit of fun this morning, wasn't it?'

All I can remember is a jab in the solar plexus and a low primal growl. 'You little Tory cunt.'

And then Labour Chief Whip Derek Foster grinning from ear to ear, saying, 'Nice fellow, isn't he?' I've been boring friends with this story for years.

But Thumper once did come a cropper in the chamber.

It was a dozy, balmy afternoon, with a dreary debate so dull that nature has excised it from my memory. The Labour front bench, including Prescott, was fairly comatose, while David Blunkett's guide dog was snoozing away. I can't remember whether it was Sadie or Offa. It was probably the one that used to let off the sort of farts that could strip wallpaper and clear whole rooms. Devastating in a TV studio, where crew staggered for the exit like soldiers in the Great War after a mustard gas attack. Anyhow, the dog had a very long lead that had entwined itself round the legs of the Labour front bench. Suddenly, a couple of well-refreshed Tory lads who had just staggered into the chamber thought it was time for a bit of sport. So they started staring into the eyes of the dog, growling and generally winding it up. In the end the poor mutt became so annoyed at having its afternoon nap disturbed that it got up and shook itself. Not good news for the Labour front bench entwined in the lead. They went down like ninepins. All very childish. But very, very funny.

Former Belfast MP Gerry Fitt was a tremendous character and enormously brave. He had been bombed out of his Belfast home and always returned. The final straw was when he fought off gunmen on the stairs. Thatcher, to her credit, made him a life peer and he returned to London.

Gerry was a prodigious drinker. He was rarely seen without an industrial-sized gin and tonic in his hand. When on the terrace he would wave to passing pleasure boats, raising his glass with the salute 'It's all free.' Sadly, it wasn't.

If he wasn't on the terrace he could be seen with his long-suffering armed detective, chugging along the Thames in his little boat, gin and tonic in hand, entreating us to join him. The trouble is that Gerry tried to insist that his detective match him drink for drink. As the man was packing a weapon he politely declined, but agreed to join him drink for drink with tonic water. A few weeks later he was rushed to hospital. It took a while for the consultants to work out what was wrong. It was an unusual condition: quinine poisoning as a result of an overdose of tonic water. Well, at least he would never suffer from malaria.

Gerry was the father-in-law of broadcaster Vincent Hanna, who sadly died before him. I once appeared on his late-night TV show just before the end of the 1992 general election. It was an interesting panel: Ben Elton, Tim Rice, Austin Mitchell and me. Austin and I were so exhausted from campaigning that we spent the first five minutes on air fast asleep. We awoke to the horror of Vincent announcing to the viewers that his guests were going to sing a song. And we did. It was all very odd.

But not as odd as the week before, when I appeared on a popular yoof programme called *The Word*, which had become notorious for the outrageous antics of its presenter, Terry Christian. I suspect that I was asked because of an appearance months before on a dreadful little show when I'd become really exasperated by a ghastly presenter trying to make a name for himself by being rude to politicians. After about five minutes of cringe-making questions I'd finally been asked, 'And what's the worst sexual experience you've ever had?'

My reply, not exactly Tolstoy, shut the little creep up.

'Your mother.'

The Word thought that they would be very clever and set up me and controversial Tottenham MP Bernie Grant with a *Generation Game* conveyor belt with everyday items on it for us to price. There was no problem until it came to a packet of condoms. I hadn't a clue. So I pleaded ignorance, saying that I only bought my condoms by the gross and with spikes on. That at least made the hooched-up teenage audience less likely to brain me.

But back to the big beasts. One of my first excursions into the Members' dining room was a chance encounter with the Reverend Ian Paisley. I saw him sitting on his own, so I thought I'd be polite, and plonked myself down. And being even more polite, I asked if he'd care to share a bottle of wine.

Not terribly bright. I learned that night that the DUP don't approve of booze.

In his drinking days, the Press Association's legendary Chris Moncrieff went to interview the big man. Clearly he smelt like a Guinness brewery. Paisley exploded, refusing to be interviewed by a man who had 'the devil's buttermilk on his breath'.

However, a few years later me and an Ulster Unionist MP decided to set the big man up. When dining together we provided him with a riddle, with the bet that in the unlikely event of him cracking it we would buy him the most expensive pudding on the Commons menu. Of course we set the riddle ridiculously easy so he couldn't lose. The prize pudding duly arrived and the big man got stuck in. About five minutes into his pud, my chum, in fits of giggles, sniffed the air.

'Ian, I can smell the devil's buttermilk on your breath.'

Then I got a fit of the giggles. Then we had to explain that the pudding that he had won was actually laced with about three liqueurs.

We looked apprehensively at the big man, but the expected explosion never came. Just a chuckle and then a booming laugh. But he never finished his pudding. I once asked him if he would ever pray for me, as I was a Catholic.

'Certainly. But not when you're dead.'

With Paisley I got away with just a polite smile every time we met, despite the fact that I had enough devil's buttermilk in me to make a rather large Satanic cheese. He probably wouldn't get on terribly well with Mike Burns, who was the larger-than-life political editor of Irish television, RTÉ. I am convinced that the man could walk on water (provided it was well diluted with Jameson's Irish whiskey). Once, he found to his horror that the train taking MPs and the press back from a Blackpool Conservative Party conference had no buffet car. Journalists retired to the hotel bar in a state of shock. Mike just rang up the chairman of British Rail and it was sorted within the hour. Not even the Minister of Transport had the power to achieve that minor miracle.

Bruce Anderson (known as the Brute) is another big beast in every way. He really has become the Michelin man of the commentariat. He has put on so much weight of late, you worry that at any moment he is going to burst out of his clothes like the Incredible Hulk. The Brute gives the impression of being a right-wing bruiser but actually his views tend to be well informed and middle-of-the-road. He once wrote a piece about me in the *Evening Standard* calling me a whinging, whining Tory. A few weeks later I bumped into him at a do in the American embassy. As we had both been drinking I thought I might have a bit of fun. I grabbed hold of his crotch and squeezed, enquiring who the whinging and whining Tory was now. At least he saw the funny side and we have been friends ever since. However, there were nearly fisticuffs when he read that I had voted against hunting with hounds.

'Hayes, you little creep, you are a traitor.' When I got out of this by saying, not entirely truthfully, that I had only done this for cynical political reasons, he smiled and bought me a drink, much relieved.

The Brute can be a bit of a handful after a few glasses. Once, we were in a television debate about the future of the EU. Before the red light came on he spotted a Eurosceptic whose wife had died in mysterious (but later fully explained) circumstances in a remote part of Europe.

'Ah,' he hissed, 'Europe is a convenient place for you to dispose of inconvenient wives, isn't it?' It did not go down well.

One of my favourite MPs was Peter Lilley. We were elected together in 1983. Charming, very bright and on the inside track, he stood out as someone who would go far. However, he was done a terrible injustice. There was an urban myth that he was having an affair with Michael Portillo. This was utterly baseless and totally untrue. But I can shed light on how this rumour came into circulation. I was having lunch with the editor of a series that I occasionally used to present. We were in the Atrium, a grim aircraft hangar of a restaurant much loved by the media as it was in 4 Millbank, where the television and radio studios are. Things were getting a little jolly and we started chatting about Members.

'I see Portillo has changed his bob for a bouffant,' my chum commented, referring to Michael's latest haircut.

'I suspect it's because he is shagging Lilley,' I joked. All very jolly banter.

A few weeks later a mate from ITN sidled up to me saying he had got some high-grade gossip. My eyes sparkled. 'You'll never believe it, but Portillo is shagging Lilley.' My face reddened. 'But that's utter bollocks,' I protested, guessing that someone had been earwigging our jokey conversation and jumped to the wrong conclusion.

Over the years, the more I've tried to explain what really

happened, the more I am just met with cynical disbelief. So, guys, I am very sorry and am fond of you both.

Sadly, there was another occasion when my mouth got me into trouble. My dear friend Paul Routledge of the *Mirror* (of whom you will read more later) and I were having what he would call a 'three-bottler lunch'. We were gossiping and joshing around and I recalled a nonsense piece of gossip involving Ann Widdecombe having a fling in the spare bedroom of David Amess's in Basildon with a 55-year-old Catholic altar boy who was also an MP. We both had a good laugh and staggered off to do some work. A few days later he sidled up to me and thanked me for a story I had given him which he had written up in his *Observer* column, Captain Moonlight. I was a bit puzzled and asked him which story.

'Oh, the Widdecombe one.'

'Blimey, you haven't written it, have you?'

'Yes, it was a cracker.'

'But it's not bloody true.'

'Shit.' To her credit, Ann let 'Routers' off fairly lightly, as he is one of the really good guys in life. He prostrated himself in abject apology and donated a sum to one of her charities.

But I am not the only person much misunderstood. My old friend Richard Benson QC dines out on a true story of when he was a student in the 1960s. He used to share a flat with a lad who had just got a coveted job as a copywriter for J. Walter Thompson. He was even more excited because he had been tasked to pitch some ideas to clients the next morning. So they went out to dinner to toss around a few suggestions.

'What's the product?' enquired Dickie.

'A vaginal deodorant,' sighed the lad. After a few hours and an awful lot of drink, Benson came up with a brainwave.

'I have a name that says what it does on the tin. You will call your deodorant SPRUNT.' After much laughter they swayed back to the flat. The next day Benson hadn't heard a word from his friend until the door opened and the lad slunk into the flat looking thoroughly miserable.

'What's the matter?'

'I've been sacked.'

'Why?'

'They didn't like my SPRUNT pitch.'

'For God's sake, it was meant to be a joke.'

Benson is a very fine advocate and has an amazing fund of stories. I once asked him why, in his *Who's Who* entry, he has put 'founder member of the THC'. I asked him what it was all about.

'Ah, one evening I was having a drunken dinner with some very pretty girls. I was playing the game 'Fiery Finger', where you dip it in a liqueur, light it and snuff it out with your mouth. One of the girls asked if I could do it with my dick. I agreed, provided one of them snuffed it out. The trouble is that dipping your dick in alcohol and lighting it is not a good idea, particularly when the girls are in such hysterical laughter they forget to snuff it out. I had to shove it in an ice bucket.'

'But the THC?'

'The Torched Hampton Club. The trouble is the bloody thing swelled to the size of an orange so I took it to my GP, who told me I didn't need a doctor but a psychiatrist.'

Many years ago Benson offered me some wise advice to help me survive the rigours of the Bar.

'Never miss the chance to have a pee. Don't trust a fart. And never waste an erection, particularly if you are on your own.' Priceless.

One of the greatest parliamentary beasts was the legendary Willie Whitelaw. God, could that man drink. In the days when he was Ted Heath's Chief Whip, it was his occasional duty to rise from his place and move 'that this House do now adjourn'. One evening after a very good dinner he misread the time. It was fast approaching ten o'clock. So he staggered to the Bar of the House, slurred the magic words and then collapsed in a heap.

Willie's idea of a light lunch was a bottle of champagne, a bottle of white, a bottle of red and a couple of large brandies. When he had his first heart attack his doctor advised that he just confined himself to one champagne before lunch. As was ordered and with much self-control, he did. Just one bottle.

Willie had a great knack of getting himself out of trouble in pre-recorded radio interviews. If he didn't know what the hell his interviewer was on about he would have a major coughing fit which made the interview unplayable. He would then politely ask what it was all about and after it had been explained in painstaking detail he would ask to start all over again. His answers would then be word perfect, mined from the information received from the hapless reporter. Willie also had a reputation for discretion. Very often in the Smoking Room you could hear him booming to a minister, 'I want to tell you something in absolute confidence.' To this day I am never quite sure whether this was a ruse to plant misinformation or just that he had a very loud voice.

Denis Healey was another class act but could be one hell

of a bully in the chamber. Watching him lock horns with Michael Heseltine when he was at Defence was very exciting theatre. It would be late at night, everyone would have been drinking and it almost got physical, with Healey, an enormous presence and a former beach master at the D-Day landings, aggressively shouting at Hezza to sit down, with 'you bastard' more *sotto voce*.

People moan today about the standard of behaviour in the chamber but it is a teddy bears' picnic compared to those days. Aggressive, alpha-male stuff from many of those who had actually fought hand-to-hand in the war. That's why the women were so tough in the 1980s. Dame Janet Fookes eventually became a Deputy Speaker, but before that she was on the Speaker's panel of chairmen. That means she chaired standing committees. Janet is charming, mild-mannered and utterly indomitable. Cross her in committee at your peril. Once, the Home Secretary, Leon Brittan (another charming man), absent-mindedly crossed her line of sight while sneaking out.

'Order, order,' boomed the great Dame. 'The Right Honourable gentleman may be Home Secretary but he will abide by the courtesies of this committee.' I have never seen a tall man shrink so visibly, go so pale nor look so utterly terrified. Today's bunch weep to the press if another Member so much as frowns at them. And the men are as bad as the women. The Wrekin MP Mark Pritchard is meant to have got rather upset because a Cabinet minister told him to fuck off. For God's sake.

Tam Dalyell was a formidable and tenacious backbencher. He once roamed the palace at the time when we were horrendously starved of accommodation and found fifty forgotten rooms. He also terrified ministers with his supplementary questions, asking a simple 'Why?' Devastating, as it doesn't give the poor things time to think. Tam is a thoroughly decent fellow although rather an eccentric, who lives in a great stately pile in Scotland called The Binns. Once he invited a group of colleagues for dinner in his great hall. Expectations were high. They dined on scrambled eggs and a glass of sherry. And disappointment.

And Tony Benn? What a joy. Wrong on just about everything, but in such a charming and elegant way that you instinctively knew he was principled. I would always go to him for advice on procedure and he would always be helpful.

And Michael Foot. Delightful, kind, thoughtful, compassionate, literary and sincere, but temperamentally unsuited for office. He was kind enough to invite me to his eightieth birthday party at the Gay Hussar as I was a 'decent Tory'. I am very proud of the Rowson cartoon of the event, with me sitting at the feet of the great man, which adorns a wall. Outside the gents. Well, you can't have everything.

The final big beast in this chapter is Ian Gow, Thatcher's delightful and effective PPS. Charming, bright, witty and murdered by terrorists who planted a bomb under his car at his home. At the by-election in Eastbourne the Tories had the brainwave of selecting my old chum Richard Hickmet, who was an excellent MP for Scunthorpe but lost his seat. What the strategists overlooked was that there is a large Greek population in Eastbourne and that Richard's second name is Saladin. He is a Turk. And he lost. Sometimes you want to weep.

So, where are the big beasts now? On the Tory side, apart

from Cameron, Osborne and May the nearest contenders are Eric Pickles and Michael Gove. Labour has more of a problem. Apart from tackling energy prices and identifying the cost of living as a major political issue, Miliband still hasn't quite found his voice. But Leaders of the Opposition rarely do. Ed Balls is probably the one big beast they have left.

Though he has been wrong on just about everything, he is a formidable opponent. Those who know him tell me that he can be quite charming. The jury is out on that one.

CHAPTER 8

THE JUNKETEERS

The House of Commons is a very hospitable place and I do not mean the friendliness of colleagues, rather the rivers of corporate hospitality that are available. Some of my more cynical chums would arrange their day by accepting a breakfast meeting, a lunch, a couple of receptions in the afternoon, a dinner and then be bought drinks by journalists until the House went up early the next morning. These were the sort of people we dubbed the Junketeers. The Members who would only put their hands in their pockets to scratch their dicks. Most of them, not surprisingly, are now dead. Buried, as a cremation would have been far too dangerous.

To accept corporate hospitality it's best to be choosy. Always accept offers from local businesses in the constituency. It's just good manners and common sense. And if you are tempted by glossy lobbyist events, make sure you only go to those that can assist job creation in your patch. That is, after all, what you are paid to do.

But in the 1980s MPs used to swarm to freebies like locusts devouring the harvest. I remember having my first lunch with International Distillers & Vintners (now Diageo), who used to have a large presence in Harlow. They remarked how abstemious I had been. This rather shocked me as it had been a splendid lunch with some great wines. Then they told me they had once invited a parliamentary committee over for a light lunch, only to discover that they were filling their pockets with the free cigarettes on the table and taking what was left of the wines and spirits for the coach back to the Commons. Their snouts were so far in the troughs that even the pigs complained.

One of my most mystifying invitations was from John King (later Lord King), the chairman of British Airways. He had assembled his board at a then popular Westminster restaurant, L'Amico. I was the guest of honour and no expense had been spared. At the end of the evening I rose to thank my hosts for their kindness and generosity, adding that I was a little bemused to be invited as I had absolutely no knowledge of airlines or airports. 'Ah,' said John, 'and we will be so honoured to teach you. After all, we are the major employer in your constituency.'

'What, Harlow? Stansted Airport is still tiny and not even in my patch.'

'Harlow? What's Harlow got to do with it? You're the MP for Hayes.'

'Actually, John, I'm Jerry Hayes. Terry Dicks is the MP for Hayes & Harlington.'

There was a brief but deadly silence and then the whole room erupted with laughter. John King and his deputy Colin Marshall became good friends. But I don't know what happened to their personal assistants.

The privatisation of BA is a story almost beyond belief and it couldn't happen today. Privatisation was a manifesto commitment, but for some reason, perhaps because the Transport Secretary Nick Ridley and John King disliked each other, no Bill had appeared. So Ian Greer, the most influential parliamentary lobbyist of all time (sadly, cash-for-questions led to his downfall), was hired. He had a cunning plan. Stick a tail on it and you could have called it a fox. What he did was rather basic, but amazingly effective. He bussed 132 Tory MPs to the Savoy. We were greeted by some of the most beautiful and alluring air hostesses, who filled us with the finest champagne and canapés. And then lunch. Mountains of smoked salmon washed down with the choicest of Montrachets. Then a saddle of lamb accompanied by a really good claret. Then a delicious pud helped by a delightful Château d'Yquem. And finally, cheese, brandy and cigars. Then the lights went down, a stirring promo for British Airways played and the Ralph Richardson figure of John King addressed us. He reminded us of our manifesto promise to privatise BA, a promise Ridley was not honouring. What were we going to do about it? I tell you what we did. We gave Ridley absolute hell. BA was privatised within the year. What endeared me particularly to John was that just before his wife died he bought her a magnificent and expensive diamond necklace which she adored. He placed it around her neck in her coffin. What a lovely old romantic.

But not all captains of industry had the charisma of John King. One of the most unpleasant and rather scary invites was from Arnold Weinstock, at the time a great industrialist and voted for many years Businessman of the Year. Well, he may have been a great businessman, but he was rather lacking on the human being front. About ten of us, including some senior people like Douglas Hogg, were invited to his corporate headquarters for dinner. The food was great, but Weinstock was a megalomaniac monster. He had surrounded himself with cooing sycophants with their tongues so far up his backside that you needed a team of sniffer dogs to remove them. He hectored, lectured and was gratuitously rude. Then he turned to one of the guests, an MP for a constituency with a large Weinstock factory. 'And how many people do I employ in your patch?' he loftily enquired. Before the lad could reply, a flunkey whispered that it was around two thousand. Weinstock smiled and barked 'Sack 'em all' to some senior bod. And smiled. On and on it went. A relentless and horrible exercise in power and manipulation.

At the end of the meal, Weinstock casually turned to his staff: 'Those men I sacked – reinstate them.'

I was almost tempted to join the Communist Party there and then. But it was an important lesson: the need to encourage a strong but responsible trade union movement. The trouble was that Thatcher gave the impression that she wanted to break the unions. After all, they had destroyed Ted Heath's and Jim Callaghan's governments. The truth is she wanted to democratise them and take them back to the principles on which they were founded: looking after the interests of their members. And while the likes of Weinstock ruled the boardrooms, they were never needed more.

One of the perks of the job is occasionally getting to see what makes the royals tick. So it was out of sheer curiosity that I accepted an invitation to lunch with Prince Charles at Buckingham Palace. Ten of us were shipped in to discuss the Prince's Trust. The trouble with meeting him is that we are so conditioned by the press that he is a bit of an odd bod who is cranky about organic farming, talks to trees and is a homeopathy nut. I found him a delight. Relaxed, unaffected and passionate about the Trust, which has improved the life chances of thousands of young men and women who would have been thrown on the junk heap of political complacency.

We were in that part of the palace where they all wave from the balcony and dining in a room decorated in the most appalling Chinese taste. So, for a joke, he gave us a Chinese meal. I hadn't appreciated how much the royals dislike the palace as it is far too big and rather over the top. A bit like Dame Shirley Porter's bathroom. Anyhow, I remarked how close we were to that famous balcony. 'Oh,' said Charles, 'has anyone got a camera? Your constituents would love a snap of you waving to them.'

Sadly, nobody did. And the iPhone was just a twinkle in Steve Jobs's eye.

However, there were events so ghastly that colleagues would prefer to eat their own spleens rather than attend. At the pinnacle of sheer torture was the annual Essex National Union of Farmers dinner. It was always held at the Farmers' Club, a solid, tweedy place for solid, tweedy people, with the walls spattered with pictures of odd-looking cows and stranger-looking sheep. The food was hearty, with slabs of beef in Desperate Dan sizes. As a precaution against what was to follow, most of us fortified ourselves with vats of red wine. After a nursery pudding, we'd be beaten, whipped and generally turned over by ruddy-faced men of the soil, berating us for reductions in their incomes, for the horrors of the Common Agricultural Policy and for what a grim lot farmers had. We would all leave at 9.30 for the ten o'clock vote even if there wasn't one.

But for every turkey (in the non-EFU sense) there could be a moment of pure joy with unexpected consequences. The British Midland Airways launch of their direct flight to Florence was one. It was held at the Goring Hotel, a favourite haunt of the royals and the place Kate Middleton and her family holed up before the royal wedding. The food was great and the ambience wonderful, probably because it is still a family-run hotel. What intrigued me was the cream envelope nestling discreetly by every place setting. Probably some blurb by the chairman. But, out of courtesy, I slipped it into my pocket and forgot about it. In fact, Ali eventually opened it when she was about to send the suit to the cleaners. She let out a whoop. It contained two club-class tickets to Florence on the new service. Nowadays the Independent Parliamentary Standards lot would have had a fit and the red tops a field day. 'MPs board plane of shame', they would scream. Yet it was all perfectly innocent. In the '80s we were paid very little. £12,000 was my first salary, with expenses for living, a secretary, a travel warrant to the constituency and a small petrol allowance. That was it. Ali had to buy a second-hand Olivetti to type the letters. Where it all went so horribly wrong was a conspiracy between the party leaders to fudge MPs' pay, as there is no popular time to announce an increase. The Faustian pact was low pay in return for generous allowances. Sadly, in 2005, when Gordon Brown was throwing money around like a drunken sailor, it got totally out of control. MPs were entitled to tax allowances for food, gardening and just about anything that an inventive and imaginative mind could make a claim for. Worse, they were encouraged to claim for the maximum that they could, on the basis that the Treasury would claw back any surpluses. The reason there were all these daft claims for duck houses, moat cleaning and manure was because they had to justify the £200 a month that they could claim for just about anything. It is not popular to say so but there was very little corruption, just MPs working a system which had been encouraged to spin out of control. Now there has been an overreaction. Hair shirts and monk-like behaviour are now de rigueur. So, will a fair balance ever be struck? No. Will MPs ever be paid sensibly? Certainly not.

People have forgotten that the issue of whether we should build a tunnel under the Channel had been rumbling on for years. And, like anything with a whiff of garlic or froggy gravy, it bitterly divided the Conservative Party. The level of intellectual debate amounted to three clichés. 'We are an island nation', 'It will open the floodgates to immigrants' and 'The Channel is nature's barrier against rabies'. Needless to say all these arguments were eventually exposed for what they were: as barking mad as the illegal, foaming, rabid French dogs that were to be let loose on a cowering British public.

At last it was built. There was to be a grand opening ceremony. And there were to be free trips for MPs and peers before the service came on line. This was going to be exciting. Perhaps more exciting than we bargained for if there had been a fire or a bomb, which had the potential of wiping out a large portion of the legislature. Actually travelling on Eurostar to Paris proved to be great fun, not just because of the great food and wine but also to witness the delightful boneheadedness of some colleagues. I was sitting next to some old boy who didn't appreciate that although we had been waved through

Waterloo Station the French would want to see our passports. He thought that I was mad, as did half the carriage. They changed their minds when Special Branch officers averted a diplomatic incident at the French end of the tunnel. Of course, the main topic of discussion was which restaurants we should visit in Paris. Remember, these were the days before you could browse the internet and book in advance. This rather confused a charmingly dim upper-crust couple who could see absolutely no point in going out for a meal in France. All that foreign food, how ghastly! 'Marigold has prepared a splendid picnic!' he hoorayed at Mach 3. It was so reassuring to see that Great Britain was being represented so well abroad.

But for sheer, opulent vulgarity which would make a Katie Price wedding seem like a finger buffet with Pope Francis, there was an event thrown by a wealthy constituent which took a lot of beating. We spent a joyous afternoon at the Newmarket races and then were bussed back to their pad, which appeared to have been designed by a combination of Liberace and David Blunkett. To our collective amazement, they had erected a succession of marquees to give the effect of a Roman banquet. Actually, it was more like a prelude to a Roman orgy. Stuffed swans were brought in by semi-naked male and female slaves. And the antechambers were petalled pools with reclining nudes of all sexes. And the splendid David Emanuel was on hand to give a little 'zhuzh' to the dress he had designed for our hostess. He was also making a programme about parties for Channel 4. 'Jerry darling, let's do an interview.' As the camera was just about to roll I noticed that one of the chaps had a rather large penis on display in one of the pools, joined by a girl who was flashing her labia like a pair of flippers. I certainly didn't want that little lot in shot: the *News of the World* would have had a field day and the local God-botherers would have been gunning for me. So, out of a sense of decency, I adorned both with a handful of petals. After a spectacular banquet and entertainment by Madame JoJo's finest (spectacularly beautiful women who were really blokes), I ended up dancing on the table with a belly dancer. This was over the top, the height of vulgarity, a parade of immense wealth which could have been given to deserving causes. But I have not enjoyed myself so much for a very long time.

The event to approach with extreme caution was the Scotch Whisky Association Christmas party. The trouble was that so many of my colleagues regarded this as 'so much to drink, so little time'. Dear old George Foulkes (now in the Lords) was very keen to sample his country's favourite drink. I dread to think how much he hoovered up that evening. And then the division bell rang and off he flew to the lobby. Sadly, George thought that it would be fun to run into St Stephen's Entrance screaming 'batman, batman' and flapping his coat tails. It would have been very amusing if he hadn't accidentally bumped into a little old lady, who fell to the ground. Mortified, he did his best to apologise and try to get her to her feet. But his feet were the problem, and he kept falling over. Unfortunately, the only officious police officer in the building intervened, which led to George spending a few hours in the cells.

If you think the Scotch Whisky Association is a worry, St Patrick's Day at the Irish embassy can be lethal. I've known journos who've spent the whole night going round and round the Circle Line after one of those shindigs. But their do at a Tory Party conference proved the undoing of the splendid

Nicholas Scott. He claimed that he had become a little unwell due to a couple of glasses of wine and painkillers for his bad back. The Irish ambassador had other views and came out with what he thought was a helpful statement that Nick was enjoying Irish hospitality so much that they kept the bar open for him.

The next day, Scott joined us in the Spanish Bar (a Blackpool watering hole in the Winter Gardens). I was with my press mates, enjoying a couple of sharpeners before lunch. 'Hi,' says Nick, not looking at his best. 'Do you know, I just can't remember how on earth I got home last night?'

That's when we showed him the front-page photo in the *Mirror* of him comatose in the back of a police car. Oh dear.

BBC hospitality can be pretty impressive too, although nothing as over the top as my Roman orgy or paddling through pools of whiskey at the Irish embassy. One lunch that sticks in my mind was with Duke Hussey, the war hero chairman of the governors. Duke was a very impressive guy and spectacularly brave. He lost a leg in battle and nearly died. Over lunch, he asked me what talent they should be looking out for. I told him that there were two young political reporters who were rather impressive, Huw Edwards and Jeremy Vine. Gentlemen, I think you owe me a drink.

At the end of the meal Duke was kind enough to lend me his car for the trip back to the Commons. As I opened the boot to put in my briefcase I noticed a long package wrapped in brown, with a little tag marked 'The Chairman'.

'What on earth is that?' I asked the driver.

'The chairman's spare leg, sir. He never travels without a spare leg in the boot.'

Bless.

The saddest invitation was lunch with the directors of Sky TV. We were having a great time and were mightily amused that none of the media moguls could work the giant, multi-screened TV in the boardroom. They had to get a lad from IT to sort it. After a lot of fiddling around, the great beast flickered into life. We all thought that it was very funny that none of these great television titans could actually switch on the TV. Well, it proved to be good background noise to some pretty interesting conversation, until there was a news flash. Something to do with an incident at a school. And then before our eyes the horror of the Dunblane massacre unfurled. It was some of the most distressing television I had ever seen. All of us were moved and most of us were choking back sobs. We decided the best thing to do was go back to our families and hug our kids. It was a very traumatic day.

CHAPTER 9

MEDIA TART

A few days after my election I received a phone call from Anglia Television asking me if I would care to pop up to Norwich and take part in a discussion programme about the death penalty.

Capital punishment used to be debated in the House once a parliament. And pretty unedifying spectacles they were too. I was never one of the hang 'em and flog 'em brigade despite the fact that my grandfather had been murdered when I was twelve. I remember that when my father first broke the news to me he wept. It was first time I had ever seen him cry. My father was in the navy during the war and had been shipwrecked three times by the time he was twenty. He didn't talk about it too much, but when you have seen your friends floating in the water, machine-gunned by German U-boat crews, and witnessed others have their skin peeled off them by superheated steam after a torpedo has slammed straight into the engine room, it must have a devastating effect upon a young man.

To make matters worse, after the murder, as my dad had been the last to see his father, he had been arrested while his mother lay critically injured in hospital. He was now a murder suspect. My grandmother still had a bullet lodged near her lung when she died many years later. As it happened, the murderer was a young thug after the takings from the family business. He had flown over from Bermuda and shot my grandfather as soon as he opened the front door, with a gun concealed behind a newspaper. He then rushed up the stairs and shot my grandmother through the chest. That was his undoing. He had grabbed one of the chrome bars on the stairway, leaving a perfect set of fingerprints. He was sentenced to death, which was commuted to life imprisonment. He was released after seven years.

My grandfather was a popular figure in the East End of London and I will never forget how our local greengrocer offered to have the murderer killed in prison. My dad declined, but the boys broke his hand in such a way that he could never fire a gun again.

This is not the sort of book for me to set out at length why I never voted for the restoration of the death penalty. In a nutshell, I was convinced that state killings only provided a recruiting sergeant for the men of terror. And as I was a barrister, I knew only too well how serious miscarriages of justice can take place.

So off I rolled to Norwich. I was to be interviewed by Anglia's political editor Malcolm Allsop; on the other side would be Eldon Griffiths, the right-wing Tory MP for Bury St Edmunds. Eldon was late, so there was no time for a rehearsal or proper introductions. He just sat down, shook me by the hand and the cameras rolled. After I'd said my anti-hanging bit, Eldon launched in. 'Well, that's the sort of view I would expect from a representative of the Labour Party.'

Malcolm and I were rather taken aback at this. When I recovered I politely pointed that we were members of the same party. Eldon, to his credit, was mortified and offered profuse apologies and suggested that we reshoot the question. I could see the pleading look in Malcolm's eyes. So I suggested we carry on as no one would notice. Well, of course they did. This was great TV and when I entered the division lobby after the programme had been transmitted there was great amusement among the Cabinet, who were slapping me on the back.

After that I had a long and happy relationship with Anglia TV. They were like a family. When you rolled up to do a programme there would always be the same crew. A joy.

My favourite programme was the Anglia TV Christmas show where Charlie Kennedy, Graham Bright, John Gummer, Clement Freud and I played the most ridiculous parlour games. The public loved it.

John Gummer is an amazingly witty and entertaining guy. But if you believe what you read in the press, he was a preachy, sanctimonious little prig. Nothing could be further from the truth. After recording one of these shows he nearly got us thrown out of an Indian restaurant because he was making us laugh so much.

Clement Freud, though, was an odd bod. Plenty of wit but not a lot of humour. Like Archie Rice, he was dead behind the eyes. Gummer and he would be team captains and both would have to think of a witty twenty-second introduction for the trail. One rehearsal and then record. Every time Gummer thought of a better promo than Freud you knew it was going to be snaffled on the real take. He just hated to lose at anything.

But fond as I was of Clem, he did have a dark side. While

being escorted down the steps to the studio he turned to the pretty researcher whose mother and father were well known in theatrical circles and asked if she would like to go to bed with him. The poor girl stammered that she was terribly flattered but had a boyfriend. Without breaking step he just said, 'Well, I fucked your mother and buggered your father; I was rather hoping for the full set.' And off he went into the night.

A few weeks later I got a call from *Nationwide*. Come on, you must remember it. The flagship BBC teatime programme in the days before John Stapleton's hair went black.

For some reason they were interested in making a frothy piece about the House of Commons gym. So I was drafted in to give it a bit of colour. All I can remember is walking into shot in a pinstriped suit, getting changed and doing a pretend work-out. Then a close shot of me back in the pinstripe, leaving the gym to perform some grave and weighty parliamentary business, then the camera pulling back to show that I was wearing no trousers, all to the chimes of Big Ben.

This, I suspect, is when my elders and betters realised that I was a serious politician.

The only other times I appeared publicly in sportswear were doing a fitness video with Heather Mills for *GMTV* and modelling Lycra with Christopher Biggins, although I suspect you will need deep counselling after picturing that.

It was all rather surreal, but not quite as bonkers as being asked to go on a photo shoot to promote what I was told was going to be a 'groundbreaking new product'. For someone as vain as me, this sounded rather exciting.

So, I was told to meet the crew on the Victoria Embankment. To my confusion, I was challenged by two rather worrying events. A lavatory had been placed on the pavement. And an almost totally naked male model was talking to the director. Some crew members were warding off Japanese tourists who thought that it was some quaint British tradition to have an outside loo and were endeavouring to pee in it. Then I heard the wail of a police siren and saw a marked car screeching to a halt and two large bobbies approaching. Their eyes darted from naked man, to lavatory in the middle of the pavement, to Japanese tourists struggling with their trousers and then to me. Heaven knows what was going through their minds. They looked at each other, shrugged and said, 'Oh, hello, Mr Hayes, it's only you then,' shook me by the hand and muttered that everything was in order, and off they went.

A few moments later I discovered that the groundbreaking product I was promoting was a laxative. The shot was of the naked man on the loo in the pose of Rodin's 'Le Penseur', with me grinning and holding a packet of the product (I really can't remember the name). Somewhere deep in a vault, this awful image exists. I hope nobody ever finds it.

So, rather than me being the face of L'Oreal or the buttocks of Calvin Klein, I had become the bottom of a laxative.

But I did do lots of serious stuff too. A regular on *Newsnight* with Paxo and, of course, the *Today* programme. However, I do have a confession to make. John Humphrys may recall interviewing me down the line from home many years ago. The broadcast was rather echoey and at one stage a short whimper could just be heard.

So here's how it went. I had been moved down the schedule and was desperate for the loo as I had had a dodgy curry the night before. So I thought I'd take advantage of the time and plonked myself down on the seat. Then the phone rang. They were ready to interview live. I had no choice but to do it *in situ*. And just as it was getting interesting (ish), my four-year-old son decided that he wanted to play. The whimper was the result of the boy receiving a playful smack.

Over the years I have been lucky enough to do a lot of work with the BBC. In fact, I started with them when news interviews were recorded on film. If you think that they are overmanned now it was nothing compared to then. For a thirty-second interview there would be a cameraman, a sound man, an electrician, a producer and the interviewer. And a motorbike would be on standby to take the film to be developed and edited at Broadcasting House. It was all slimmed down by the time I was asked appear on *Children in Need*. Would I be prepared to paraglide over Harlow? Of course, not a problem. So I rolled up at North Weald aerodrome, where the cloud base was rather low. 'Your costume is over there, Jerry,' smiled a helpful young member of the crew.

Costume? Nobody mentioned anything about a costume, but what the hell, it's for the kiddies. So, dressed as a chicken with big clawed feet and a big flappy beak, I soared up into the sky, eventually to come crashing down to earth. An assistant thought it would add a touch of humour to come bounding up with a packet of sage-and-onion stuffing.

But the live appearance a few days later was the most unnerving. Walking down the corridors of Elstree Studios dressed as a chicken doesn't do a lot for one's dignity. Until I noticed that the cast of *EastEnders* were dressed as elves and fairies, which made me feel a lot better. Eventually, I was interviewed by Rob Curley, with one claw crossed over the other and a large gin and tonic in my hand.

However, I do want to put the record straight over a little misunderstanding with the comedian Mark Thomas. The party thought that it would be a good idea if I was interviewed on his then famous *Mark Thomas Comedy Product*. So I trekked down to the studios, just off Carnaby Street. The lights were on but there wasn't a camera in sight. But there was Mark, sitting on a sofa, dressed as a bear. He asked if I'd care to peep behind the sofa, see my costume and put it on. Well, I had a peep and didn't like what I saw: a six-foot penis costume with a big blue vein down the side, two little eye holes, and slits for my arms to come through.

Well, you can imagine the conversation. 'You must be fucking joking … *The Sun* will have a field day … everyone sniggering that Hayes doesn't need to dress as a prick … blah, blah, blah.' Little did I know that I had been tricked by the producer, a ghastly, tubby, humourless man called Dom Joly (yes, that one from *Trigger Happy TV* and *I'm a Celebrity*) who had planted hidden cameras to record my expletives and eventually played them on air. He tried to convince Michael Grade, then CEO of Channel 4, that by signing the release form I had consented to be secretly filmed. He failed. But I never put that damn penis suit on.

Some of my happiest broadcasting experiences were working with my old friend Ed Boyle. Ed is a creative genius but should be locked away in a darkened room and kept well away from management, whom he despised. He was the first political editor of Independent Radio News, a brilliant writer, a fantastic producer, but quite, quite bonkers. I was lucky enough, with Charlie Kennedy, Ken Livingstone and Tony Banks, to be part of his parliamentary repertory company. He wrote and produced two wonderful series for us: *Party Pieces* on Capital Radio and a nightly live TV show, *Left, Right and Centre* on BSB (the first UK extraterrestrial broadcasting company, later bought by News International and rolled up with Sky). It was thanks to Ed that I learned to write, and read an autocue. I owe him a very great debt.

However, he did have a penchant for getting into scrapes. As political editor of Independent Radio News, he had to put together packages for the regions. These were the days before digital. Every studio had an enormous tape deck and as soon as you made your microphone live by pushing your fader forward, the tape recorder would swing into action. Obviously, you only lifted those clips you wanted for the package and that was done by marking the tape with a chinagraph pencil, cutting it, splicing it together and putting it in a beta cassette. This would be 'fired' by putting it in a slot and pushing the fader forward. That's how the first jingles were made. And darn time-consuming it was too. But imagine putting together a budget package region by region with each clip being different. And only one guy to do it, Ed Boyle. It used to drive him totally crazy, or rather even *more* crazy. And as he was doing the voice-overs he would be shouting, swearing and generally cursing … always being careful to make sure that those bits were cut out. Until a grateful nation heard Ed's wonderful nationally networked Budget round-up. It ended rather oddly: 'Fuck, fuck, oh God … wankers … shit, shit, bollocks.'

But rather than being sacked, the great man was given an

assistant, the equally bonkers Max Cotton, who went on to do rather well at the BBC.

Ed and I put together a great quiz show called *A Kick in the Ballots*. It was from a germ of an idea by me, and Ed's genius did the rest. Charlie Kennedy was in the chair, with Neil Kinnock and a few others on the two competing panels. One of the games Ed devised was called 'U-turn'. A politician would start speaking in favour of an idea and then the chair would press a buzzer and they had to oppose it. So I would start off opposing the death penalty until Charlie pressed the buzzer, shouting, 'U-turn.' I would then, in mid-sentence, say, 'on the other hand…' and launch into an argument in favour. The trouble was that MPs could do this so seamlessly as to make the programme popular with the public but hated by MPs. They gave me a lot of stick over it. 'Your damned programme is making us a laughing stock,' huffed some ancient grandee. Oddly, I thought that many of them were doing that without any help from me.

Sadly, we only did three programmes on nationally networked LWT. There were rows over money and they wanted to put in teams of writers and completely mess it up.

Ed is a great practical joker. You had to be prepared for just about anything if he was about. Once, when the House was debating the Dangerous Dogs Act, I was asked to pop over to IRN to do a live interview on it down the line. It started quite well until I heard barking in the studio and then felt a scuffling around my ankles. And then something biting my ankles. Of course it was Ed on his hands and knees. I completely fell apart and pretended that there were technical problems. Heaven knows what the poor fellow who was trying to interview me in another studio thought was going on.

Also when I am around Ed, particularly at parties, I have to watch out for my hair. He has a habit of creeping up behind me with a lighter and setting fire to it. A lovely, lovely man who has forgotten more about broadcasting than I shall ever know.

I do have a great deal of affection for LBC. I cut my teeth there in the old Gough Square offices with Pete Murray. Pete was the very first DJ in Europe, if not the world. He started on Radio Luxembourg in the 1950s. He was playing music for the kids well before the pirate ships, let alone Radio 1. But he did have a disconcerting habit of popping off to the loo when the news came on, leaving his teeth on the table. He'd always come back with ten seconds to go, reinsert his gnashers and we'd restart the programme.

Next (actually it was about ten years later), Ed Boyle's parliamentary rep got a rather interesting offer. Every Tuesday at 11 a.m., Charlie and Ken and I would appear on an LBC round table. Our host was the phenomenally famous Michael Parkinson. The programme proved to be very popular, particularly with taxi drivers.

The reason that we, along with Tony Banks, were hoovering up the media opportunities is because, for politicians, we were pretty truthful. We told it as it was and if that got in the way of the party line (which used to change like the weather anyway) it didn't really matter too much. What we didn't do, which seems to be the norm today, is make personal attacks on our leaders.

Parky was great fun and obviously the consummate professional. It would be amazing to roll up at ten and get chatting to those megastars he would be interviewing. Most were a delight. I once bumped into a wheelchair-bound Ginger Rogers. For those of you under fifty, let me explain that she was once the dancing partner of Fred Astaire and the most famous actress in the world. I asked Parky what it was like interviewing her.

'Bloody nightmare. I'd prefer to do ten rounds with Cassius Clay than interview her.'

It is worth remembering that Parky was a distinguished journalist well before he became famous as a chat-show host. He covered the Korean War and slept in the bath for safety. He was also a brilliant sports journalist and really passionate about sport, particularly cricket. He found it utterly incomprehensible that Charlie, Ken and I had about as much interest in sport as in eating our own spleens.

Parky is a very entertaining, warm guy. We had great fun, the deep well of his stories seemingly bottomless, and he was a generous host. Every so often he would take us out for lunch. Being old school, Parky's idea of lunch was the same as ours: start at about 12.30 and finish sometime around six, if it was a short one. He used to take us to Langan's when it was a proper restaurant and not some gastronomic wilderness infested with Essex scrap metal merchants and their bottle-blonde mistresses. He was always given a side table so everyone knew he was there. This was rather handy, as every time he was noticed a bottle of champagne would arrive. And there was a hell of a lot of champagne. Once, Parky thought he would lay on a treat for Charlie Kennedy. There was a very beautiful television actress (whose blushes I will spare), and Charlie was always banging on about how much he fancied her. So, just after pud, this vision of pulchritude sat down with us for one of the bottles of champagne that were beginning to queue up for our attention. What should have been love at first sight, or at least a shag, turned into a disaster. The poor girl had just come from one of many consultations with her gynaecologist and spared us none of the grisly detail. Charlie should have been creaming in his jeans rather than being on the verge of throwing up. For the rest of us it was great entertainment.

It is difficult to choose my favourite Parky story, as there are so many. But I still dine out on the one when he was the first British journalist to interview Cassius Clay after winning the world heavyweight title. Parky is waiting nervously inside the trailer while the champ is having a shower. 'Suddenly, Clay was standing in front of me stark bollock naked.'

'And?' we asked aghast.

'And he had the smallest cock I have ever seen.'

'What did you say?'

'Nothing, he's the bloody world heavyweight champion.'

Parky, what a great man.

Sadly, he went on to greener pastures and left us in the hands of the ghastly Richard Littlejohn. We took an instant dislike to each other. I think he saw me as a cocky little clever-dick. I saw him as an arrogant bully with the brain the size of a pea. I didn't last more than a few weeks before he booted me out. Littlejohn was not very popular with the staff. His driver, a tough little Scot, became thoroughly fed up with his boorish behaviour after a drink. He once had to pick Littlejohn up after a session in the pub when he was at his most irritating, needling the poor guy mercilessly. This was unwise as the driver did a little bit of debt collecting on the side and was not afraid to give a stern warning that if he kept it up he would lamp him. Well, it never came to that. Littlejohn just passed out, and his limp form was laid in the back of the limo like a snoring Jabba the Hut. It was eventually dumped outside his front door, with the driver ringing the doorbell to alert Mrs L.

Well, Littlejohn didn't last all that long. The chair was taken by a former Radio 1 DJ, the thoroughly likeable Simon Bates, and I was reinstated. Simon is another one of the great gods of radio. My affectionate memory of him is him taking out his chrome stopwatch and talking live for ten minutes without a note. 'Luv, it's amazing, this gift I have for being able to witter on about absolute shit.'

Simon is a fascinating guy with a gift for gossip which makes me look positively discreet. He started off work in a slaughterhouse, which he hated after he was offered fresh blood sandwiches for lunch. He then moved to New Zealand as a cattle inseminator. He gave up sitting in the back of a small truck masturbating horny bulls for broadcasting ... tough choice.

The wonderful thing about Simon is that he is great fun. One evening we had all been out on the town and the next morning we had the eleven o'clock show to roll out, with the alcohol still coursing through our veins. In those days I rented a flat in St George's Drive in Pimlico. I staggered out of bed to pick up the morning paper. As I was completely naked, I carefully opened the front door and slowly inched my arm out to collect *The Times* on the doorstep. Unfortunately, I slipped, fell onto the pavement and heard the depressing sound of the front door slamming shut. So there I was, starkers on the pavement with only a newspaper covering my modesty. Thank heavens it was a broadsheet. It goes without saying that I didn't have a key on me. What on earth would I do? Then I remembered that there was a retired professor, an elderly spinster, on the top floor. I pressed the bell.

'Yes?'

'Er, Professor, this is Jerry Hayes from downstairs; unfortunately, I've locked myself out.'

'I'll be down straight away.'

'Only one slight problem. I have no clothes on.'

Bless her, she didn't bat an eyelid.

I rang up our producer to ask if the car could come a little later as I needed to shower and get dressed. I explained why. Five minutes later the phone rang and I received a tirade of abuse from a madman accusing me of being a pervert. It took a minute for me to realise that this was Bates winding me up.

Trevor McDonald also sat in the host chair for a while. One of the most pleasant and unassuming people that I have ever worked with. One day, off air, he remarked that he couldn't understand why so many presenters opened their homes to *Hello!* magazine. I explained that it was because they were paid about £100k. This rather shocked him. But two months later, guess whose house appeared in *Hello!*?

Finally, that great Australian broadcaster Mike Carlton briefly took over the show. He wasn't well known over here but in his own country he was a legend. And, at twenty-one, he was the youngest reporter to cover the Vietnam War. He once took me out for what I can only describe as a marathon lunch at the Ritz. When we both staggered out I suggested we go and have a drink in Annie's Bar at the Commons. By this time Mike was in full Aussie mode. He was on great form. He fell off a bar stool, thumped a fellow journo and was escorted off the premises. It was a wonderful afternoon.

The next day, the boys thought it might be a good idea to wind him up. So, on House of Commons notepaper they drew up some mad admonishment from the Speaker for his clear contempt of Parliament which could carry the penalty of imprisonment in the Tower of London. When Mike received it he was petrified. What should he do? I explained that there was an ancient ceremony by which he could purge his contempt. So I took him back, where he expected terrible humiliation. But it was just the boys in fun mode, ready to buy him drinks and slap him on the back. That, mercifully, was the only violence that happened that day.

Probably the weirdest experience in television is working with puppets. I used to do quite a bit for *The Big Breakfast* and was once asked to do a slot with Zig and Zag. I hadn't got a clue what to do and just sauntered into the studio to see two Irishmen lying under trellises with the famous puppets on their hands. I suppose simulating a conversation with imaginary friends is something I had been well trained for.

CHAPTER 10

SHE

If you think that David Cameron is deeply unpopular with some of his backbenchers, it's as nothing compared to the visceral loathing that Margaret Thatcher suffered in her early years. As is the case with most leadership elections, the party did not elect her because they thought that she would be a fantastic success, but rather because all the other candidates were tainted with the past. Try to remember the traumas of the Heath government. He wasn't expected to win in 1970. His victory came as a shock, particularly to Harold Wilson, who found himself with nowhere to live, virtually penniless. Heath had a horror of the same fate and allowed Wilson to stay at Chequers until he could find a home and, more importantly, he passed legislation granting a car and a pension for all former prime ministers.

Probably the biggest disaster to befall Heath was bad luck. His heavyweight and cerebral Chancellor, Iain Macleod, died at No. 11 within a few months of taking office. He was replaced by a comparative lightweight, Tony Barber. And when a massive hike in oil prices and an explosion of greed among the trade unions began wrecking the economy, Heath made a fatal error of judgement by turning his economic policy on its head.

The famous U-turn. That was the beginning of the end, with the 'Who governs Britain?' election blowing up in his face.

Heath became bitter, brooding and remote, and Thatcher, a horse so dark as to be almost invisible, had the courage to stand for the leadership and win. Harold Wilson, now ensconced back in No. 10, cracked open the champagne.

More fool him.

But Thatcher was a pretty hopeless Leader of the Opposition. Shrill and humourless at the despatch box, out of step with her male, patrician shadow Cabinet and genuinely hated by many of her backbenchers. Those who were in the Whips' Office at the time told me how she would seek solace with them, often in floods of tears. Even when she won the 1979 election, most backbenchers wanted her to fail. Even when the fleet sailed to liberate the Falklands, few believed there would be a fight; rather a capitulation. Many were willing her to get it wrong. God, Tory backbenchers can be a ghastly, self-centred, mutinous bunch. Things don't change.

According to Ferdinand Mount, who worked closely with her, even that consummate patrician gentleman Lord Carrington privately referred to her as 'that fucking petit bourgeois woman'. Compared to that, Cameron has had it pretty easy.

And, like most Leaders of the Opposition, she didn't know too much about foreign policy. Jonathan Aitken, who blotted his copy book with her for dumping her daughter Carol, once said that she knew so little about the Middle East that she thought Sinai was the plural of sinus.

But through sheer drive, determination and force of will she moulded her party and the country (although not all of it) to her very simple beliefs of thrift, hard work, sound money and aspiration. She was the very first anti-Establishment Prime Minister who had a direct line to the public. Thatcher destroyed the cosy Conservative/Labour arrangement where everybody knew their place in society and everybody trusted that the political elite knew what was best for them. She believed in the individual. The importance of aspiration. The importance of hard work and education as a way out of poverty. That any 'place' in society should come not through birth, but through ability. And, most important of all, that owning a home and a business was now open to everyone.

Today, we all take that for granted. In the 1970s it was considered revolutionary, if not downright subversive.

Sadly, Thatcher and I didn't get on from our very first meeting. I was brought up in the days of Macmillan and Heath. Macmillan was my great hero. He was the man who coined the phrase 'banksters', who wanted to turn the Conservative Party into something more socially democratic, who believed in building homes for the poor. He was haunted by the horrors of the Great War, where so many young men died and he survived.

He famously wrote to his director of policy saying, 'The middle classes clearly want something, please jot down whatever it is on a couple of sides of notepaper and I'll see if I can give it to them.' Macmillan once briefed the press after a meeting with Thatcher, saying she made him feel that he had just failed in Geography. They did not get on.

Thatcher's real problem was that she was devoid of any sense of humour. I was at the Young Conservative conference when she laid out her stall to be leader. Her biggest applause and laughter came when she told a story about how, during a game of golf, Willie Whitelaw 'had me at the eighteenth hole'. She hadn't a clue why we were laughing. And that was the trouble. The Commons is a very clubbable place, but she wanted none of it. Not because she was a woman; it's just that she never did small talk. When she lost the leadership there was a dread of standing next to her in the division lobby simply because she attempted it. And not very well. It was like Edward Scissorhands trying to make balloon animals. Some locked themselves in the loo till she had passed.

And yet Denis was great fun. He once came down to Harlow to speak on my behalf. The first thing he did was tell my guys that he'd given security the slip but had 'pranged' the Cortina. 'Anyone here got a garage?' We sorted him out.

He was also hoovering up the gins and noticed a local reporter taking a picture. 'Be a good chap and bin that, will you? I'm president of a few rugby clubs and the boys would be a bit upset to see a drink in my hand.' Utterly preposterous, of course, but the press bought it and loved it. That man had charm in buckets.

One of the perks of being a government MP was being invited to the No. 10 summer party. The trouble was that the Lady made us queue up and shake her by the hand before we could get a drink. If she liked you, she would grasp you and hang on forever. She used to use this to great effect at funerals. On the death of some prominent Russian she grabbed Brezhnev by the hand and wouldn't let go. She knew how to milk a photo opportunity.

But if she didn't like you she would give your hand a quick twist and give your shin a slight tap. She did that to me once and I ended up sprawled in front of Denis (I had had a couple of sharpeners). 'Looks like the old girl doesn't like you, old boy,' he grinned.

There was a wonderful No. 10 do when Norman Lamont (then Trade Minister) had been splashed all over the papers for shagging Olga Polizzi. The boyfriend had returned home and found Norman in the boyfriend's monogrammed silk jimjams. As a result, Norman sported a beautiful black eye. Suddenly the word went round that he was coming up the stairs. So, just as he'd finished the handshake and got the disapproving look, a few of us were dancing behind Thatcher with one hand over an eye. I know, I know, it was very childish. But it was fun.

I remember uncomfortable meetings with her in the early days as Leader. As a YC area chairman I would be summoned into the shadow Cabinet room for lectures. We totally disagreed on monetarism (although she was proved to be right) and in one of the newly released documents she had written by our names 'and each one more ghastly than the other'. I think I fitted the bill rather well.

The trouble is I always managed to say the wrong thing to her. I had just come out of Annie's Bar one day when she was in full sail in one of the corridors with a flotilla of flunkeys trailing in her wake. She gave me a steely stare with those piercing blue eyes drilling into me. 'Jerry, have you voted?' A good time for a joke, I thought.

'Well, Prime Minister, I've been in Annie's all afternoon and I really can't remember.' If looks could kill.

On our first meeting after the 1983 election she invited us to No. 10 for a celebration drink. As we all staggered out I was chatting to Cecil Parkinson, newly appointed Secretary of State for Trade and Industry. It was at this point that the ghastly Mark appeared and obviously wanted to button-hole Cecil for some deal or other. I should remind you that Mark had been in a car rally in the Sahara and had got lost. So much so that Mum had persuaded the RAF to find him. Unfortunately, they did. Anyhow, Cecil politely indicated that he would rather eat his own spleen than talk to Mark Thatcher. So he used the oldest trick in the book. 'Mark, have you met Jerry Hayes?' Of course he bloody hadn't and wouldn't want to unless I owned some floozy-infested club. So I thought this was a good time for an icebreaker. 'Hi, Mark, did you find your way here all right?' It did not go down well.

One of the most unnerving experiences was walking into the Members' dining room to discover that the middle table had chairs leaning against it in the same way that Germans placed their towels on sun loungers. This meant only one thing: Thatcher was coming in for dinner and her PPS would be trawling the corridors for blood sacrifices. I was about to make my escape when the delightful Michael Alison nabbed me. 'How lovely to see you. Would you care to have dinner with the Prime Minister?' What could I say? 'No, I'd rather have a consultation with Dr Shipman after having sex with Teresa Gorman and a BSE barbecue with the Gummers'?

God, they were grim affairs. Do you have a drink or do you sip mineral water? And if you decide to tipple, how much? Anyhow, when I could take no more of some little creep dribbling all over her, the division bell rang. Glorious relief. But this was my second parliament and I was a 'senior' back-bencher (what a joke!), so we took a leisurely pace in these matters. This seriously irked madam. In full Lady Bracknell mode she addressed the dining room: 'Is anybody going to vote?' To a man and a woman we all trooped into the lobbies. Even the Labour Party.

The first meeting at the PM's office behind the Speaker's chair was another nightmare. She knew how to put you at ease. 'Whatever you do, don't line up.' I was talking to Giles Shaw, the Minister for Police, when our turn had come for an audience. 'Good to see you, Giles, how are things at Environment?'

'Actually, Prime Minister, I'm at the Home Office.'

'Don't be ridiculous,' she hissed. And that was it.

When she made her little speech at the end, she pointed to an alcove. 'That's where Marcia used to sit,' she said with considerable distaste. She was referring to Marcia Falkender, the great friend and gatekeeper of Harold Wilson and author of the famous 'lavender list' of baubles for his resignation honours.

Michael Alison once again nabbed me in the lobby one evening. 'The Prime Minister would love you to pop in for a drink and a chat at No. 10. Seven o'clock OK?' My heart sank. I had been particularly rebellious during the last few weeks, so this was going to be a hairdryer-meets-handbag event.

I arrived at seven o'clock sharp and was led up the grand staircase and into the white drawing room. 'I'm afraid the Prime Minister will be a little late. May I offer a gin and tonic?' said the butler. How could I refuse? And it would give me time to think of a cunning strategy to weasel my way into her affections. What could I do? Aha, a little bulb glowed above my head. There was much talk about President Reagan launching a bombing attack on Tripoli and the party line was diplomacy. That's the right message. She'll love it.

Eventually, she arrived and I launched myself into full oleaginous mode. 'Prime Minister, you are so right not to allow Reagan to use our island as an aircraft carrier.' At that she tugged at her pearls and gave me a stare. 'The reason that I am late is that I have just given the order for the F111s to bomb Tripoli.'

So I thought it wise to change tack. 'Douglas [Hurd, then Home Secretary] did a great job this afternoon on relaxing the Sunday trading laws.'

She smiled. So I warmed to my theme. 'He even promised a free vote at third reading.' The smile withered; her neck went red.

'He did what?' she shouted, then brought it down an octave (mustn't be disloyal about a Cabinet minister to a little oik like me). 'He did what?' she purred, but was not amused, as Hurd must have taken a gamble to get the second reading through.

Finally, I thought, I'm now so totally stuffed I might as well tell the truth.

'Prime Minister, don't you think that sometimes people perceive you as inflexible and insensitive?' This did not go down well and she reached to press a button in the wall. What flashed through my mind was: Oh God, my chair is like Sweeney Todd's. I'm going to be hurtled down to a pie factory in the basement.

Actually, she was just calling the butler. 'Mr Hayes will have one more gin and tonic and will be leaving us.' The next ten minutes were not easy.

So off I went to the Smoking Room for a quick drink. The mood was sombre. We all thought that the bombing of Tripoli was a disaster. Then a young sprog bounced in. He was in a terrible state. 'I've just read the tapes [the Press Association news wire outside every room]. Terrible news. The Americans have just accidentally bombed the French embassy.' An almighty cheer went up. The champagne was uncorked and a very good evening was had by all.

To be fair, she did her best to be kind in difficult situations. One former governor of the Bank of England wrote that he could take the bollocking but being forced to eat the cream bun afterwards was more difficult.

But back to the humour-free zone. Everyone knows about 'every Prime Minister needs a Willie'. It is worth trawling back through the newsreels to see some classics. I hope they are on YouTube. During the 1979 election she pops into a hardware shop, picks up a drill and comments, 'This is the biggest tool I have ever had in my hand.' The camera crew cracked up. She was bemused.

And then after the Iraq War (the first one), she sat astride an enormous field gun and asked the assembled press, 'Do you think this will jerk me off?'

Finally, my favourite. The Lib Dems had just changed their logo to a bird. Aha, think the speech-writers, we work in the dead parrot joke from Monty Python. Of course she had never heard of it and even when it was explained she just didn't understand. So she read it out and got rapturous applause. She was rather impressed and a little confused. So she went up to her speech-writers and said, 'This Monty Python, is he one of us?'

But she could be very grumpy. It is no secret that she liked a drink, as did Denis. One evening I was on board a City of London boat with a crowd to watch her switch on the lights on a newly tarted-up Tower Bridge. One of the officials came up to me in despair.

'The old girl is in a filthy mood. We've given her the finest champagne but she's still spitting tacks.' And there lay the problem.

'Look, it's after 9 p.m. She likes a glug of whisky. Call up a police launch, send them to Majestic and buy a bottle of J&B.'

And that's what they did, to delighted smiles.

In another chapter I will describe the downfall. But for this one, let us end on a happy note. I last saw her when she had begun to lose the plot, a few years ago at Jeffrey Archer's seventieth birthday party in Grantchester. It was a magnificent affair. They always are. Jeffrey and Mary are delightful and generous hosts. Most of the Cabinet were there, along with John Major. After a wonderful afternoon, Kit and the Widow came out to entertain us. Suddenly, a sheet was unrolled and we found ourselves singing an Indian takeaway menu to the tune of 'Nessun Dorma'. It was riotous. It was fun.

Margaret had a smile on her face. For once, I think she got the joke. I was never a great fan, but it was deeply distressing to see her in her final years.

CHAPTER 11

THE MINERS' STRIKE

Margaret Thatcher was extraordinarily fortunate in her opponents. General Galtieri, the President of Argentina, who invaded the Falklands; Michael Foot, whose 1983 election manifesto was described by Gerald Kaufman as 'the longest suicide note in history'; and miners' leader Arthur Scargill. If you really want to understand the appalling vanity and extraordinary lack of judgement of this man, it is well worth reading Paul Routledge's brilliant and insightful biography. Some people say that it was Thatcher who destroyed the miners. In reality it was Scargill.

Industrial relations destroyed the Heath and Callaghan governments. Ironically, Margaret Thatcher would probably never have come to power if Barbara Castle's plans for the unions had come to fruition. Promoted to the Cabinet by Harold Wilson, Castle was a fiery, diminutive redhead. And a determined, forceful politician. As determined and as forceful as Thatcher. She too was a force of nature. She realised that the unions had to be tamed and democratised. So she came up with a plan. The notorious 'In Place of Strife'.

Harold Walker, her Minister of State at Employment, told me the real story in Annie's Bar one day. Castle had been secretly drawing up the plans for months. Even he, as her deputy, had been deliberately kept in the dark.

The relationship between the unions and Labour had always been fraught with difficulties. This plan must not leak or else it would be dead in the water. And never forget how closely the unions worked with Labour in those days. There were regular beer-and-sandwiches meetings in the Cabinet room. And they had a snout in the trough of every major government decision. However, most of them preferred a decent glass of wine, in the same way that Wilson smoked cigars rather than a pipe. Don't be fooled into thinking that the age of spin began with Alastair Campbell. Walker got wind of Castle's plans and began to challenge her. She always denied that 'In Place of Strife' existed. Until one day he had had enough and directly asked her about it.

'No such document exists,' she spat.

This was an unfortunate and fatal remark because Walker opened his briefcase and threw the document across her desk. The print unions had smuggled him a copy. After all, they had printed it.

It was the end of Labour's attempts to tame the unions. As soon as Jim Callaghan got wind of it, it was dead in the water. This one act to curry favour with the unions proved to be his nemesis and the making of Margaret Thatcher.

Callaghan never forgave Castle for attempting a policy that could have begun to set the economy on the right track and saved the Labour Party from itself. She was Health Secretary when Callaghan became Prime Minister. She was the very first to go. Her parting words were, 'Jim, I don't mind being sacked, but to be replaced with David Ennals is an insult.'

The way in which Callaghan's minority government was 'run' is a masterclass of how not to govern and a warning to the lederhosen brigade on the Tory back benches who think that you can push through any sort of legislative programme relying on the tiny parties. You can't. They will grab what gifts you have to offer and then stab you in the back.

I once asked Merlyn Rees, Callaghan's Home Secretary, how they managed to keep afloat for such a long time. He just chuckled and he told me how he and Jim used to patrol the Tea Room and bars and 'give the boys what they wanted'. So Plaid Cymru got their own TV channel in Welsh, and the Northern Ireland and Scots nationalists got a few gerrymandered seats. Predictably, they all stabbed Callaghan in the back. This is always the price of minority government.

I was very fond of Merlyn. A really charming and caring man. He told me the story of how a man in a cloak appeared late at night out of the mist surrounding the Commons and so scared a driver that he accidentally ran the man over. The driver swore he 'looked like Dracula'. Before the police arrived, the unconscious Dracula lookalike mumbled that he was an MP called Rees. The police cheered. Here was the Home Secretary being rushed to hospital. The police never like Home Secretaries. But their joy was short-lived, as the man in the ambulance was actually Billy Rees Davies QC, the 'one-armed bandit' and thoroughly dodgy Tory MP for Thanet.

His nickname came from the fact that he only had one arm and was as trustworthy as a nine-bob note. He claimed that he lost his arm as a hero in the war. Like most of his life, this was fiction. He crashed a fuel tanker stolen from the Germans that he was trying to sell on the black market – the arm went missing in action.

He was also a thoroughly corrupt barrister. I know; I was briefly in his chambers. Once, he was on his feet in the Court of Appeal when he asked the bench to excuse him for a moment as his client had passed him a billet-doux. One of the judges remarked loudly that this was probably a 'Billy, don't'.

The one lesson that Thatcher learned after the horror of the miners' strike that destroyed the Heath government was to be prepared and choose your battleground carefully. In those days, the National Union of Mineworkers enjoyed power unconfined. They could bring the country to a standstill. Industry could be shut down and the lights switched off. They had done it before. They had slain a Tory government. But their leaders like Joe Gormley and Mick McGahey were a canny bunch of political operators. They knew what they could get away with and just how far to go – unlike Arthur Scargill, who was addicted to power and showed seriously flawed judgement.

In Thatcher's first term, she was wise to back down after a skirmish with the miners. Following the 1983 election she drew up plans to roll out a programme of industrial reform – but slowly and cautiously. She also hired Ian MacGregor, an old American strike-breaker, to run the Coal Board and made Peter Walker, that consummate political operator, Secretary of State for Energy. Walker had been very close to Heath at the time of his downfall and appreciated the need for coal stocks to be built up. He also understood that his department worked seamlessly with the NUM and that any plans he might be developing would be on Scargill's desk within the hour. Walker countered this by bypassing the Whitehall machine, ensuring his private office dealt directly only with fellow Cabinet members' private offices. Secret and confidential papers were biked to them directly. He took his department completely out of the insecure Whitehall loop.

Peter was the first Cabinet minister to invite backbenchers to lunch in his office. I mean a proper lunch, with decent booze, laid on by private caterers at the department. Pretty young girls who had been to finishing school served us and he was wealthy enough to pay for them out of his own pocket, which he did. Politically, this was a very clever move, as he was able to keep backbenchers up to speed in private. Or as private as gossiping politicians ever can be.

One day he was a little late and insisted that he caught us up on the booze front. He let slip that MI5 had just told him that they had intercepted a container-load of cash from the Russians to support the miners' strike. He then said that he had insisted that the container be allowed to get to Scargill's people.

This rather confused us.

'Why?' we asked.

'Oh, we did a deal with the Russians. They send money in fraternal solidarity to the NUM and sell us cheap Russian coal so we can break the strike.' And I thought I was pretty cynical.

Once, when I was travelling back to Energy Questions, the cab driver performed the usual trick.

''Ere, you'll never believe who I've just had in the back of the cab.'

'Try me.'

'That Wedgie Benn.'

'Mmm.'

'You'll never guess what question he's got lined up for your Walker guy.'

'Go on, mate.' And he told me.

I immediately rang up Peter's PPS to forewarn him. Poor old Tony Benn wasn't prepared for what hit him an hour later in the chamber.

The awful thing was that the miners were a thoroughly decent bunch. Never mind all the terrible pictures of violence on the picket line. Whole communities were under threat, not just jobs. And still in the old pit-villages some family members will not speak to each other for their past roles in the strike. It didn't just divide the country. It divided families and broke communities.

At the height of the strike I was wandering back to the Commons after a gossipy lunch with a journo. It was the day the miners were lobbying Parliament. And suddenly, in front of me was a platform, with some loudspeakers and about a thousand miners listening to rabble-rousing speeches. My beard and blond curly hair were spotted.

'It's that Tory MP off the telly!' went up the cry. Oh dear. I was going to be lynched. 'You gonna come and talk to us?' one jeered.

What on earth should I do? Try and do a runner, get thumped and end up on the news as a cowardly imbecile? There was only one course open to me. So I strode forward, hand outstretched, pretending that I was cool as a cucumber and not bricking it. The crowd parted only to swallow me up.

'Of course I will speak to you,' I quavered.

And for the next hour I listened to their grievances and did my best to explain that it was no longer economically viable to mine deep coal. We didn't agree, but they were polite. I saw in the flesh that these were some of Britain's finest, wanting to earn their living in the way their families had done for generations. Destroy this and their communities would collapse.

The miners were so let down by Scargill. He refused to ballot them on a strike. He turned down a billion-pound package to save jobs and start retraining. And he called the strike for the summer, when coal stocks were high. Insane, vainglorious fool.

In many ways, the miners' strike was the first whiff of the beginning of the end of Thatcher. It was a great victory for her personally and politically, but it rather upset the comfortable middle classes. If she treats the miners like that, what could she do to us? More prescient than they could possibly know.

CHAPTER 12

FACT FINDING

Some MPs manage to turn overseas travel into an art form. One Labour guy from Liverpool was nicknamed Gulliver, and a Tory, Neville Trotter (to be fair, he had a constituency interest in airlines), was known as Globe Trotter. But before anyone gets all hot and bothered about how taxpayers' money is wasted on MPs' junkets, it is important to differentiate between select committee trips, where you are sent abroad to report on a specific issue, and all-party committee jaunts. The former are paid by the taxpayer and are all business and little play. The latter are funded privately and are designed to persuade MPs to go native – and they are all play.

In those days, BAA provided a free airport parking pass for all MPs. And when on government business we were allowed to travel business class and clock up air miles for our own use. In these straitened times this would be regarded as a terrible abuse. But in truth the taxpayer wasn't footing the bill, so what the hell. Nowadays the *Daily Mail* expects all MPs to behave like monks. It may be why Yvette Cooper dresses like a nun on holiday.

I'll deal with select committee trips a little later on. In the meantime it is worth having a look at the all-party groups. In those days they hadn't multiplied in the way they have today. To be a member of an APG was breathtakingly simple. I once blundered into a committee room looking for my old mate Derek Conway. He was there with three others.

'Hi Jerry, this is the AGM for the APG on Morocco. We are missing a secretary. Are you interested? No work and a few free trips? Interested?' Of course. But I wasn't quite sure precisely where Morocco was. Despite this minor handicap I became the secretary. A week later I received a lovely carpet from the King and six months later, as the great expert, I was invited to the state banquet in his honour. All very strange, particularly as he was very late and had all his food cooked for him on a portable stove. But it was fun. Until I realised that the reception at the Guildhall was not one of those where they fill you with champagne until you are ready to burst, but a queue to be clapped in by the Common Council. But, thirsty as I was, the City of London always makes up for it on the booze front.

The king of APGs which involved overseas travel was Dr John Blackburn, a former policeman and all-round good guy. Unfortunately, he had a bit of a weakness. He could not resist chatting up (in a totally platonic way) any woman who crossed his path. If you entered the central lobby with a woman who could have won the Turner Prize for ugliness John would glide up in slow motion with hand outstretched. He would grasp the lady's hand, make a great show of kissing it and then launch into his famous opening gambit. 'My dear, how are your feet?' This used to cause said woman much confusion until he offered an explanation. 'I was so worried that you might have hurt them when you fell from heaven.' For reasons beyond my comprehension, they all loved it. And this was followed by one-liner after one-liner. He didn't just lay flattery on with a trowel; you could almost hear the cement mixer chugging along in the corner. His favourite trick was to put his arm round some old duck with a face that would have sunk a thousand ships simply to get away from it, and call them his daughter, niece, younger sister or whatever he could get away with without making anyone not involved with this treacly love bombing violently sick. And when it came to love bombing John had earned his wings and a chestful of medals that would make Colonel Gaddafi blush. But oozing faux love to the wives of an African dictator or pawing a member of a Middle Eastern royal family doesn't always make for good diplomacy. On at least two occasions he was nearly bundled into a plane bound for home. But John's little vignettes provided us with endless entertainment. He was fortunate he wasn't stoned to death, missing a limb, or even worse.

One of my early trips was to South Africa and was fascinating and a little scary. It was organised by John Carlisle, the Tory MP for Luton West, whom we dubbed the Member for Johannesburg West. The idea was to send out a few Tories who would be totally besotted with the wonderful concept of apartheid. Unfortunately, I had broken my index finger in a car accident so I insisted that my doctor strapped it up in such a way so that in every official photograph I look as if I am giving the finger. Which of course I was. Although on the plane over I had rather an embarrassing experience. I was seated next to a very pretty girl from Cape Town. She asked about my finger and offered her sympathy.

'But how do you have a wank, then?' she politely asked,

causing my two parliamentary colleagues Michael Knowles and Richard Hickmet, who were sitting in the row behind, to take an interest.

'Ahem, well, erm…' I stammered.

'Let me give you a hand then,' she kindly offered. The front page of the *News of the World* flashed before me: 'MP joins mile-high club'. I made my excuses and feigned sleep. I think.

God, the Afrikaners were a ghastly bunch. Before each meal was a prayer. And then, when we were politely asked if we required something to drink, the splendid Michael Knowles would always save the day.

'A large Scotch, please.'

Satan had entered the room, thank heavens or whatever. At one time we met ultra-right leader Jaap Marais, who looked a bit like a budgerigar with a squashed beak. His views were utterly vile. And his secretaries gave the impression of being a horrible Mengele experiment in breeding Aeroflot hostesses with Belsen guards. A deeply unpleasant experience.

One day I thought it might be a good idea to shake off our minders. Why not pop into Soweto? Why not slip into a church service with Desmond Tutu? So I looked him up in the telephone directory and gave him a ring.

'Hi, Archbishop. I'm Jerry Hayes with a parliamentary delegation from Britain. Tomorrow is Sunday, any chance of us meeting up after your church service tomorrow for a chat?' There was a sharp intake of breath then that famous Tutu chuckle.

'Of course, but it is very dangerous.'

Dangerous? But we were British MPs. What could they do to us?

That line of thought was dangerously stupid, although I didn't think so at the time. I had forgotten that Soweto was a serious trouble spot. Cars with white people were regularly attacked. The necklace, a tyre filled with burning petrol, was a favourite and barbaric means of execution.

Tutu told me where we could find him. Now, this will shock you. Nobody wanted to take us. So we bribed a driver and lurched through the rubble-strewn streets of Soweto with not a signpost in sight. They had all been torn down. Eventually we reached the church. It was packed. We were the only white faces, like the white spots on a domino. The organ swelled with the great hymns of the C. of E. tradition. 'All People that on Earth Do Dwell' sticks in my mind. It was not sung in English but in Xhosa. And then we all started to dance. An enormous African conga line towards (oh dear) the collection plate. I had only the equivalent of a South African £50 note. Sod it. I wasn't going to be lynched. In it popped.

Afterwards I spoke to Tutu.

'What message do you have for our Prime Minister Margaret Thatcher?'

He smiled and in that beautiful, melodious voice he just said this: 'Tell her to listen to the victims of apartheid not the perpetrators.'

The man is a living saint.

Of course we tried to visit Mandela. Quite impossible. Although we did manage to have a chat with his lawyer. But I remember, years later, being at a reception given for him as President in Westminster Hall. He was being led down the steps by our Speaker, Betty Boothroyd. I could see the look of wonder in her eyes. Here was she, a former mill town girl, now

Speaker of the House of Commons, with the man she had fought so hard to free. And there she was arm in arm with this man who been imprisoned for twenty-seven years by an evil regime, urging peace and forgiveness. On that day we were all star-struck.

I remember the day Mandela was freed with great clarity. Ken Livingstone, Charlie Kennedy and I were doing our LBC slot, with Simon Bates in the chair. We were filling time with banter before the moment when Mandela strode to freedom. When it happened I was at the microphone and described it something like this:

> And now the moment has come. This great man, imprisoned for more than twenty-seven years, now walks into the sunlight not as a bitter man but with the air of someone born to rule. He looks almost presidential. This is remarkable and a moment in history we will treasure. Ken Livingstone has tears of emotion coursing down his cheeks.

To which Ken replied in his South London nasal twang, 'Nah, it's my hay fever.' Bless.

Next on our travels we were off to see Chief Buthelezi, hereditary leader (not king, that was King Welcome) of the Zulus. Oxford-educated and highly intelligent, he lent us his plane to fly us to his fortress in Ulundi. I remember three things. He was charm personified. He gave me a pair of cufflinks. And our plane was guided down on a red dirt runway by one hundred bare-breasted Zulu women with red flags. You couldn't make it up.

Then we went into Bophuthatswana. And what a dodgy

bunch they were. Ministers lived in the lap of luxury and travelled their impoverished land in shiny black Mercedes. This was a faux South African experiment in letting the blacks rule a homeland. In reality the government was just a puppet regime whose purpose was to supply black labourers to the south.

One evening, ministers invited us to a lavish dinner. We were all awash with drink and it was now time for dreary speeches. The trouble was that our host was not only very drunk, he was also very cross-eyed. I think he was intending to call someone else to speak, so Richard Hickmet and I had to guess which eye (one was pointing in his direction, the other in mine) was to be the victim. I took the challenge. Actually, it wasn't too bad a speech, but it wasn't that good either. I'm afraid I got a little carried away, ending up heaping praise on these ghastly crooks for 'good governance ... belief in democracy ... blah, blah, blah'. Awful, hypocritical crap. But I didn't want to end up fed to the crocs. My pièce de résistance was '... and nobody could accuse you of being corrupt whisky ministers swanning round your land in bulletproof Mercedes.'

I slumped down after polite applause to notice the table strewn with empty whisky bottles and, in the corner of my eye, the car park groaning with shiny bulletproof Mercedes. My lasting memory of South Africa then was of cowed black men who were too afraid to look white men in the eye. But what really shocked me was lunch with someone who was considered to be a progressive white woman. I had been rather impressed by what I had thought were her quite liberal views. Until she came out with a little tirade against her maid. 'The trouble with the blacks,' she confided, 'is that they are born liars and thieves. They just can't help it.' And that was from a liberal. Utterly depressing.

However, I will never forget how humour was the most effective tool of the liberal press to undermine the deeply unpleasant South African government. In the middle pages of a Cape Town broadsheet was a picture of soldiers with night sticks and assault rifles marching through a township. Women and children were cowering back in sheer terror. The headline cleverly escaped the censors.

'Colonel "Blackie" Stewart takes his men on a "getting to know you" exercise.'

One day I received a message from the whips. President Reagan was flying to Britain; would I (with a few others like Fatty Soames and Steve Norris) like to go and meet him? Of course! So off we were bussed to the beautiful Regent's Park residence of the American ambassador, Winfield House. It used to belong to a nymphomaniac Woolworth heiress unkindly known as 'the mint with the hole'.

Meeting Reagan was fascinating. You could tell in those days the rank of each secret service officer by the size of their earpiece. They got smaller and smaller as the great man approached. Reagan was tall and affable, but read everything off a card. Like an actor with mini idiot boards. But the man oozed charm and charisma. Like a good actor, he stood on his marks and recited his lines, often written by his legendary speech-writer Peggy Noonan.

Reagan had the gift to move an audience, make them laugh and – something so rare in a politician – make them feel good about themselves. And that's how he conquered America after the disaster that was the well-meaning, but utterly hopeless, peanut farmer Jimmy Carter. It is a popular myth that Reagan was a bit dim. According to my friend Stephen Masty, who used to write his party speeches, this was way off-beam. Most of the really memorable lines were penned by Reagan himself.

The relationship between him and Thatcher was remarkable. They sang off the same hymn sheet. If any two people changed the course of history with the fall of the Berlin Wall and Soviet arms reduction, it was their partnership. And they were not without affection for each other. It was rather moving that at his funeral she kissed his coffin. But she wouldn't take any nonsense from him. Charles Moore's brilliant biography of her shows her sheer force of will persuading him not to give in to the State Department's policy of us doing a deal with the Argentinians during the Falklands War.

So here am I in an intimate setting with the most powerful man in the world. And can I remember a word he said to me? Sadly not. I really should have kept a diary.

A few weeks later I received a call from the embassy. Would I like to go on an all-expenses trip to the States for a month? Of course! But the trouble I had with the pairing whip, the delightful Tim Sainsbury (he of the supermarket), was remarkable. Remember, we had a tiny majority of 140. I fought and fought and fought to get on this once-in-a-lifetime trip and finally won.

It was my first time Stateside and I had a tremendous time, travelling enormous distances. I had a wonderful tour of the White House and in the West Wing hatched a plot with the neocon head of protocol. Neil Kinnock was due to meet the President, so how could we screw it up? The answer was: no moving pictures and black-and-white photos only.

Sorry, Neil.

But I did meet Senator Dan Quayle who became, rather extraordinarily, Vice-President a few years later. He was devastatingly handsome (think Robert Redford crossed with Brad Pitt). He had only one serious drawback. He was a master of talking total gobbledegook with great charm. Obviously nothing compared to the batshit-crazy, hog-whimperingly dumb ignorance of Sarah Palin. That is an aberration of nature in itself.

No, dear Dan was just run-of-the-mill dim. But at least he wasn't dangerous. When I left his office, a senior aide summed it up rather well. 'Nice guy, huh? Just darn stupid.'

I found a great bar in DC, at the Ritz Carlton. I was first taken there by the head of the election commission. He invited me for tea, which I thought was a rather genteel idea. Ten Black Russians later (don't worry, it was a drink), I realised that the old boy liked to tope. I haven't a clue what we discussed. But the bar was a magnet for some serious characters. Dodgy judges and the cream of organised crime. Often they arrived together. I became friendly with an enormous guy of Italian descent called Joe. On my last day he invited me to lunch at one of his restaurants. A stretch limo, with a large muscly guy in attendance, drove me and Joe downtown to an Italian restaurant. When we entered, the waiters stood to attention, but never quite relaxed. All through the meal, dodgy-looking fellows would come up to pay their respects to Joe. Just passing the time of day, I brightly enquired if there really was such a thing as the Mafia any more. The restaurant went deathly silent and waiters shiftily eyed each other. Until Joe spoke.

'Jerry, you are a good guy, but if you cut your linguine again I will have you rubbed out.' Then he smiled, slapped me on the back and everyone laughed. A little nervously. I never mentioned the subject again. I presented Joe with a splendid House of Commons keyring. It is probably now embedded in some poor fellow's eye socket.

Then off to San Francisco. Wonderful. There was only one minor hiccup. At the bar I was approached by a number of ladies in need of a shag. I was rather flattered until I realised that they were more interested in the bulge in my wallet than anywhere else. Uncle Sam had put me up in a brothel. I made my excuses and went to my room and locked the door. Yup, I'm pretty sure about that.

The next stop was Minnesota. I was to stay with a family on a farm. It was a nightmare. I first realised that there were going to be problems when I noticed that there was a large Pat Robertson (a mad gospeller of the right) magnet on the fridge. And when, after dinner (not a whiff of alcohol in sight), their idea of entertainment was the non-stop showing of hellfire sermon videos.

They were a charming family, but were creationists and believed that the Bible was a manual to life that could be used for everything. Literally. They told me with a straight face that if the devil deprived you of money the Lord would recompense you seven-fold. I nodded politely. They saw my scepticism. So they gave me an example of the Bible in action. Here was their story. A few months before, they had received what they believed was an unfair tax demand. So they consulted the Bible and prayed with their community. Guess what? A few weeks later they received a tax rebate. The amount?

Seven-fold what had been demanded of them. Jesus! Or maybe not.

Then off to Florida, where I had a volunteer driver called Felix who was a rocket scientist at Cape Canaveral. He drove me to an engagement with the Episcopal Church stuffed full of daughters of the revolution who were utterly convinced that they were related to royalty. They were a pretty grim bunch. The plan was that there was to be a finger buffet, after which I would make a jolly speech. All went well until Felix walked in after parking the car. There was a stunned silence. Felix was black. When they had recovered from the shock I suggested that he join us for the buffet. It was as if I had offered them a gynaecological examination with a used knife and fork. With a fake smile that revealed expensive plastic surgery, the head daughter, through perfectly formed gritted teeth, gave me the full Southern hospitality treatment. 'We are delighted to feed Felix,' she drawled, 'but I am afraid he will have to eat in the kitchen.' I was puzzled.

'Why? There is no table plan and Felix is being kind enough to drive me around for nothing.'

'I am afraid that it would be inappropriate.'

'I'll tell you what, I'll do my speech as long as Felix joins us for supper.'

'I'm afraid that will not be possible.'

'Then thank you and good night.'

So Felix and I drove off into the night. We dumped the car and spent a wonderful time singing blues round the piano in a bar. It was depressing that even at the end of the '80s racism was still alive and well in some parts of the United States.

Last on the list was Boston. A great place. I was invited to the President of the State Senate Billy Bulger's St Patrick's Day lunch. This was a very Irish, very pro-Irish Republican event, where the dogs were painted green, as was the beer and the food. With Noraid raising funds in the shadows. What's more, Billy was a man who took great pleasure in ripping the guts out of his guests, who included Vice-President Bush, Governor of Massachusetts and presidential candidate Mike Dukakis, Joe Kennedy and me. A Brit MP and a Tory at one of these events was not dissimilar to lions having a pleasant chat with a Christian at the Colosseum. I was going to be creamed. So I came prepared. I appeared on the platform in a green leprechaun hat and an enormous badge emblazoned 'Irish is beautiful'. I then ripped the piss out of Billy ('It is always a pleasure to see you on TV so I can switch you off') and told a load of off-colour Thatcher jokes. It was a high wire act.

Mercifully, they loved it. My miserable skin was saved and I became a good friend of Bulger.

Hollywood later made a film based on Billy's brother Whitey. It starred Jack Nicholson and was called *The Departed*. Whitey was a gangster and was the FBI's most wanted man. He is now behind bars. We never met. I think.

Next, a trip to Israel, where Sir Ivan Lawrence and I read the Beatitudes on the spot where Christ would have given them: at the bottom, by the Sea of Galilee, where the acoustics are amazing, as the hills provide the perfect amphitheatre.

Later we had an uncomfortable meeting with the Prime Minister and former Stern Gang member Yitzhak Shamir of Likud. A sinister little man.

Then, a wonderful chat with Shimon Peres (now President).

What a great man. What a fantastic and charming sense of humour. This was his icebreaker. In his thick Middle European accent he said this: 'Gentlemen. We in Israel have an incompetent government and more Arab firepower against us than that of NATO. But it is not as serious as your poll tax.'

We also had an opportunity to meet with the Palestinians, which was invaluable. The way it worked was like this. The British ambassador dealt with the Israelis, while the consul had great contacts with the Palestinians. However, at the dinner the Defence Secretary, Tom King, came in for a slagging-off. Andrew MacKay, who was on the trip, was not amused. He, after all, was Tom's PPS.

Then a little trip to the Dead Sea. My old chum David Amess, a fellow Essex MP, was a little concerned. 'I don't want to go in, I can't swim,' he moaned. We gently explained to him that swimming wasn't relevant as one tended to float. The Israelis always called him Mr A. Mess. Well, we thought it was funny.

The good thing about select committee trips is that this is the only time you really get to know your colleagues from other parties. It is a great bonding exercise. This is what makes these committees invaluable to democracy and potentially lethal to the executive. By and large, reports are delivered that grapple with the issues rather than with the party politics. It keeps ministers on their toes.

I thoroughly enjoyed my time on the Health and latterly the Heritage (now DCMS) Committees. We had three wonderful chairmen, Frank Field, Nicholas Winterton and Gerald Kaufman. All dedicated, all bright and all great fun. It would be far too dull to log every trip, but two come to mind.

One was a visit to Holland to investigate childbirth. It was all rather scary and very Calvinistic. Women in the late 1980s and early '90s were encouraged to give birth at home rather than at a hospital, and a white bedstead would be set up in the living room. We asked a senior consultant about the sort of pain relief that was available. He looked (it would have had to be a he) at us with total incredulity.

'Pain relief in childbirth is not part of our culture,' he snorted. 'Our women believe that once they have had the pleasure they then have to take the pain.' I made sure that when my wife Alison was pregnant we didn't travel anywhere near Holland.

Then, a lovely trip to the USA with Kaufman. For anyone interested, the way to his heart is ice cream, as he is a serious connoisseur.

His tales about the days in Harold Wilson's kitchen Cabinet could fill a library. I once asked him about Joe Haines, Harold Wilson's notorious press secretary. 'Introducing him to Harold was the biggest mistake of my life.' They despise each other.

This trip was just before the 1997 electoral slaughter. Gerald predicted the overall Blair majority within a couple of seats. He asked me what I would do when I was flushed down the political pan. I remarked that I would rather like to write a column.

'If you do, use it to destroy your enemies and promote your friends.' Mmm.

My only recollection of that trip was going to Salem (where the witch trials were held) and its famous maritime museum. There, in pride of place, was an enormous ear trumpet. I asked its provenance.

'Ah, it is made out of a whale's penis,' intoned a straight-faced curator. Of course. What else could it made of? As it was America, I thought it best not to attempt any Dictaphone jokes.

Sometimes it is necessary to milk your contacts to arrange an overseas trip for political advantage. The 1987 election was bound to be a tricky one, particularly in a marginal seat like Harlow. So the splendid Ann Widdecombe came up with a wheeze. Why don't the Catholic MPs get an audience with the Pope? So we all contacted our local bishops and it was sorted. Wonderful. Particularly as it was John Paul II; a proper Pope and now a saint. So off we popped to Rome, lined up and got a hug and a blessing from the old boy. Within an hour and minus six quid, photos of the great event arrived at our hotel rooms. To milk the whole affair for all that it was worth, I filled my pockets with rosaries so that I could distribute them to Catholic Harlow voters like some Chaucerian indulgence seller. After all, they had been blessed by the Pope. Then I ensured that the photo was splashed on the front pages of my local newspapers. Harlow was awash with Catholics and the cherry on the cake was that I had helped the local Catholic club get their booze licence back. In the 1987 election I doubled my majority to over 6,000. No wonder the man is a saint. That was probably his first miracle.

My last little jaunt abroad before being taken to the electoral vet and put down by the people of Harlow was to Paris. This was a group of Labour and Tory MPs who had a large French company based in their constituencies. This was pure indulgence and fantastic fun. On the last day, after a magnificent lunch, our beautiful hostess asked in her perfumed, delightfully French and hormone-fuelled accent what we wanted to do next. She listed a number of cultural attractions. To this day I still tease my mate Bill Olner and remind him of his request. In his broad Yorkshire accent he asked this insightful question: 'Merci, madame, mais où est le knocking shop?' What a star. Of course, we never found it.

CHAPTER 13

THE WHIPS

Of all the government jobs, the one I really coveted was a place in the Whips' Office. But as I am an inveterate gossip and as discreet as Katie Price in full *Hello!* mode, I was never a candidate.

The job of the whip is to fade into the background and sniff out what Members are up to. They are a sponge to soak up all the gossip, intrigue and backstabbing and report back to the Chief about who is trustworthy and who is a total shit. The Chief is the Prime Minister's Beria. The job of the Whips' Office is not to bully or threaten but to flatter and cajole. Lots of carrot and just a little bit of stick when absolutely necessary. Their power is knowledge. MPs love to gossip and plot. To gain brownie points there are always those who will quite happily stitch up their colleagues in the hope of personal advancement. Very few MPs don't have one or two skeletons rattling around in the cupboard. And before they step out of line there is always the fear that the whips might just know about them. The chances are that they won't, but one of the great strengths of the Whips' Office is that it is shrouded in mystery. Break that mystique and they lose their authority. And the Chief's official title is not Patronage Secretary for nothing. He can determine the future of even the grandest of ministers.

Once, when I was PPS to Robert Atkins (Ratkins) when he was Minister of State in Northern Ireland, there was a three-line whip on some nondescript and eminently forgettable piece of legislation. Ratkins couldn't be arsed to fly over from Belfast as he had a full diary the next day. So I was despatched to negotiate with the whips. As Ratkins was a close friend of John Major, then Prime Minister, I thought that this would be easy. Unfortunately, the whip in charge of this vote was my old adversary, the 'caring whip' David Lightbown. I could hear the low growl of his twenty-five stone lumbering into action down the phone. 'I imagine your monkey enjoys being a minister? If so he'd better be at the vote tonight.' And the phone was slammed down. That was that.

Ratkins did like to chance his arm. He once asked Major if he could have a few weeks off so he could go to Australia and watch the cricket. John realised that if he allowed this it would open the flood gates to daft requests from ministers and play very badly in the press. So Ratkins had his request denied, but his disappointment was rewarded with elevation to the Privy Council. He was styled The Right Honourable Sir Robert Atkins MP. The jammy devil.

There seems to be a misunderstanding by some of the 2010 intake about what the role of the Whips' Office really is. One poor dear was moaning in the press recently that his whip never took him to one side, bought him a cup of coffee and listened to his woes and brilliant policy ideas. The whips are not the Samaritans. Their overriding responsibility is to push through the government's business. If you find yourself in a spot of bother, like being found with a cold woman, a hot boy or a serious drink problem, they will advise you how to minimise the damage. But they are primarily doing this to protect the government. Not you.

I recall two very sad cases when the whips took their eye off the ball. John Heddle, the delightful Member for Lichfield, took his own life rather than face the horror of bankruptcy. He was a lovely chirpy man. It was awful going to his memorial service and witnessing the distress of his widow and two little boys.

Then there was the tragedy of Iain Mills. He had been missing for days. He had had a messy divorce and had taken to drink. His body was found in a bottle-strewn flat. He had been dead for three days. Alone.

Mind you, some of the guys did take advantage when we were effectively in a minority government in the '90s. The last thing anyone wanted was a by-election. It came to the attention of the whips that an MP was facing bankruptcy due to gambling debts. A donor was found. But rather than pay off his debts this MP took the family off on an expensive holiday. He was not flavour of the month.

The whips tend to classify their little charges as 'troublesome … shit … absolute shit … insane'. The worst offence is not rebellion; it is not playing the game. This means letting them know if you have problems with a vote. In other words, if you feel very strongly on an issue and particularly if it affects the constituency, let them know well in advance. They will arrange a meeting with the minister, who will do his best to persuade you that the slaying of the firstborn male child is very much in the interests of the economy and an

overburdened health service. If you have listened to the arguments and are still concerned then they will do everything
they can to persuade you to support the government. But if
you really want to incur serious anger, just roll up to the vote
and go into the wrong lobby without having the courtesy to
let them know. They need to know the numbers.

On one successful rebellion which I was part of, to ensure
that child benefit should be paid to the mother rather than
the father, the minister (the lovely Tony Newton) had two
speeches prepared. One conceding, the other battling on. He
had to choose the former when the whip on duty told him
that we didn't have the numbers ... one minute before Tony
got to his feet.

On his death, John Major said of him that if someone
robbed Tony of his coat he would chase after them and offer
them his shirt. He was a great human being.

During the Teeth and Eyes rebellion (over the government's plan to save £30 million by abolishing the free sight
test and dental check-up) I asked my old chum Tim Devlin
how he was going to vote.

'Oh, with you,' he said in his charmingly laid-back way.

'So long as you tell the whips.'

'Oh, really? Oh, not to worry.'

Well, he did need to, as he was torn limb from limb. But at
least his heart was in the right place.

Veteran *Telegraph* sketch-writer Ed Pearce gave me a tip
on how to impress the whips and get a job. 'Make a speech
defending the utterly indefensible. Read Michael Howard on
the economic case for not allowing local authorities to spend
all of their council house sales receipts on new builds. He will

get a job in the next reshuffle.' And he did. It was the beginning of a meteoric and distinguished career.

Ed is an interesting fellow. After university he won a writing competition organised by the *Sunday Express* and was hired, on a piece-by-piece basis, by the legendary John Junor. When I was first elected Ed was a parliamentary sketch-writer for the *Telegraph*. I say 'a' because he shared the job with Godfrey Barker. In those days, Prime Minister's Questions were fifteen-minute slots on Tuesdays and Thursdays. For reasons beyond human understanding, the two of them would race to sit in the *Telegraph* perch in the press gallery overlooking the chamber. Sometimes this led to unpleasantness. I will never forget seeing Ed fighting with Godfrey for the seat. Mercifully, this was before the cameras were permitted in the chamber, otherwise viewers would have been entertained by Godfrey getting perilously close to being flung over the railings.

The clamour for whips to get information knew no bounds. They would attend all committee meetings, patrol the bars, sit in the Tea Room and strategically plonk themselves in the Members' dining room. They also kept a close eye on the two biggest enemies of the executive: the lavatories and the photocopier. If ever you wanted to have an indiscreet chat in the loo, you always had to check that the cubicles were empty. More often than not one would be occupied by the 'toilet whip', some poor devil sitting there for a couple of hours in the hope of eavesdropping a tasty morsel of gossip. The photocopier was also a source of indiscretion. All governments arrange for questions to be planted, and the whips distribute helpful suggestions for supplementary questions and 'lines to take'. Every now and again some hapless aide would leave the original plants on the photocopier. They would then be found by an Opposition aide, who would re-photocopy them and distribute them throughout the chamber to embarrass the government.

In those days the Members' dining room was configured along strict party lines. Government at the bottom, Lib Dems and minority parties in the middle and the Opposition at the far end. The government Chief Whip's table had one special feature: the chair for the great man had arms. The only chair with arms in the whole dining room. Heaven knows why. Every so often, Labour would send over a raiding party to occupy the Chief's table. All very public school.

I always used to enjoy a drink with Walter Harrison, the iconic Labour Deputy Chief Whip under Wilson and Callaghan. His stories of how his Whips' Office kept the minority government in office were scarily fascinating.

On one clincher vote Walter and his opposite number, John Stradling Thomas, went down to the courtyard to inspect a Labour Member on a trolley connected to a spaghetti of wires and tubes. Those were the terrible days when even the most mortally ill had to be 'nodded' through.

Stradling Thomas looked at the poor inert patient who had clearly popped his clogs.

'You can't count him, Walter, he's dead.'

'No, he isn't,' says Walter and kicks the life-support machine, making the corpse convulse. 'There you are. I told you he's alive.'

And he was duly nodded through. In those days even the dead voted.

The Tory whips were known for their cunning subtlety, like hiding MPs in cupboards and calling surprise votes.

Violence was rare. Sir Spencer Le Marchant was a legendary
Tory whip. His job was to ensure that his MPs stayed to vote.
One evening out of the corner of his eye he spotted a Tory MP
creeping down the steps to slink out of a vote. This seriously
angered the old boy and he aimed a kick which sent the
MP flying, with the shout of, 'And you can fuck off, you lazy
bastard.'

However, there was a slight problem. The kickee wasn't a
Tory at all. Nor an MP. It was the Peruvian ambassador on his
way home from a drinks party. This caused the Foreign Office
one or two difficulties.

Spencer was a popular whip on the Finance Committee.
This was the standing committee by whom every dot and
comma of the Budget would be pored over. The sessions
went on long into the night. So, to keep the troops happy,
Spencer would lay on vast quantities of free booze in an
adjoining committee room and allowed his little charges
access on a rota basis.

But back to Walter Harrison. The acclaimed play *The House*
was based on his antics. Sadly, he was too unwell to see it.
He wasn't exactly the most subtle of operators. After all, he
and his boss, Michael Cocks, had to keep hard-drinking, very
tough working men on the reasonably straight and narrow. He
told me that he would not tolerate shagging on overseas trips
and would order room inspections every night after ten.

One week there was a desperately tight vote and Walter
could not find one of his Members. His government could fall
if they lost. Eventually, a lackey passed him the phone.

'Where the fuck are you?'

'Er, just taking a short break in Crete.'

'Well, if you're not back in time for the vote you'll be in fucking concrete.' And he meant it.

Another time Walter was concerned for the whereabouts of one of his confirmed bachelors, who had a keen interest in rent boys. He wouldn't answer his telephone (there were no mobiles in those days) and hadn't been seen for days. So Walter despatched a junior whip to go to the old boy's flat. He sat outside in his car for a day and a night. Nobody answered the door but there was a steady stream of young men who were let in. After a while the whip could take no more and broke the door down. He entered the bedroom to find the MP sitting up in bed with a smile on his face – stone dead. He rang Walter.

'Found him, but I'm afraid he's dead.'

There was a growl at the other end of the phone.

'I said find him, not fucking kill him.'

Peter (now Lord) Snape was a newly appointed whip and received a call from Michael Cocks. Labour MP Maurice Edelman's voting record at the dying embers of the Callaghan government was woeful, so Snape was sent round to give the slacker a serious bollocking. Off he trundled to Edelman's magnificent old house in Belgravia and read the riot act. That night, Edelman came in to vote. Sadly, the next day he died. Cocks rang Snape.

'Overkill, boy, overkill.' And slammed the phone down, to the hoots of laughter in the Whips' Office.

Jack Weatherill was a thoroughly decent Deputy Chief Whip and a great Speaker. When he was Speaker he used to pop into the Labour Whips' Office to keep them up to date with the gossip. One day he told them that he had just received a report from the Papua New Guinea Parliament that its Speaker had been sacked for being drunk and urinating on the floor of the parliamentary press gallery. I can imagine how tempting this might be for John Bercow.

When Jack was Speaker he would always host a reception if any Member's child was christened. In 1984 my daughter, Francesca, was baptised by my old friend Tommy McMahon, the Bishop of Brentwood. Usually, before the Speaker entered, his train bearer would formally shout 'Speaker' and we would all stand as the great man walked in. On this occasion he sent in his five-year-old grandson wearing his full wig, which trailed on the floor.

Jack used to organise prayer suppers from time to time and invite a guest speaker to address us. One evening the famous American evangelist Billy Graham was invited to give a talk in the state apartments. Billy was an imposing, lantern-jawed charismatic used to wowing stadiums of 100,000. So addressing thirty of us ought to have been a piece of cake. But at the last moment a familiar figure seated herself on the front row: Margaret Thatcher. Her steely blue eyes pierced into him all evening. The poor man fell apart.

It is remarkable the lengths some Members go to in order to be called to make a speech. Labour old guard and Glaswegian hard man Jimmy Wray once complained to his Chief Whip, Derek Foster, that Betty Boothroyd wouldn't call him in debates.

'I canny catch the Speaker's eye, but I think I've cracked it.'

The next day he came into the chamber wearing a bright pink suit.

'She'll fucking see me now,' he grinned.

She did, but she still didn't call him.

The only other MP I have ever seen wearing a pink suit regularly was Nigel Lawson when he was Chancellor. And very fetching it was too.

I had a habit in the summer of wearing a blue-and-white seersucker suit which I had bought in New York. After a couple of years I gave it up after endless ribbing by the likes of Fatty Soames, asking me for an ice cream. Not unlike my good mate Ian Twinn, who always insisted on being called Dr Twinn by staff. We used to have great fun at his expense, pretending to be unwell and persuading secretaries to consult him on gynaecological matters. Ian, of course, was a doctor of planning.

My old friend Roger Pope (Popey), for years press officer to various Energy Secretaries, told me about the time he went to work as special adviser to Derek Foster, the newly appointed Labour Chief Whip. Michael Cocks called him in.

'You're going to work for the Chief Whip. I've only got one piece of advice. Never forget the strategic value of two words: "fuck" and "off".'

Actually, I always got on rather well with the whips because although I was independent-minded I would never take them by surprise.

One day, when I had been particularly well behaved for a few weeks, I was summoned by the then Chief, David Waddington. I was intrigued. A pat on the back? Perhaps my first slither up the greasy pole? Sadly not. David was in a foul mood.

'The chairman of the party was in his bath this morning and was listening to the *Today* programme,' he boomed.

The image of Peter Brooke naked in a bath up to his ears in soap suds and rubber ducks was not something I wanted to hold for too long.

'And then he heard some bloody socialist sounding off.'

'How awful,' I empathised.

'And then he realised it was you!'

This mystified me, as I had been vaguely supportive of the government that morning. But he would have none of it.

Eventually I managed to get a transcript and I sent it to him. To his credit, he sent me a charming letter saying, 'I must have sounded more ferocious than I meant.' He really is a lovely guy.

A few weeks later I ran into a charming lady in the lift.

'How are things, Jerry?' she politely enquired.

I asked how she knew me.

'Ah, I keep a particular interest in your career.'

She saw that this puzzled me.

'I'm Gill, David Waddington's wife,' she grinned.

Peter Brooke was a funny old cove. He only seemed able to have a conversation about his only two interests, Balliol and cricket. As I had not been to the former and didn't have much interest in the latter, we didn't have an awful lot in common. One time, when he was the Secretary of State for Northern Ireland, he unfortunately tried to show a little humanity by singing 'Oh My Darling, Clementine' on *The Gay Byrne Show* on Irish TV. He was not to know that a few moments earlier a bomb had gone off in Belfast. The media rather unfairly creamed him.

One of his civil servants once told me that when Brooke was given his first-day briefing as Secretary of State he was shown the colour-coded map setting out the political allegiances. He cottoned on fairly quickly.

'So that blue bit is where all the Conservatives are, I suppose?'

'Not quite, Secretary of State. That's the loch.'

Tim Renton was briefly Chief Whip but, for reasons that I never quite understood, was never a great success. He was witty, educated and very well read. An all-round good bloke. In the days when the Whips' Office was based at 12 Downing Street, I used to drop in to have a chat to my mate Murdo Maclean. Murdo's official title was Secretary to the Chief Whip. In reality he was 'usual channels', one of the most powerful men in government, with the rank of Permanent Secretary. His job was to do deals with all parties to ensure that the government ran smoothly. He had loyally served Wilson, Callaghan, Thatcher and Major. He was trusted by everybody and was one of the most popular figures in Westminster. I greatly enjoyed his company. Sadly, the Blair machine took a dislike to him (heaven knows why) and he took early retirement. Their loss.

When I was waiting to have a gossip with Murdo I would drop in to have a cup of tea and a chat with Dot, the No. 12 tea lady.

One day we were sitting in her cubbyhole when Tim Renton appeared. He was not in good spirits.

'Dot, am I really such a hopeless Chief?'

'I'm afraid so,' she said without a blink.

Those Downing Street tea ladies were a formidable lot. Sometimes, if Blair's mob had done something really daft the Cabinet would find themselves without tea or biscuits. Cross a Downing Street tea lady at your peril.

As No. 12 was the whips' lair and therefore by its nature very political, it was used for party functions. These were very often ghastly affairs where people who had donated a few quid could rub shoulders with MPs and ministers over a glass of warm white wine. I remember going to one these ordeals and being confronted by a terrifying lady in a veil whose views made the BNP seem rather left. And she had the easy charm of Miss Havisham. I introduced myself and asked if she had any concerns about policy.

'Don't you think that there are too many Jews in the Cabinet?' she hissed. This rather stumped me.

'Actually, I've never counted,' I chirped.

Through her veil I could see a look that would have melted an iceberg as she rattled through the bloodlines of ministers, spitting venom.

Time for a conversation change.

'Anyhow, we have loads of Catholics. Look, there's Chris Patten.'

The word 'Catholic' didn't have the desired effect. It was like one of those projectile vomiting moments in *Little Britain* whenever the word 'homosexual' is mentioned. And in no way was I going to mention *that* group of ministers.

So I did something quite unforgivable.

I beckoned over Chris Patten.

'Hi, Chris, here's a lady who'd love to speak to you.' And I made my excuses and left. He is probably still in counselling.

Lord (Bertie) Denham was a delightful Chief Whip in the Lords. This is a very difficult job and relies totally on charm, as there are neither threats nor inducements worth the paper they are not written on.

Once, he was splashed all over *The Sun* for an alleged dalliance with a very pretty young lady. It was sadly totally untrue. Nevertheless he was summoned to John Gummer, who was then chairman of the party.

'John, do you think people will believe this nonsense? I certainly hope so.'

In the '60s he once took Peter Carrington to the Bunny Club. They were agog at the amount of female flesh on display. They thought that they were being very, very wicked.

Those were innocent days.

CHAPTER 14

HER MAJESTY'S PRESS

My first bromance with Her Majesty's press started way back in 1981. I had just been selected as the candidate for Harlow, but I had one more hurdle to jump and that was to get on the official candidates list. And that meant spending a weekend at a dreary hotel just off a roundabout at Potters Bar. The idea was that you would be taught how to use a knife and fork properly, engage in debate and be grilled by a few captains of industry. It was a bit like being on *The Apprentice* but with nicer people (not a high bar) and loads of drink. As I was in the wonderful and unique position of having been selected for a seat already, so as long as I didn't appear splashed across the tabloids in a 'Top Tory shags royal corgi' story, I would sail through. Which I did. It was at Potters Bar that I made three lifelong friends, Gerry Bowden, Steve Day and Ian Twinn (who still does a very passable Ted Heath routine).

But if you think the modern-day back benches are infested by bonkeroons, you should have been a fly on the wall there. There were so many alien life forms on display it was like appearing in an episode of *Doctor Who*. One fellow spent the whole time walking around the place leaning on a shepherd's crook. And outside in the rain stood a small and solitary figure sniffing around for a story, with whom I used to chat. It was that titan of journalism, the Press Association's political editor Chris Moncrieff. One of the reasons he always managed the scoops was because he was omnipresent. I suspect that he rarely went home. When elected I became part of his Monday morning round-up for a quote about whatever political issue was exciting the chattering classes. And as PA fed every national and regional newspaper, it led to TV and radio appearances and hoovering up print. All right, many of my colleagues looked down their noses at me for being a rent-a-quote, which I was, but it made me stand out from the pack and 1983 was one of the largest Tory intakes in generations.

Politics is like broadcasting. Don't do vanilla. And don't try to be too cerebral, either. And on no account ever try irony. The punters want their politicians to look as normal as possible. Sometimes that is a very tall order. Nowadays, it's rather difficult because so many seem lobotomised with an on-message chip implanted in their brains.

The 1980s were when Charlie Kennedy, Tony Banks, Ken Livingstone and I mastered the art of the sound bite. In any news clip, ten seconds is as long as you're ever going to get. In a pre-record, think of your pithy bites and repeat them over and over again. They can't be edited against you as long as rambling interviews can. And it makes for easier editing. I remember walking across the Members' lobby when Mike Brunson, political editor of ITN, called over to tell me that Nigel Lawson, the Chancellor, had just resigned: 'Get over to the studio ASAP in time for a pre-record for the *News at Ten*.' It was 9.45.

I arrived at the studio with not an interviewer in sight. Only a camera and sound man. 'Mike's tied up, you'll have to interview yourself, mate.' So I gave them three ten-second bites to choose from. And the one that fitted in with their spin was used. You may think that all this is very cynical, but really it's quite practical. Broadcasters are on a deadline and if you can deliver the goods in one take they will use you again. It also means you get your message across crisply and clearly. There is nothing worse than seeing politicians ducking questions or equivocating. It makes them look shifty and dishonest.

In politics there is a caste system. Those on the inside track who have advised ministers and who will rocket their way to jobs; those who are desperate to please the whips; and then people like me who were elected purely by accident. George Osborne refers to the former as the Guild. I was never an insider. I had to plough another furrow.

I don't wish to be unkind to my former colleagues but some were a pretty dull bunch. Have dinner with them and they would only give you their views (most of which had been given to them by the whips) on a need-to-know basis, for fear that you might somehow use it against them. They would scuttle away to issue unreadable press releases and never ever speak to a journalist. The press was considered the enemy. That was so wrong and counterproductive. But there is an element of truth here. As far as the news desk is concerned, trust them as far as you can throw them. They have a different agenda. Everything you say is on the record even if you use the magic words 'off the record' first. And as they are never likely to speak to you again, who cares if they burn their source so long as they have the story?

The lobby system is very different. Everything you say is off the record unless you say to the contrary. They want stories and the background to stories. They want to sniff the wind and gauge the mood. Some criticise this as too cosy a relationship. Actually, it's not. It's a good working relationship. But if you are a scheming little shit who lies to them, word will get round and you will never be trusted again. They will destroy you, because there will be a time when you need their help and it won't be there.

Politicians should remember that journalists are gossips because that's how they get the germ of a story. I was lucky enough to have worked with the very finest. Gordon Greig at the *Mail*, Ian Aitken of *The Guardian*, Trevor Kavanagh of *The Sun*, Geoffrey Parkhouse of *The Herald* and David English, saviour of the *Mail* group. These guys were giants. It is just not possible to do a roll-call of all the great men and women of the lobby, but two of my closest friends are Nigel Nelson, veteran political editor of *The People*, and Ian Hernon, now deputy editor of *The Tribune*. Ian trained up so many distinguished Fleet Street names that they are affectionately called Hernon's Heroes. With that other old leftie, *Mirror* columnist Paul Routledge, I would trust those three with my life.

One evening, Nelson invited Darkie (Anthony Beaumont-Dark), Gerry Bermingham, Barry Porter and me to the *People* Christmas bash. It was to be at the Café de Paris so we thought it was going to be a bit posh. Mmm. When we got there the place was throbbing. A little bit too throbbing for our liking. For reasons I still don't understand, crowds of totally over the top and delightfully outrageous transvestites had been hired to entertain us. The real fear was that we had been set up (we hadn't) and that we would be splashed as 'MPs in tranny shame' (we weren't). But we did huddle together in terror. It was all very funny. But not at the time.

One day in Annie's Bar, Hernon received a call from Anglia TV. He was told to get one MP from Labour and one from the Tories to discuss the Rate Support Grant. Ipswich MP Jamie Cann and I were propping up the bar. 'Come on, lads,' pleaded Hernon.

Jamie was keen. After all, he had been leader of Ipswich Council and he understood this impenetrable mechanism. And I had as much interest in local government as studying to be a mortician. Worse, I hadn't a clue how the settlement would affect Harlow. So we did a deal. I would do the head-to-head provided Jamie gave me some sound bites. So after another drink we headed to College Green for the interview. Well, we both knocked nine bells out of each other and thanks to Jamie I didn't look too much of a fool. But it was all a bit Salvador Dalí.

Sometimes your mates in the press rally round to help. Just before the 1992 general election I received a phone call from the Chief Whip, a lovely guy called Richard Ryder. By this time I had become a bit of an expert on health matters and as this was going to be the last conference before the election, would I make a rabble-rousing speech, since the NHS was a major public concern? You bet. I had always got on well with Romola Christopherson, who was head of press at the Department of Health, and I knew she was pushing for me to be a junior minister if we won the election. This was my moment.

So Nelson and Hernon worked with me until three in the

morning perfecting the speech of my life. The only drawback was that this little masterpiece, which would have made Socrates green with envy, was put together in the hotel bar. The next morning my big moment arrived.

'I now call Mr Jerry Hayes MP.'

Thinking about what happened next still makes me nauseous. I swaggered up to the podium without a note. I'll show 'em. And I did. But not in the way that I expected. It actually started off rather well and I got a few cheers. And when I got into my main theme I was on fire. I was just approaching the part when I would reveal to the world the horrors of Labour. So I built up to my climax. 'And the Labour Party do ... [at this stage alcoholic amnesia swung towards me and my mind went blank] terrible things to people.'

Oh, God. It was gut-wrenchingly awful. So I tried to save the day with a joke.

'Sorry about that. I had a heavy night last night.' There were cheers, as half the audience were nursing hangovers. But I was dying on my feet. I was Archie Rice without the aid of half a bottle of vodka. It's hard to believe, but I got into a worse muddle by calling the chairman of the debate Madam Mr Chairman and saw my political career crash and burn, with the chances of a red box a distant joke. It made the *Titanic* look like a minor boating accident, except that the only person who died was me.

The next morning I slunk into the bar to be joined by Hernon and Nelson. They bought me a large Bloody Mary to calm me down.

'Well, at least it escaped the notice of the press,' I smiled. Until, grinning from ear to ear, they produced the tabloid front pages with my alcohol-induced sweaty face plastered all over them.

Years later, for my fortieth birthday, they hijacked a TV studio and made a spoof documentary about great speeches of the world. The Gettysburg Address, I Have a Dream, the Sermon on the Mount and of course That Bloody Speech. Thanks, boys.

Another journalist to whom I am devoted is Glaswegian *Mirror* Rottweiler Don Mackay. Editor Piers Morgan once brought Tony Blair into the newsroom for a stately tour. They paused at Mackay's desk.

'Don, have you met the Prime Minister?'

Don looked up at the great man and growled, 'Hello Blair, you cunt.'

At least he didn't take his teeth out, which was always a sure sign that somebody was going to get thumped.

On the death of John Smith, Don was put on the story. And in true Fleet Street fashion he borrowed a doctor's coat and stethoscope just to make certain that the fellow really was dead and not faking.

But Don really became iconic during the donkey wars. Just to remind you, a few years ago there was a great tabloid story about a ceremony in some tiny village in Spain where once a year a donkey was thrown from a church tower and caught in a blanket. Fleet Street felt that the British public wouldn't like this one little bit and so there was a tabloid war to find the donkey, rescue it and bring it back to Blighty, where it would live for the rest of its life in donkey luxury. All the red tops sent hacks to find the damn thing. In the best traditions of Fleet Street cheque-book journalism, the *Mail* won and the donkey was on its way to Britain. Don was distraught.

Until he thought of a plan of genius and cunning. The *Mirror* would splash a photo of the donkey's girlfriend looking wistfully across the Channel, waiting for her beloved. So the art department was tasked with finding a suitable photo. All went swimmingly until the mock front page showed something that really shouldn't have been there. Girlfriend donkey had an enormous cock. Luckily Don got it airbrushed out in the nick of time.

When the *Mirror* won Newspaper of the Year, Piers thought it was fitting for Don to pick up the award, an expensive piece of cut glass. The trouble was that he was rather refreshed, slipped over and the award smashed into a thousand pieces. Piers, to his credit, thought it was all rather funny. Despite what is said about him in the press, he is a really nice guy. You will hear more about him later.

I always got on rather well with the *News of the World* crowd. Rebekah Wade (now Brooks) was great fun, as was Tom Crone, the in-house lawyer. Once, she invited me to lunch at Queen's. She was with her then partner Ross Kemp and his screen Mitchell brother Steve McFadden. Sadly, I had never watched *EastEnders* so I hadn't a clue who they were. Queues of fans were lining up for their autographs. So, over lunch I asked why they were so famous. For the next twenty minutes they royally wound me up.

'Actually, we keep a rather famous pub.'

'Oh, really? What's it called?'

'The Queen Victoria. It's in the East End.' In the end, as everyone else round the table was crying with laughter, they let me in on the joke.

Another memorable lunch was with *News of the World* news

editor Alex Marunchak. A crowd of us were taken to Rules in Covent Garden. We had such a good time and the wine flowed in such quantity that the second brigade of waiters clapped us out. And then I remembered I was due to speak at the Oxford Union that night against Bill Cash and David Heathcoat-Amory in a debate on Europe. Now, as much as I like Bill, he is not the most exciting of speakers. Attendants would be sent round removing all sharp objects, ties, shoe-laces and anything else that could be used by people to top themselves. As I was well oiled, I decided to play it for laughs. Bill got rather annoyed and complained through the President that this was the most outrageous speech he had ever heard. I admitted guilt. The audience cheered. We won the vote.

I once had a very interesting lunch with a *Sunday Times* correspondent. He had rather a lot to drink and thought it would be a good idea to play with the traffic on Fleet Street. I went out to rescue him, tripped and found it difficult to walk. I thought that I had broken my ankle, so I called an ambulance. It suddenly dawned on me that I was not injured at all and had just lost my heel. We fled to one of those dodgy clubs that had a liquor licence all day. There were quite a few of those then, as the pubs had to close at 2.30. This was the Presscala Club. There used to be a large mat on the door with WELCOME written on it. The trick was if you were not a member you'd jump over it or else an alarm would sound. The Presscala was not exactly a fine drinking establishment. This would be the place where newspaper executives would take their secretaries for a few swifties before a pre-going-home-to-the-wife shag. The barmaid was a lady of a certain age who had a cleavage that could have raised the *Titanic*. When she bent over to pick up a mixer she would be in the habit of emitting a sphincter-rattling fart followed by the ladylike comment, 'Well, better out than in, loves.' A truly classy joint.

Private Eye lunches were always splendid occasions. The idea was that Ian Hislop and his hounds would get you roaring drunk in the hope of a couple of hours of indiscreet gossip. Just up my street. They were held in a scruffy upstairs room in the Coach and Horses when the splendid Norman ran the place. We used to have a drink in the bar with Jeffrey Bernard and then up for steak, chips and vats of red wine. The journos and politicians would sit at editor Ian Hislop's end of the table and down the far end sat a tweedy Richard Ingrams with equally tweedy literary types. He always referred to me as The Beard. I never cared for him too much and always found him rather snooty. But to be fair to him, he probably was quite entitled to view me a cocky little sod, as humility was never my middle name. But at Hislop's end the gossip would flow. I have always found him to be very good news. At Leveson, he was one of the few editors to behave with absolute integrity. It was a powerful performance.

But since Norman left, the Coach and Horses is a dreadful little place. I never bother to go in any more.

The *Mail on Sunday* lunches for the 'Black Dog' column were the most entertaining. Peter Dobbie, the political editor, was a rough diamond, but could squeeze a story out of a stone. Or, as we still say, polish a turd. Once, on my mate Adrian Lithgow's first day in the Commons as a journalist, Dobbie introduced me to him with these words: 'This is that twat Jerry Hayes who hasn't given me a story in a week,' as he gently kicked me in the gonads.

Adrian was a serious ladies' man. His penis reached iconic status when it was described in a Julie Burchill novel as 'the silken cosh'. I recall one famous Black Dog Christmas lunch when we shared a restaurant with the sports department, which got a little out of hand. I dimly remember being assaulted with a rubber chicken. Quite why, I can't remember.

Dobbie had a habit at the end of every party conference of apologising to each politician he bumped into. I asked him why.

'Well, I probably twatted him, called him a cunt or both.'

Dobbie was a star.

But today it has all changed. The Commons bars are rarely full, Annie's is closed and journalists' expenses for a decent lunch are long-distant memories. Now pasty-faced youngsters are stuck in front of their screens picking up feeds and press releases from the internet. And apart from a few old-school MPs, the idea of going drinking with a journalist is too terrifying for some of them to contemplate. Clem Attlee used to advise all new MPs to stay clear of the bars and journalists. And what a dull little man he was.

The rot set in when Ali Campbell, as Blair's brilliant press secretary, pretty well lobotomised the press. They were prepared to be spoon-fed with press releases, as in those days the Tories were a hopeless shambles. Very few went in search of real political stories. There was also an element of fear. If Blair's chief fixer, Peter Mandelson, took exception to a story or what he thought might turn out to be a story, he would threaten and bully a journalist into submission. The veiled threat would be that he would go to the editor and have the journo sacked. Whether this ever actually happened we will never know.

In those days only the most secure journalists dared cross Mandelson. He was a terrifying and venomous figure. And nobody was safe. For an ambitious junior hack, these were very dark days. *The Thick of It* is not far off the mark. The only journalist who really had the courage to fight Mandelson was my old friend from the *Mirror*, Paul Routledge. But more of him later.

For now, a brief word about the legendary David Healey, a rough Glaswegian bruiser of the old school, but with a heart of gold. One day he told me of one of his first kick-in-the-door assignments as a young reporter. He had to go and interview some old duck who had had a bereavement. David, still suffering from the night before, slumped heavily down on the sofa and felt a bit of a crunch. The old duck came back rather distraught because she couldn't find her little dog. And off she popped to have a look round the house. Healey then looked at what he had sat on. Sadly, it was the dog. He popped it in his pocket, let himself out, and dumped it in a rubbish bin.

CHAPTER 15

THE FALL

The 1987 election had secured Margaret Thatcher another large majority and she wielded absolute control over her party. Or so she thought. It is a fatal error for successful leaders to start believing their own propaganda. And when you have a 50 per cent approval rating, have routed your opponents in the party, defeated the miners and are faced by a weak and divided Labour Party there is a danger of becoming a cult figure rather than a leader. And if you surround yourself with sycophants who cocoon you in your own political la-la land and you humiliate and ignore your senior ministers it is inevitable that it will all come to a sticky end.

I always think that that overused phrase of David Maxwell Fyfe that 'the secret weapon of the Conservative Party is loyalty' is as hopelessly inaccurate as it is laughable. What makes it even more risible is that he coined this phrase two weeks before he was unfairly sacrificed by Macmillan in the Night of the Long Knives.

The secret weapon of the Conservative Party is adaptability. We will borrow or even steal policies, perhaps even dogmas, provided that they achieve the party's default setting: power. And if any leader, however revered and feted, proves to be an obstacle to re-election they will be destroyed. The Conservative Party has always been the cannibal of the political jungle. We eat our own and we do it swiftly.

Many commentators cast the poll tax as the beginning of the end of Thatcher. This was only contributory. Her real problems began when her political secretary, Stephen Sherbourne (now Lord Sherbourne), left her side. He was one of the few people who would politely stand up to her and tell her when she was wrong. And she would listen. Her sensible and cerebral adviser, Ferdinand Mount, tried honesty. But it cost him his job.

Stephen would have counselled her against the worst excesses of the poll tax and might just have saved her from her arrogance and hectoring. 'Never explain, never apologise' wears a little thin after a while. He might also have saved her from some seriously mad advisers, in particular the odious former Communist machine gunner in the Spanish Civil War, Alfred Sherman.

Determination and grit go a long way in politics. But if it transforms into arrogance, it is lethal. Grim as it is, a party leader has to keep the team on side, listen to the moans of senior ministers, flatter backbenchers and at least pretend to consult the party.

By 1989, Margaret Thatcher and her worshippers believed that she would (as she said to the press) 'go on and on'. Coupled with attending a Guildhall banquet dressed not unlike Queen Elizabeth I, then, after the birth of a grandchild, the almost royal 'we have become a grandmother' utterance struck a sour chord with ministers and the public.

An alternative to the rates had always been high in the public's mind. It is instructive to consider the origins of the poll tax (it was actually the community charge, but we stupidly allowed the name to be hijacked). At every public and party meeting there was a strong feeling that the rating system was unfair. Why should a family of five in an identical house to their pensioner neighbour pay exactly the same as her when they used five times more services?

So there was a groundswell for change. The theory was to let the local tax be levied on the individual rather than the household, with exemptions. This was a very good and very popular idea. Sadly, in reality it gave the impression of being administered by the inmates of Bedlam. Pensioners, students and those on benefits would have discounts or total exemption. But they would have to pay first and reclaim the money. Totally crackers and a political nightmare.

And another barmy idea was to try it out in Scotland first and, to compound the lunacy, couple it with a property revaluation. So any financial gains were immediately lost. Our sensible theory to make the system fairer now looked punitive and expensive. It was a public relations disaster. And the punters didn't like it one little bit.

Of course, many of the poll tax riots were manipulated by the far left. But when 18 million refused to pay the community charge and 100,000 marched on Trafalgar Square, alarm bells should have been ringing in No. 10 that this was time for a compromise. But that was not the Lady's style. To her, compromise equalled weakness.

In those days we used to talk about the need for consensus politics. The look that you would get from her at the C word (far more offensive than the other one) was as if you had just served a rat sandwich garnished with Arthur Scargill's blood as a jus. So, all criticism had to be in coded language. There was nothing wrong with our policies, oh no. It's just we need to present them more clearly and we must listen. It sounds awfully familiar. Utter bollocks, of course, but it was the best we could get away with.

So, party chairman Ken Baker joined the 1922 executive to troop into No. 10 to tell madam what needed to be done. I'm still not sure what they talked about or even if anyone got a word in edgeways, but there was a clear crossing of wires. The delightful Ken, grinning like the Cheshire Cat, appeared on the steps saying that she was 'in listening mode'. A day or so later when the Lady was asked in an interview about this she looked rather puzzled: 'Is that what he said?' Things began to get worse.

It is worth remembering that although Nigel Lawson was one of the finest and most reforming of Chancellors, his reflationary 1988 Budget stored up a whole raft of economic difficulties. The hike in property prices made and broke the loadsamoney classes. By 1990, inflation was running at 9.7 per cent and interest rates nudging 14 per cent. Worse, the deficit was beginning to soar. With unemployment still high and the country reeling from the poll tax riots, the mood was getting very ugly on the back benches. There was much speculation of a stalking horse. Eventually, we settled for the stalking donkey, a charming old toff called Sir Anthony Meyer. He was never going to win but the idea was to encourage a real candidate later. But the No. 10 rubbish machine was cranked into action. *The Sun* was tipped off that the old boy had been up to naughties involving a bit of S&M with a comely black lady. He and his equally elderly wife Barbadee were ambushed by a hack one Sunday morning after attending church.

'Any truth in the rumour that you have been engaging with a lady in bondage sessions, Sir Anthony?'

Without breaking step and still arm-in-arm with Barbadee, he replied – not quite as they were expecting.

'Oh, you mean Simone? Barbadee knows all about that, dear boy. Good day.'

The now stalking stallion obtained thirty-three votes. A clear victory for Thatcher. But the writing was on the wall. Sadly, I didn't have the courage to abstain or vote for him. The machine would have destroyed me.

Then something came along that catapulted me into the media: the ambulance dispute. Pay has always been hotly fought over in the public sector and in the NHS in particular. Ambulance care was very different from now and my dear old mate Ken Clarke did not help matters by suggesting that they were 'professional drivers'. In fact (obviously), they weren't. Ken was getting muddled with the people who dropped off the old dears to outpatients.

But this ignited a volatile situation. These guys were clearly underpaid and undervalued. Then, by chance, I was invited onto *The Time, The Place*, an ITV programme which was the forerunner to *Kilroy*, *Vanessa* and now *Jeremy Kyle*. In those days it was hosted by John Stapleton. Needless to say, despite my support for the ambulance men's cause I was creamed simply because I was a Tory. Two days later I was approached by two trade union leaders, Roger Poole of the National Union of Public Employees (NUPE) and Bob Abberley of the Confederation of Health Service Employees (COHSE). Would I be an honest broker between them and the government to break the deadlock? Of course.

And what a decent bunch of guys, in the old-fashioned trade union sense of not playing party politics but just trying to get the best possible deal for their members. We became good friends.

But it was a white-knuckle ride. Extraordinarily, Clarke, through no fault of his own, had never met any of the union leaders. The Department of Health, through their own depressing incompetence, were swapping round senior executives to negotiate. Ministers were left out of the loop.

I was able to sort this. Well, it was hardly political brain surgery.

The ambulance dispute was a massive political disaster. Four and a half million people signed a petition in favour of the ambulance men and according to opinion polls the majority of Conservatives supported them too. The strike lasted for months and concluded reasonably amicably in March 1990. I was trying to do a deal for a pay review body, which the Treasury was resisting. To be honest, in hindsight they had good reason to: these bodies were fair but uncertain. The Treasury is obsessed with certainty. Mostly their obsession is misdirected.

For months I had the media camping outside my house. I did my best to give a daily briefing about how it was all going. But my favourite experience was in December 1989. I was invited on a Friday to a very boozy lunch at a Chinese restaurant near where I lived. Negotiations were at a sensitive point. But it was the Friday just before Christmas. Nothing will happen, I thought. Wrong.

It all went a bit mad. No. 10 wanted a chat. The chairman's office wanted to be updated and so did Clarke's office. So I am trying to balance all of this by talking with the health unions. I wanted everyone to be in the loop.

So, what's the big deal, you might ask. The big deal was that I could only get a signal in the gents' toilets. And this was before the days of mobiles, just a cordless. So trying to get a deal with the unions, Thatcher, Clarke and Baker had a rather surreal backdrop. Drunks falling around, out of their brains and swearing. Boozers throwing up. Kevin having very noisy sex in the cubicles with Kali from Accounts and, the pièce de résistance, a German oompah band playing in the background. Well, we were in Essex.

In March, the strike was over. No pay review body, but a commitment to paramedics and a promise to treat them as true professionals. Ken Clarke deserves much of the credit for this. He is a tough old warhorse. And he got it about right.

I am very proud of my small part in this, as my son Lawrence is a paramedic. And he reminded me of the dispute when he looked it up on the internet.

As a decent sort, John Stapleton invited me back to *The Time, The Place*. After the credits rolled, John opened something like this:

'Well, a few months ago you howled at Tory MP Jerry Hayes. Now he has helped broker a deal. What would you say to him now?' he asked, with a smile that expected an orgasmic televisual ovation for me. Needless to say, they howled at me far worse than Gordon Brown under a full moon with a warm Nokia in his hand and an adviser perched precariously on the stairs.

But there was more trouble in store for us. The economy was overheating. I used to come up on the train to London with a senior Bank of England official called Ben Gunn. This was one of those joyous times when everyone was feeling happy. I had a smile on my face and not a political care in the world.

'But don't you get it, Jerry? It will all go tits up. Too much money chasing too few goods. Classic cause of inflation.'

All the other guys in the carriage nodded. They were all bankers.

But nobody in government seemed to get it. It was party time.

Interestingly, Ben had another complaint. Nobody ever accepted his cheques because his was a Bank of England cheque book. They all thought it was a scam. The man who advised government on credit just couldn't get any himself.

In those days the NHS was even more of a poisoned chalice than it is now. In 1990, 83 per cent believed that the Conservatives weren't the people to trust with it. I've written earlier about the effect of Geoffrey Howe's resignation speech. We all knew it was the end of the Lady. The question was when.

A few weeks later I was on a speaking engagement with Hezza. He gave me a lift back to the Commons.

'Why on earth don't you stand? Have you lost all ambition?' I asked.

'Dear boy, this has nothing to do with ambition. It is timing.' A few days later he threw his hat in the ring.

The Thatcher campaign was a disaster. It reeked of complacency. John Moore was 'running' it yet spent most of his time in the States. One day, Michael Forsyth (who has since become a big beast) sidled up to me and casually asked if I was 'on board'.

'Not on board the *Titanic*,' was my reply.

Michael just smiled. There was no way the Lady could possibly be defeated.

Probably the biggest mistake she made was not enlisting the services of Tristan Garel-Jones. He was the über puppet master who made Mandelson and Machiavelli look like gifted amateurs. He offered help. But he was not 'one of us' as he was to the left of the party and a pro-European.

He could have swung it for her. Just.

Fleet Street understandably went into overdrive. Mike Brunson and I sat down to work out the sums with a few bottles of wine. As old hands, we ignored the number crunchers. They were all talking about left and right, wets and dries. We knew better. Those whom she had never promoted, had slighted and sacked, no matter what their views, would vote against her in droves. Party elections are based on malice and malcontent rather than dogma. Mike and I were about three votes out.

But after her resignation and with Major in play, Hezza knew that he was doomed. He came up to me in the lobby and assumed that I was going over to the winning side.

'Michael, you will not win and John Major is a friend. But I was one of those who urged you to stand. I will not be disloyal. But it is the end.'

And I wrote to John Major saying that despite our friendship it would be a shitty thing to drop Hezza in the lurch. But wished him well.

Oh, and if you are not convinced by now of my brilliant political judgement, you should have been a fly on the wall when, early one morning, I strode into the Commons with Sir Eldon Griffiths. He asked for my view as to what she would do.

'I have no doubt that she will fight on,' I said confidently. She resigned within the hour. At the very end I bumped into Cecil Parkinson at LBC.

'Do realise what you have done?' he asked with a pained expression. Sadly, I did.

Margaret Thatcher had saved the country, defeated the Argentinians, democratised the unions and helped free the Soviet Union. But she was leading the Conservative Party into electoral disaster. She had to go or else Neil Kinnock would have been the next Prime Minister. But it has bitterly divided the Conservative Party. I suspect that it will take at least another ten years before her political ghost will be finally laid to rest.

CHAPTER 16

JOHN MAJOR

History will treat John Major one hell of a lot better than his party did. By the time of the 1997 election the Euro-obsessive Amish wing of the Tories had put government into suspended animation, giving Norman Lamont's bitter speech that we were 'in office not in power' more than a whiff of credibility. Despite the fact that the economy was booming and the deficit under control, people had bitter memories of crippling interest rates, bankruptcies and Tory MPs on the take. Couple this with the young modernising and charismatic Tony Blair and people weren't afraid of Labour any more. Like vaginal deodorant and flares, the Tories had gone out of fashion.

But when John Major became Prime Minister in 1990 he didn't have an enemy in the world. Despite a few frustrating years in the Whips' Office his rise was meteoric. From Minister of State to Foreign Secretary to Chancellor to Prime Minister in a couple of years is a remarkable achievement. And he didn't achieve this through endless scheming, plotting and trampling over the bloodied bodies of his political rivals. He did it through ability and charm. When he first became Prime Minister he was a little star-struck.

'Well, now you're Prime Minister you can have dinner with whomever you want.'

'Really? Even Joanna Lumley?' And his wish was her command. She came, bless her.

The trouble is that many people confused being a nice guy with being weak. Anyone who saw him in action knew that he was anything but. Challenging John Redwood to put up or shut up and having to sack his campaign manager, friend and Chancellor, Norman Lamont, were signs of enormous courage. The sad fact was that by 1997, seven years after the fall of a now worshipped Margaret Thatcher, nobody could have led the Conservatives to victory.

His early days were a fascinating insight into his mindset. During the leadership campaign one young MP rolled up on a Saturday morning to No. 11 (Major was Chancellor). He had brought his toddler son with him. Major could see that there was going to be trouble so he suggested that the little boy play in another room. It wasn't long before the young MP set out his demands. He would vote for him provided that he was given a government job and a ring road round his constituency. John just smiled. 'Thank you for your support, but I think it's time for you to fuck off.'

The weird thing was the right thought Major was of their persuasion. I tried to explain to Gerald Howarth (now Sir Gerald and a former Defence Minister) that his views were not much different from mine. Gerald thought that I was quite mad. The fact that Ken Livingstone had once described Major as the most enlightened Tory chairman of housing he had ever met, when they served together on Lambeth Council, should have been a bit of a clue.

No doubt the unfortunate 'I will be a back-seat driver' from the Lady stiffened the sinews of the Wagnerian wing. In fact, the right thought that under his premiership there would be a glorious continuation of the mythical land of milk and honey provided by Margaret Thatcher. They were in for a bit of a shock. Although Tony Blair eventually gave us Thatcherism with a smile, Major gave it to us with a heart. Rather than plough on with the poll tax, its excesses and lunacies were ironed out.

One of the first visitors to No. 10 was Sir George Gardiner, a cadaverous old right-winger who was one of Thatcher's earliest supporters and guardian of the True Flame of the Blessed Blue Shrine, the 92. Actually, although we lived on different political planets, I rather liked old George, a former *Express* journalist. We were having dinner one evening and I let it slip that it was my fortieth birthday. Suddenly he became wistful.

'Ah, forty. That was when I had one of my finest mistresses,' he sighed.

It is worth remembering that the right wing of the Conservative Party is utterly ruthless. They see compromise as weakness, a U-turn as a failure and being reasonable as a personality defect. Worse, they looked at everything through the prism of dogma which basically meant: the unions have to be smashed, healthcare should be insurance-based if we can get away with it, the unemployed should have to work for their benefits and we should have left the EU years ago. And they would be prepared to destroy anything that got in their way, including their leader and their party. Sounds awfully familiar. So Major was under no illusion about what this meeting with George was really all about. The conversation went rather like this:

'Congratulations, Prime Minister, we are all behind you.'

'Thank you, George.'

'Obviously we want to help as much we can. But it would be much easier if you did it our way. If not, things could become difficult.'

'Thank you, George, now why don't you just fuck off.'

This was the beginning of the poisonous, corrosive, destructive relationship with the right. But even if Major had said, 'Sure, George, you guys just tell me what to do,' it would have made no difference. The right take no prisoners.

Graham Bright (now Sir Graham and police commissioner for Cambridgeshire, and a very old friend) became Major's PPS. And a very effective one he was too. The trouble with being an affable fellow was that his enemies confused this with stupidity. The right nicknamed him Graham Dim. And he was anything but.

But Graham has a great sense of humour. I remember when Major had to make a decision on who to vote for as chairman of the European Commission. I asked Graham who he thought it might be. He paused and grinned. 'Well, it won't be the big fat sweating Belgian.' And it wasn't.

One of John Major's earliest tests was in February 1991. I was in the Tea Room at lunchtime when he came and joined a crowd of us with a plate full of sliced tomatoes. We asked what had happened and he explained rather matter-of-factly that the Downing Street kitchens were out as the Provisional IRA had just bombed Downing Street and he needed his lunch. He was remarkably relaxed after what had happened. Not too many people realise how close the Prime Minister and senior members of the War Cabinet (first Gulf War) came to being murdered on that day. The IRA had launched three mortar bombs, two of which failed to detonate and one of which exploded in the Downing Street garden, causing a massive crater. If there had been a direct hit they would have all been killed. But Major had another stroke of luck. A few weeks earlier the bombproofing of the Cabinet Room windows and the French windows that lead down to the garden had been completed. If they hadn't then I suspect that there would have been some serious injuries, if not deaths.

The Cabinet followed the standard procedure and sheltered under the Cabinet table, which is specially reinforced. I remember speaking to John Wakeham that day, then Leader of the House, who had been horribly injured and lost his wife in the Brighton bombing. He told me how impressed he was with Major's unflappability. While they were all crouching under the table waiting to be taken to a safer place he calmly commented that he thought that it would be a good idea to reconvene somewhere else. But what really impressed Wakeham was that Major gave strict instructions that as soon as they left the room they should telephone their wives and loved ones to tell them that they were safe before the news broke.

But my old friend Graham Bright, the Prime Minister's PPS, had an even narrower escape. He was sitting in his Downing Street office, which did not have bombproof windows, just bomb-resistant curtains. He came into the Tea Room covered in glass. He was very lucky to be alive, as was Murdo Maclean, the private secretary to the Chief Whip.

In the early days of Thatcher, Graham asked me to sponsor his Video Recordings Bill. This was to get rid of the anomaly that there was a classification of sex and violence for films but absolutely none for the newly emerging video market. The idea was to protect children. This had all-party support. Unfortunately, the lead minister at the Home Office was David Mellor. To be fair, Mellor can be a nice enough guy on occasion, but the air around him used to crackle with his ambition. He promised us that in no way would this Bill be hijacked to revamp the Obscene Publications Act, which was an unworkable piece of legislation put on the statute book in 1959. That is, until the Lady brought him in for a chat. She had been got at by Mary Whitehouse, founder of the National Viewers' and Listeners' Association. Mary, a former sex education teacher, was a lovely old duck but was on a crusade to clean up what she believed to be the filth on the television and radio. There were daily nipple and buttock counts, all lovingly researched by her outraged members. At the next standing committee meeting, Mellor came armed with amendments which had Whitehouse's fingerprints smeared all over them. This was nothing more than an attempt to harden the Obscene Publications Act, with Parliament deciding what the public was allowed to hear, view or read. There was a bit of a row. We made it clear that the Bill would fall if there were any plans to tighten the Obscene Publications Act, as any all-party support would wither on the vine. Eventually, common sense prevailed and Bright, with me as his whip, pushed it through the Commons. David, to his credit, stood up to the Lady.

It is worth remembering that the Obscene Publications Act is rarely used nowadays. The offence was possessing material that tended to 'deprave and corrupt', which is very much in the eye of the beholder. In those days, selling magazines depicting basic sex or an erect penis could attract a prison sentence. But the moral right wanted to make the sentences even stiffer. If you know what I mean.

But the Video Recordings Bill was not without its bizarre moments. Sitting in the ministers' room in the Home Office watching *The Texas Chainsaw Massacre* and such cinematic triumphs as *I Spit on Your Grave*, where a woman graphically cuts off the penises of all those who have raped her, bordered on the bizarre. One day, Graham told me that he had been doing some research on telephone porn lines. He was so animated about regaling us with what he had heard that he spent most of the time wheezing into his inhaler. I suspect that it was all pretty tame by today's standards. But I feared for dear old Graham's health when he was on the line to some potty-mouthed granny doing her ironing while pretending to be an orgasmic Swedish nurse.

After winning the 1992 election, everyone expected backbenchers to be a happy, united little family. In their dreams. After reeling from the shock waves of Black Wednesday we had to endure the horrors of the Maastricht wars, with the right wallowing in ripping the party apart. Despite the fact that Major had won serious concessions from Brussels, keeping us out of the euro and the Social Chapter, nothing would ever be enough for them except a referendum, a no vote and a withdrawal. Preferably yesterday.

It was open civil war. The depressing thing was that these guys were so obsessed with the purity of their arguments they genuinely didn't care if the Tories lost the election and let in a pro-Brussels Labour. Many were muttering that it would have been be better had we lost the 1992 election. And some genuinely believed that it would be in the party's interests to lose the 1997 election, as we could regroup with a Thatcherite leader and come out invigorated and refreshed. By this time, the argument went, voters would have sussed that Blair was a red-in-tooth-and-claw socialist and kicked him out. It goes without saying that this sort of Euro Wahhabism was aggressively promoted by those who had rock-solid majorities. Whoever won the next election would not affect them one jot. No wonder, Major confided to Mike Brunson, that they were bastards. Well, it was meant to be confidential except nobody had thought to tell him that his microphone was still live.

It is not easy to describe how poisonous the atmosphere was. There was almost a rerun in early 2013 when Euroloonery and Cameron vilification nearly ripped the party apart again. Post-1992, the usual suspects were in full throttle. Bill Cash, Teresa Gorman and John Redwood seemed never to be off the news, while, in the background, Michael Portillo was secretly preparing to ascend into prime ministerial heaven. Things were coming to a head.

One day I received a call from Graham asking me to join a few decent sorts for lunch at No. 10. These were always convivial affairs and while we were waiting for John we downed a few industrial-sized gin and tonics. This was at a time when *Spitting Image* was at the height of its popularity and the sketch of the PM being obsessed with eating peas off the end of a knife was very well known. Eventually he arrived, had a couple of gins and sat down for lunch. There on the table was an enormous tureen of peas.

'Oh God, not peas again,' he moaned. 'Don't they realise it's a joke? I can't stand the bloody things.'

At the end there was just John, Graham and me. We were despairing at the way the right was behaving. I cut to the chase.

'If you don't fuck them, they will certainly fuck you.' A few weeks later he issued his put-up-or-shut-up challenge and in October 1995 John Redwood resigned from the Cabinet and threw his hat into the ring for the leadership. In turn Major resigned as party leader but remained as Prime Minister. It was a remarkably brave thing to do and one hell of a gamble. The battle for the leadership had begun. And in the space of just a few years the Conservative Party indulged itself in a destructive civil war. What was a little surprising was that Redwood and the rest of the Cabinet had undertaken not to stand. Most of us expected that the challenger would be Norman Lamont.

Norman Tebbit and Norman Lamont were the heavyweight Redwood supporters. The trouble with Redwood is that he is great company, highly intelligent and very pleasant, but on camera he looks completed deranged. He has the knack of making some of the most sensible proposals sound completely bonkers. It didn't help that in his campaign launch he was surrounded by Teresa Gorman, Richard Body, Bill Cash and Tony Marlow (nicknamed Von Marloff) – not the sort of people you would necessarily choose to stand next to when there is a full moon. Dear old Richard Body once prompted Major to comment, 'Why is it whenever I hear the name Body I always think of flapping white coats?' And in India, Gorman would be considered sacred. They all looked madder than a box of frogs. Gorman's was the first call I received after losing my seat in 1997.

'Jerry, my supporters are very upset that my majority has

been significantly reduced. They think it may have something to do with you blaming me for our defeat.'

Considering that this ghastly woman spent most of the time undermining the Prime Minister and destroying any chance of a Conservative victory, I gave her short shrift. I suggested that she fuck off, and never spoke to her again.

It is strange how a hard core of Tory backbenchers regularly conspire against their leadership. Heath, Thatcher, Major, Duncan Smith and now Cameron. The trick is to try and keep as many on side as possible. It is easier to herd cats. The worry in 1995 was not that Major would lose the leadership but what the numbers would be. There was considerable speculation that real challenges would come if Major failed to get the 50 per cent of the vote or, like Thatcher, was holed below the waterline. And in the true Tory tradition of 'never kick a man unless he is down and there are at least five of you', Michael Portillo was on manoeuvres, installing a bank of telephones at a secret campaign headquarters. Just in case. Except that nothing in Westminster is secret for very long. He, of course, professed nothing but utter loyalty to Major. But it was the end of his career. Nobody trusts underhand behaviour if it is coupled with a lack of courage. It was a shame because deep down he is quite a decent soul. But it is very deep down. I just wish he had told us before he lost his seat in 1997 that he was a compassionate Tory.

A few days after the telephone business I was particularly exercised about Portillo's disloyalty. I was chatting to a chum near the Members' taxi rank and exclaimed my frustration with a shout of 'Portillo. What a total cunt.' It was then that I noticed the diminutive shape of the delightful Ann

Widdecombe. I was mortified that I had used the C word in her presence and profusely apologised.

'There is absolutely no need to,' she smiled. 'The only word that I objected to was "Portillo".'

I am very fond of Ann. Feisty, opinionated and a heart of gold. Although we don't always agree.

Well, Major received 218 votes with Redwood at 89, 12 abstentions and 8 spoilt papers. I was appointed as one of the scrutineers. It was all rather peculiar. I would be sitting in Committee Room 14 and ballot papers were handed out. Loyalists would flourish them while those who were going to vote for Redwood would scamper into the shadows. Needless to say the names were all noted. We all hoped that this would be the end of the matter and that the troops would realise how close they had come to destroying the party and behave.

Wrong. The right seemed to get another wind. And after Black Wednesday the press was gunning for us. The *Mail* and *The Sun* had been charmed by Blair and Mandelson and were moving over to New Labour.

I remember when Blair stood for the leadership. I bumped into him with a member of my constituency executive. After a brief hello from Tony, my supporter wished him well, 'but I hope you don't win the leadership because you will win the election'. A year later I bumped into him in a corridor. 'Why don't you join me in New Labour?'

'Tony, I'd love to but you're a bit too right-wing for me.'

He grinned.

But everyone was out to get us now. At one time, Major came down to Harlow and asked me to mind the local press. I remember one interview with ITV's Tim Ewart, who behaved with aloof condescension, bordering on the downright rude. It was a very unpleasant interview. John appeared charming and affable, but inside he was fuming.

'How can he talk to the Prime Minister like that?' he said after Ewart, now the royal correspondent for ITV, had departed in a cloud of televisual glory. If he was made of chocolate that man would eat himself.

It is a horrendous job being Prime Minister even at the best of times. When your party is ripping itself apart and the press has turned against you, it must be the worst job in the world. I suspect that he hated it. And yet he transformed the economy and, because of his special relationship with Albert Reynolds, he started the peace process in Northern Ireland with the Downing Street Declaration, which culminated in a ceasefire, setting us on the road to peace.

I was particularly fond of Major's brother Terry. We met at events and various TV programmes. A very kind and decent man with a great sense of humour. But he had hardly any money. Not that he cared. One day I asked John why he didn't sort out a job for him. He looked at me with incredulity.

'You really don't understand our family. Terry would be mortified. When I needed a room to study for my A levels he left home to live in a flat so I could have his room. Except he wasn't in a flat; he was living in a lock-up garage.'

The press was wicked towards Major. Kelvin MacKenzie, the *Sun* editor, was really beyond appalling, ringing him up and, when asked how the next day's front page would be treating the government, replying, 'Prime Minister, on my desk I have a large bucket of shit and tomorrow I'm going to pour it all over you.' Simon Heffer (then of the *Telegraph*) and Peter

Hitchens (*Mail on Sunday*) were particularly vicious. That always caused me a problem, as personally I like them both. Aha, you might say, how can you like these guys when they are slagging off your party and your friends? Easy. You can like someone socially but professionally you could quite cheerfully murder them. And sometimes I could, particularly over the appalling rubbish they write about Cameron, whom I like and admire.

The worst thing in politics is to bear grudges. This helped me tremendously when I became a journalist.

On one rare occasion I actually found a Hitchens column that I quite liked, which must be a collector's item, I told him. Peter was horrified.

'People like you are not meant to like my column,' he sighed.

At one occasion I bumped into John at one of Jeffrey Archer's sparkling summer parties. We spied Heffer in the distance.

'Shall I hold him down and you kick him in the balls or would you prefer it the other way round?' I suggested. He just smiled enigmatically.

Apart from the normal cut-and-thrust of politics there were some very exciting moments which I will never forget. For a few years I had been a PPS in the Northern Ireland Office and knew the territory well. One late night I received a call from No. 10 saying that the PM wanted to see me in his office behind the Speaker's chair. A crowd of Northern Ireland hands were seated around the table. Major was ashen with anger. He wanted to brief us about the front page of the next day's *Times*, where Matthew d'Ancona had obtained what he thought were the government plans for the Unionists in the peace process. Actually, it was a very early draft which had been rejected. But it was very, very inflammatory. I remember Major banging his fist on the desk. He felt that this could derail months of hard work. He wanted us to blitz the media to say that this document did not represent government policy. Robert Cranborne, leader of the Lords and staunch Unionist, was in the room. There was an uneasy feeling that he might have had something to do with the article. Major turned to him: 'Robert, are you content?'

'Prime Minister, I am content.' From that moment we knew that Robert was on side and that he had had absolutely nothing to do with the story. Robert may have been sacked later by William Hague after he put together a lifeboat under the radar to save ninety-two hereditary peers from Labour's reforms, but I have always found him to be utterly trustworthy and loyal. In the Lords he was revered.

On the way out I bumped into shadow Northern Ireland Secretary Mo Mowlam. We had been friends for years so I told her what was going on.

'Ah, well,' she said, sensing a great bi-party media opportunity. 'I had better do my hair, then.' And off she flounced. What a great lady with a tremendous sense of fun and mischief.

I was once having lunch in L'Amico, then a popular Westminster troughery, when she as City spokesman was doing her prawn cocktail charm offensive. She was with some pretty wide-looking City types whom she got rid of fairly quickly and came over to join us. She kicked off her shoes, lit a fag and had a long slurp of wine.

'God, I'm fucking bored.'

The rest of the afternoon was a bit of a blur, but it would have been a complete gossip fest.

—

I have always done my very best not to be bitter. The world of politics and journalism is full of bitter men and women whose disappointment disfigures their souls and eats away at their humanity. So the Tory right wing have not made me bitter, just angry. Their total selfish indulgence destroyed what history will eventually record as a great Prime Minister in John Major. He was no flash-in-the-pan Prime Minister either. People forget that he was in office for seven years. He achieved great things for his country while his party kicked him in the teeth. When you see him in long interviews with Andrew Marr, you realise what the nation has lost. Judgement, compassion and a single-minded determination to put the country back on its feet. He bequeathed Labour a thriving economy, low debt and low unemployment. Sadly, Gordon Brown and Ed Miliband's Treasury trashed it.

And history is in danger of repeating itself. Thatcher worship is often accompanied by Cameron hatred. These same people who sabotaged their own party in the '90s are at it again. On the Tory back benches, treachery is never more than a shadow away.

CHAPTER 17

PARLIAMENTARY AIDE

The 2010 intake, particularly those with marginal seats, really don't know how lucky they are. I used to dread the dawn chorus every morning. It heralded the beginning of spring and that could be the countdown to a summer election. Now that the next election date is set in stone, those who will be the parliamentary roadkill of 2015 at least will know when they will be crushed under the wheels of the electoral charabanc.

I know that most politicians are far better at self-delusion rather than mass deception, but I was pretty sure that I was going to win the 1992 election. The clue is on the doorstep. If people are unwilling to say how they will vote or there is a slight flicker in the eye when you mention the C word (Conservative), you can be pretty sure that there is not a cat's chance in hell that they will vote for you. But the key indicator is the 'knocking up' just before the polls close. Electioneering is about finding your voters and making sure that they actually turn out and do the business. When your supporters are either ringing or knocking on the doors of those who said they will vote for you, you know what the lie of the land is by the response. If they've turned out and voted you have a reasonable chance of success. But if they are giving excuses you know that the chances are that you have been stuffed.

In 1992 the reception on the doorstep was pretty good and those who promised to support were voting in droves. And yet strangely the opinion polls were telling us this was going to be a Labour victory.

Mike Brunson rang me up on election night and told me that he was getting similar responses from all over the country. I told him that the polls were just plain wrong. That night, in his final broadcast before the polls closed, he kept his options open by declaring that that 'tonight could hold some surprises'. Well, it did.

John Major's Conservatives achieved the highest vote of any political party in history, but because of the quirks of our system he won a parliamentary majority of just twenty-one. And my majority was halved at just over 3,000. But we had survived. For now.

The *Mail on Sunday*'s political editor, Peter Dobbie, warned me that the next five years were going to be complete and utter boredom. 'There'll be nothing to get my political dick into at all,' he moaned. As it happened it was one of the most fraught and poisonous parliaments in living memory. But that's for another chapter.

But what was going to happen to me? I'd had to leave the Health Select Committee under a cloud before the election as I was suspected of leaking a draft report. The truth of the matter, which I have never admitted before, was that I did. I had no choice. To be honest, I felt very uncomfortable about it as Nick Winterton was both a good friend and an excellent chairman. But he had a very big bee in his bonnet about the government's health policy. And this draft report was so damning and so wrong that, due to be published just before a general election, it would have destroyed any chance of a return of a Major government. A government that I believed in and was utterly loyal to.

My days of rebellion ended the moment John Major became Prime Minister. To let his premiership be destroyed by Labour was not something I could possibly contemplate. And in the 1992 election the NHS was being used cynically by Labour as a political football, with the most wicked scaremongering tactics over the War of Jennifer's Ear, about a little girl and her lack of a grommet operation. So I made sure that the government had a copy of the first draft so that it could be neutralised.

Soon after the election I received a call from the Chief Whip, Richard Ryder. Would I like to be PPS to Robert Atkins in the Northern Ireland Office? Of course.

I had always got on rather well with Ryder, a fellow member of Major's East Anglian mafia, who used to bring me in once a week for a one-to-one to discuss the political climate. The trouble was that I didn't know Ratkins very well at all, and we got off to rather an unfortunate start when my mates at the *Mail on Sunday* wrote what they thought was a helpful piece, saying that Ratkins would be grateful for my input as I was so much brighter than him. This meant that our first meeting was distinctly chilly, with him chucking a copy of the paper at me and warning that if I thought I was going to be leaking everything that went on in his department to my mates in the press then I should fuck off now. It was sound advice which I took to heart.

Ratkins turned out to be a seriously bright and astute political operator and we became great friends. They nicknamed us Hale and Pace, as we used to roam the bars to sort out backbenchers, particularly the Euronutters, usually with charm which could sometimes be a bit quirky. And sometimes with a snarl.

One day we were on manoeuvres in one of the lobbies and were having an amusing discussion about a well-known Eurotwunt.

'God, that man is a total cunt,' chirped Ratkins to me, not realising that the Eurotwunt was standing right next to us.

I discreetly coughed and without breaking step Ratkins turned to the guy, put his arm round him, smiled and said, 'Good to see you, old boy, we were just talking about you!' And off we sniggered to a bar, where we collapsed in hoots of laughter.

One of my responsibilities was to be his minder at 'gang bang' lunches. These sorts of affairs were when two senior journalists from different newspapers would take a minister to lunch and share the spoils of their indiscretions. As Ratkins was a close personal friend of John Major, he tasked me to ensure that he never let any tasty morsels slip into their hands. For the first time in my life I was to be the arbiter of discretion.

We had a code. I would kick him under the table if I thought he was heading into dangerous waters.

Once, we were being gang-banged by Trevor Kavanagh (*The Sun*) and Simon Walters (then of the *Sunday Express*). Both are masters of mining gold nuggets which may seem innocuous at the time but could lead to embarrassing headlines. In the trade we call this 'polishing turds'. And these guys' turds would gleam so brightly that you would have to wear welding goggles.

Lunch was going well, with Ratkins at his most discreet, and then suddenly I could see that they were gently corralling him into a corner. I delivered a series of rapid kicks, to no avail. Afterwards I asked him why he'd ignored my signal.

'But you never bloody kicked me!' he roared. And then the penny dropped. I had been kicking the long, gangly legs of Trevor Kavanagh. Heaven knows what he thought.

A couple of hours later I bumped into Trevor in the Members' lobby. He looked distressed.

'Quick, quick, pretend we're having a private discussion,' he pleaded.

I gave him a puzzled look. He pointed to the man who bores for Britain on all matters Brussels hot-footing it for Trevor with a stack of papers. So Trevor and I engaged in very serious conversation, and Bill Cash swerved towards another prospective lobby victim.

In those days the Northern Ireland Office was even more fascinating than it is now. It was based in the Old Admiralty Building just off Horse Guards Parade. Now it is in the MI5 building.

The Secretary of State's room was Churchill's office as First Lord of the Admiralty. We used to open the map case for visitors which still had the pins to show where the British convoys were in the Atlantic. And at the Trooping of the Colour we would hold a party for the good and the great overlooking the ceremony presided over by the Queen.

One day, we were sitting in Paddy Mayhew (the Secretary of State)'s office when we heard loud footsteps and the even louder voice of the Reverend Ian Paisley, whose tone rather shocked us as it was in the form of a rallying prayer.

'Oh Lord, bring down that wanker Mayhew from his lofty throne and cast our enemies to eternal damnation,' it went. This meant serious trouble. Paisley cursing? Catastrophe. Suddenly the footsteps stopped and the door flung open to reveal not the big man, but the junior minister Jeremy Hanley, who is a very talented mimic. There was a sigh of relief and a lot of laughter.

Despite the appalling difficulties, the NIO was a great place. And the people in the Province were absolutely warm and wonderful. My first job was to trail Ratkins round the various departments, as his responsibility included the economy, employment, tourism and just about everything apart from health and security. It was a mammoth job and a terrible strain on the liver. Whatever time of day you visited a departmental head, a bottle of Jameson's special crested whiskey would be cracked open. The North may have been a deeply troubled and dangerous place, but it was very convivial.

Another job was to bring MPs over and give them a great dinner at Stormont Castle with the various factions. These always ran like clockwork. Industrial-sized spirits beforehand, gallons of wine during the meal, all sweetness and light until the brandy was poured and then animated argument, dates and general acrimony.

The next morning we would give the MPs a political briefing and colour photos of the atrocities. Which usually made some of them chuck up their breakfasts. Then we would take them round to see the peace walls, show them the state-of-the-art council housing and trot them off to Derry.

One of the strangest requests I had was from the adorable Lady Olga Maitland, who sweetly asked if she could pop into the Falls Road to see a few antique shops. I explained that this was a hotbed of Republicanism and if she was spotted as a Brit MP I couldn't guarantee her safety.

'Ah, don't worry. I could always get a black cab.'

I reminded her that black cabs in Belfast tended to be run by the IRA. The trip in search of knick-knacks was duly abandoned.

Olga once told me how, many years ago, Norman Lamont serenaded her outside her bedroom window. Another time, she regaled us with the story of how she was once approached by a flasher and remarked to her husband that he had taken out 'Mr Mouse'. She is a quality act.

Derry was the original name of the city until it was anglicised to Londonderry. When Chris Patten was a minister he changed it back, upsetting some of the Unionists. When he became Governor of Hong Kong, the standing joke was that he would rename it Kong.

We had put a former IRA man in charge of the rebuilding. Both his sons had been killed in the Troubles and he had turned his back on violence. I once asked him if he had ever met the Security Minister, Michael Mates, who had once served in the Province at the height of the Troubles, as an army colonel. His eyes narrowed to slit trenches.

'Aye, I once had him in the sights of my rifle.'

I didn't pursue it.

Poor old Mates came terribly unstuck by giving Asil Nadir a watch inscribed with the words 'Don't let the buggers get you down'. Nadir was the Polly Peck boss accused of fraud who had fled UK jurisdiction and is now in prison. Looking back now, it seems an awful fuss about nothing. A minister of the Crown giving some moral support to a man accused of serious offences when the minister is not in any department that can assist seems rather tame. But in those days the press was out to get him, and the situation from a news management point of view had spun out of control. The view that he was going to have to go was gaining currency simply because the story was drowning out any good news that the government wanted to present.

Michael asked me what he should do. My advice was that he should resign with dignity and a grateful Prime Minister would reward him after a decent interval. He nodded. So I assumed that was it. I sent word back that that was what he would probably do.

That night I was watching the six o'clock news and there was Michael standing in front of a bomb crater condemning the Provisional IRA. Then the interviewer asked him if he was thinking of resigning. He replied that he wasn't and had the full confidence of the Prime Minister. My jaw dropped, as did my chum's at No. 10, who rang me with a 'What the fuck?' The next day Mates got the chop.

One of the PPS jobs is to get the troops prepared for departmental questions, which happens every few weeks. Luckily there was all-party consensus on Northern Ireland so it was fairly easy. But questions had to be planted, as otherwise there would not be much of a Question Time. God, it was tiresome, and not unlike selling insurance or encyclopaedias.

First you had to think of something that would put the department and your minister in a good light. Then you wrote it out on a yellow form. After that, it was begging your mates to table it. That was the easy bit. You then had to await the ballot to see who had a reasonable chance of being called, write to the poor unfortunate devils who had succeeded and politely suggest a supplementary question, which, in effect, you wrote out. Such great incisive questioning along the lines of 'In the light of my Right Honourable friend's careful stewardship of the Northern Ireland economy, is he not encouraged that this is one of the first steps on the road to peace?' And other such mindless tripe. Then you had to go into the chamber, ensure that your plants were in their places and read the right script, and then drop them a note of thanks afterwards. This is what is whimsically called holding the executive to account. But it keeps the kids on the playground happy.

You have to remember that this this was all before devolution, so ministers were effectively responsible for everything from vitally important matters such as the economy and security down to the utterly daft, such as car parking. But even car parking had its sectarian implications. In fact, everything did. I remember hosting a dinner to get MPs to know the DUP (Paisley's lot). Just before the guests arrived, I noticed that some bright spark had laid a green tablecloth. On the mainland, this would be of mind-erasing irrelevance. In the Province you could start a riot for less. I quickly got the staff to put a few bowls of oranges on the table. And not a word was said.

Politics in Northern Ireland has changed a great deal over the years – and very much for the better. The Ulster Unionists used to be the largest party and when I was in the NIO David Trimble had become their leader. I am very fond of David and he eventually became an effective First Minister, but in the early days he was hard work and would be easily offended, particularly by Paddy Mayhew. When he became really angry a vein used to throb on his left temple, which is how officials gave him the nickname Penis Head.

Paddy was always good news. Tall, patrician and a very effective Secretary of State. Our Permanent Secretary was John Chilcot, later chairman of the Iraq War inquiry.

One evening I received a call from Paddy on the day that Jacques Delors was due to pay a visit to Hillsborough Castle for a reception.

'Bloody Delors has got the flu, come and help me with the food.'

So Ratkins, Paddy and I spent the evening at Hillsborough, sitting on the floor of the Throne Room watching the telly and hoovering up all those wasted canapés and a few bottles of wine.

The video link, quite a modern innovation in those days, kept us all in touch. If in London, we would go into a leaky basement and chat on what we hoped was a secure link. After all, we remembered Richard Needham as a junior minister a few years earlier mentioning on his mobile that he was having to entertain the 'old cow' the next day. The IRA monitored all mobile phone traffic and released the tape. And the 'old cow' in question was Margaret Thatcher, who was decidedly frosty when Needham escorted her round Belfast town centre.

One day, on the link, Paddy made an announcement. 'Gentlemen, we have been less than honest with you recently, but for good reason. We have received a message from the Provisional IRA that they want to end the war.'

This was the beginning of the peace process.

Relations with the Irish were friendly but fraught. One of the difficulties was that every now and again there would be suspicions that we were leading them up the garden path, usually over something that had been said by John Hume.

John is a very great man, the leader of the civil rights movement and a hardworking and decent bloke who did more than many to secure peace in the North. But he could be a little erratic after a drink. He would tell a journalist that there was about to be some breakthrough and then perhaps mention it to one of his mates in the Irish government. John would then disappear for a few days and none of us knew where the hell he was. So the Irish would ask us what the great breakthrough was and we would tell them the truth. We didn't know. He hadn't told us. And no, we hadn't a clue where he was. They often didn't believe a word of it. But we muddled through in the end.

But the Irish were always great fun to deal with, although sometimes a little quirky. Poor old Paddy was totally exasperated by one Irish Foreign Minister who had agreed to keep silent about some recent progress and then went out to give a press conference on it. When asked why the agreement was broken, the minister looked rather confused. 'Sometimes when you need to be silent you have to say something.' Mmm.

And in the Province the politicians can be delightfully dopey too. I once had to trek up country to a remote village to listen to the chairman of a local authority make a speech which he had clearly not bothered to read before delivery as he ended with, 'And Mr Chairman should you have any questions about the content of this speech please contact me on…' Wonderful.

There was a time when I was a member of the Anglo-Irish parliamentary body. Now that was serious fun. You have to remember that the Irish government is designed to get you drunk and then sober you up. We would land, be tanked up in the VIP lounge, go for a reception and then have dinner up at the Castle with the President. The next morning would be a plenary session. Then at 11.30 a.m. we would troop off to the bar, laden with bucket-sized Bloody Marys. And the first question they would always ask me was never about politics, but what was James Whale really like. But those drinkathons were useful in that we formed good friendships, and with that comes trust.

There was a time when Ireland always used to keep winning the Eurovision Song Contest, which they hated as they had to stump up the cost of the next one. In the early hours of the morning I was drinking with a crowd in some grand Dublin hotel. Suddenly some unshaven guy reeking of drink staggered over to us, recognised John Hume and plonked himself down. We thought he was a derelict who had just wandered in off the street. Anyhow, we bought him a drink. After a while we asked why he was in the hotel.

'De Eurovision Saang Contest,' he slurred in an impenetrable accent. We asked him how he got a ticket, to which he explained that he was representing Ireland. We raised our eyes heavenward in disbelief.

'Come on, mate, you've had a drink, time to bugger off,' said one of the lads. And off he went.

At the weekend I switched on the news. There was the derelict, greatly smartened up. The winner of the Eurovision Song Contest.

I was really enjoying the NIO. Then one day I received a phone call from Ratkins.

'Tim Yeo has just resigned. We're off to the Department of the Environment.'

So, with a heavy heart we left the joy that was the Province and headed for a building in central London so ugly and so unfit for purpose that it should never have been built. These were the Marsham Street twin towers, which have now been mercifully razed to the ground. Each tower housed a separate empire: Transport and the DoE. And each department was within spitting distance of the other. This was appropriate as both were at war.

Poor old Tim Yeo had to resign as Minister of State for the Environment as he had been exposed by some grubby tabloid as having a 'love child' with some woman. Nowadays people would just shrug this off as an entirely private matter and unless it compromised his job he would have stayed in post. But these were the fetid days of 'sleaze', and an idiotic Tim Collins, a Downing Street spinner, had briefed that 'Back to Basics' was about morality rather than getting government stripped back to the basics that mattered.

So Ratkins and I arrived at the Department of the Environment expecting to be bored out of existence. We were not disappointed. But the views were wonderful. We didn't need a clock in our office as we could see Big Ben so clearly. The scary bit was that in the morning you could see the clouds of polluted air sweeping into London, for which we were technically responsible.

The Secretary of State was John Gummer and our Permanent Secretary Richard Wilson, who went on to become Cabinet

Secretary. The parliamentary secretary was Sir Paul Beresford, whom Major had allowed to practise as a dentist at the same time as being a minister, which we all thought was rather odd. The joke was that apart from my chum Steve Norris, he was the only minister who pulled. Ratkins and Beresford did not get on terribly well, probably because Beresford was a dyed-in-the-wool Thatcherite and had run Wandsworth Council.

The Minister for Housing was my old mate David Curry. We live within a mile of each other and used to come back on the train together. One day when he was at Agriculture he told me that the worst part of his job was visiting abattoirs, which was 'like descending into hell'. He was told at the last Major reshuffle by the Chief that he was to be promoted to Cabinet as Minister of Agriculture. Sure enough, the No. 10 switchboard rang, asking him to wait for a phone call from the Prime Minister. I bumped into him on the train recently and he told me that he is still waiting. Reshuffles tend to be chaotic affairs.

Gummer was a brilliant minister. He had this reputation for being pious simply because he believed in God, and was eventually brought into the Catholic Church by the splendid Michael Seed, a priest based in Westminster Cathedral. Seed also brought Tony Blair into the Catholic Church and told me that when he went to say Mass at No. 10 (for Cherie) he refused to put the communion water and wine on George W. Bush-personalised coasters. Michael is a great character. Once, we were having lunch at the Savile Club and he asked me when I'd last gone to Mass. I said I couldn't remember.

'What about confession, then?'

'Blimey, thirty years.'

So he led me into the snooker room for confession. Probably a Savile first.

I have mentioned earlier that Gummer is great fun with an impish sense of humour. At our first morning ministerial meeting at the DoE, which, unlike other Secretaries of State, he refused to call 'prayers', he drew our attention to a report that the department had commissioned, at enormous public expense. The conclusion was delightfully barmy: 'that the majority of people that fell out of windows did so because they were left open'. Ratkins and I looked at each other in utter amazement. 'Jerry,' said Gummer, 'any view on this?'

'Complete bollocks and an appalling waste of money.'

Gummer nodded and smiled.

'Richard, could you ensure that this sort of nonsense never happens again?' The Permanent Secretary agreed.

One day, the news that Tesco heiress Dame Shirley Porter was accused of moving Labour voters out of their council houses to ensure a Conservative victory was discussed. Gummer was very clear.

'If these allegations are true they are appalling and just not Conservative. But I don't want a single word of support for her, from anyone in this department. Nothing must jeopardise the inquiry.'

A few days later I received an invitation to attend an 'at home' with Shirley. I had never met her before or since, but as I had absolutely nothing to do with the inquiry I went just out of sheer curiosity. Not surprisingly, she was charm personified and showed me her portrait in full Lord Mayor of Westminster regalia. In the corner of the picture was a shop sign that she had specially commissioned. She was very proud of it. It said 'fuck off'. All in the best possible taste. Years later she was fined £30 million by the district auditor.

You would have thought that as ministries are staffed by politicians, policy decisions would be very political. Well, not at the DoE.

The amazing thing about the DoE was how apolitical it was. Everyone really wanted to make a difference without scoring too many party points. One day, we were discussing what to do with £30 million worth of grants. I suggested that we look at the best projects and if two were of the same value we'd give it to a Tory marginal. There was a sharp intake of breath.

'That is far too political.'

And that wasn't from officials. It wasn't from Ratkins, either.

Gummer was very politically canny. He had done deals with Alan Beith, offering support for his Bill on saving energy. He had given his word. Then, the Treasury had a change of heart and we found ourselves in a bit of a mess. There was a way round it if a few clauses were redrafted. Richard Wilson told us that there weren't enough parliamentary draftsmen to amend it in time for Friday. Gummer made it quite clear that he wasn't going to be hung out to dry on this and that as Permanent Secretary Richard would have to find one. This is always the problem in government: it is rarely joined up.

We were tasked to come up with a housing policy that cost nothing. So we spent an away day at David Curry's home trying to sort something out. A well-meaning total waste of time, because every good idea we had cost money and the Treasury would be certain to block it. When I spoke to David the other day I reminded him of this and asked him what eventually our housing policy was in 1997. He looked at me blankly and then both of us laughed. We hadn't got a clue, and we had written it.

Then the sad day came when Ratkins invited me out to dinner to break the news that he was leaving government to nurse his marginal seat. As we had such fun together I saw no point in staying on at Environment, so we both left together.

But then another opportunity came along which would change my life: *The James Whale Show.*

CHAPTER 18

THE JAMES WHALE SHOW

One day, a badge messenger (the guys in white tie who search you out) handed me a green slip with 'Please ring Mike Mansfield'. To be honest, I wasn't quite sure who he was, but assumed it was the well-known criminal barrister. Well, it wasn't. It was a delightfully camp television director whose claim to fame was *Cue the Music*. He was the guy who at the beginning of every programme would have a close-up of himself giving the imperial television order, 'Cue the music, darling.'

Mike had a TV project involving radio legend James Whale. Was I interested and if so could we have a chat? Of course.

So I rolled up to his offices. The project was a very wacky weekly television show for a youth audience late on a Friday night. Would I consider doing a regular political slot which would involve James asking me some light-hearted questions about the political issues of the day? Why not?

So I found myself one Tuesday evening in a tiny studio just off Carnaby Street for the first recording. By the magic of television, everyone thought it was live, but we recorded two shows on a Tuesday back-to-back every fortnight. I was on with solicitor Gary Jacobs, *Daily Mail* showbiz columnist Baz Bamigboye and an attractive black lady who was always dressed in the scantiest of clothes, called Cookie. She was a model who traded off some very large assets. We were to be the regulars and the show would be nationally networked for ITV by London Weekend Television at midnight every Friday. It became an immediate hit, pulling in about three million viewers a week, and now it is regarded as a cult show. Even today, twenty years after it came off air, I am still recognised on the street by catering staff, drunks and druggies. In fact, it was aimed at students and those who had just arrived home bombed out of their brains. They loved it.

A year or so ago a black-cab driver took one look at me and said,

"Ere, you're that Jerry Hayes, aren't you? Answer me just one question. Did you ever shag that black bird, Cookie?'

'Er, no.'

'Well, you're more of a twat than I thought you were. Where do you want to go, guv?'

And then there was that very weird experience standing outside El Vino in Fleet Street late at night, waiting for a number 23 bus. After a long wait one appeared. The doors opened and the driver yelled, 'James Whaaaale! Hop on, Jerry, where are you going, mate?'

I thought this was all a little strange as, after all, this was a bus. But nevertheless I told him I was trying to get to Liverpool Street. And off we went, swerving around corners and not stopping for anybody. Then I noticed some other odd goings-on. There were no other passengers. The lights weren't on and there was a very strong whiff of alcohol. It was only when we finally screeched to a stop outside the station and the driver fell out of his seat that it finally dawned on me that he had nicked the bus. I made my excuses and got off as quickly as possible.

James Whale had the reputation of being a hard-nosed and thoroughly objectionable sod. But that was his media persona. The truth is he is a bit of a pussycat but, like everybody else, can't stand it when people in authority seem incapable of telling the truth. So he would give them a hard time.

At first we couldn't quite get the measure of each other. I was waiting for the killer below-the-belt question, he for the slimy political evasions. When neither happened we relaxed and became good friends.

I would be dressed in what would be now called skinny jeans, with a waistcoat made by one of Tom Gilbey's students. The waistcoat would be wackier by the week. But the show was done on the cheap. I and the other regulars were paid the princely sum of £50 a show. But nobody cared as the publicity was amazing and it was a fantastic buzz to be part of groundbreaking TV. Nowadays television executives would never allow a show to go on air in the manner we did. There was no script and no rehearsal. We knew the structure of the show in so far as who would be coming on, but that was it. One guest was Hollywood legend Neil Sedaka, who loved the spontaneity. As did Kiki Dee, Simon Le Bon and many others. We had some great guests because everyone wanted to appear.

One of things I would do before we started was warm up the audience. The trouble was we didn't always have one, so runners, sometimes accompanied by me, would do a dash round the pubs and drag people in. And we pulled in some pretty strange characters, some of whom were sober. One night, I noticed a young lad sitting in the audience dressed solely in latex. I haven't a clue where they'd found him. I thought it best not to ask. On another occasion, a leather-clad woman came in off the streets with a remarkable contraption full of zips, leggings, rubber and electric wiring. She explained that this was a simulated sex machine. Would I care to try it on? She would plug it in for me. As I wasn't entirely sure where it would be plugged in, I politely declined.

But it is a really good idea if you are doing a show as live to warm the audience up yourself. It gives you a rapport and pointers as to what will make them react when the cameras roll.

James was notorious for playing tricks on me. We had been interviewing some fellow who had written a book about the wonders of urine. Great for your health, your complexion and, if you drank it, your gums. Although it probably wasn't so good for your breath. The idea was that at the end of it all James and I would toast each other with the stuff, have a long slurp and grin at the camera. Of course, it would be cider. Just before my slurp I noticed that James's glass had a tiny black dot at the bottom. Alarm bells rang. I had been given a glass of the real McCoy. No way was I going to put that to my lips. And thoughts of a *Sun* headline – 'Tory MP takes the piss' – flashed before my eyes. So Whaley and I had a mock fight.

Not as bad as the bit of fun I had with a former *Blue Peter* presenter, the lovely Michaela Strachan. It was one of those daft evenings where the dream girls were playing strip poker with the dream boys and we had about thirty seconds to kill before the end of the show. The floor manager whispered, 'Do something.' So, with great presence of mind, I picked up a whip (as you do) and chased a giggling Michaela around the studio, giving her the odd swish. I thought nothing of it until

I read the tabloid headline afterwards: 'Tory MP spanks *Blue Peter* presenter'. Actually, it was all rather innocent.

I once got into trouble for an off-the-cuff remark that I made while filling some time with a black cat on a fishing line. It was a skit on the then famous 'astrologer' Mystic Meg. I called it Mystic Mog. And in a moment of devilment I grinned at Cookie and leered, 'Well, we like a bit of black pussy, don't we?' She gave me a playful slap and that was it. LWT were not amused. Three (!) people had complained about my 'racist' remark. Of course, nothing happened.

On one occasion Adrian (AA) Gill of the *Sunday Times* wanted to see a recording and do a profile of me. I implored James to behave, but it's like waving a red flag at a bull or saying to Eric Joyce MP, 'You don't want a drink, do you?' It becomes a challenge.

All was going rather well until we came to the bit where there was a scene involving a set of stocks. I was to put my head in, then quickly jump away, and a poor member of the audience would be locked in while we all threw gunge at them. Well, you can guess what happened. As soon as my head was in, James clicked the lock shut. And a custard pie came flying in my direction. Gill couldn't believe his luck. He stitched me up like a kipper the next Sunday, complete with a video grab of me being custard-pied. To be honest, I could hardly blame him; if our roles had been reversed I would have done exactly the same thing.

Then one Tuesday I noticed that some beauty from *Baywatch* was on. I was handed a pair of Speedos and was told that she was going to rescue me from drowning in a nearby swimming pool and we'd all pretend to do it in slow motion. The trouble was it was then midwinter, with the snow still on the ground. So I was chucked in the pool, dragged out, and laid by the side of the road while this woman with child-bearing lips and implants that could raise the *Costa Concordia* proceeded to attempt mouth-to-mouth resuscitation. This caused great amusement to the straggle of drunks and druggies who had gathered, wondering what on earth was going on. It took three takes. God, it was cold. Which is probably just as well.

It is difficult to decide who the most bizarre guests were. There was a fellow who would bounce up and down dressed as a penis, who called himself Knobby the Knob. Or some guy who had twenty-two piercings in his todger, whom James had to interview. This caused a dilemma, as he could hardly whip the thing out on camera. Luckily, the guy was wearing a kilt. So James just shoved a microphone underneath and asked him to jump up and down. It sounded like a seedy and eerily perverted 'Jingle Bells'. But it was great television.

Then there was a couple who claimed to be turned on by the smell of baking bread. That interview was done in bed, with every bloomer/French stick pun imaginable. And then there was a very disturbing group of men who got their kicks by being dressed as babies; worse, wanted to be treated like them. Creepy.

The only time that I really came unstuck was when we were meant to be chatting with the Vice-President of Iceland. I had just had to leave for a vote, which was always a treat for my parliamentary colleagues, as I would be trooping through the lobbies in full TV make-up and a weird waistcoat. Although where the myth came from that I was once dressed as a French maid still perplexes me. This was mischievously raised in the chamber by Labour MP Ann Clwyd, who, on a point of order, said that she couldn't take anything seriously from a man who appeared on the TV dressed as a French maid. Madam Speaker came to the rescue by saying that with my golden curls (the *Telegraph* used to refer to me as the golden golly) she was sure that I would look very pretty in the outfit.

After the vote, I came back to the studio without having had time to read the notes. So I complimented the blonde and beautiful Vice-President of Iceland, whom James was interviewing, on her English. She looked perplexed. Then the penny dropped.

'Not the country, the frozen food company,' she sweetly smiled.

After each show we would pop into a lovely Italian restaurant just off St Martin's Lane called Giovanni's. The owner, a great guy called Pino, used to keep the place open for us until the early hours so we could let off steam. And more often than not, after a few bottles of Sicilian red wine we would take down a couple of unwieldy ceremonial swords from the wall and have mock fights, usually with actors who had just finished their shows and were in need of a little light relief.

On one show we had a few guys from Madame JoJo's dressed as very pretty girls. At the end, one of them said that as he had never been to the Commons would I give him a tour? My pleasure. So, on the appointed day I searched the central lobby for him. No luck. But there in the corner was a tranny in full rig. It was him. I had foolishly assumed that he would come as a bloke. He really was a very charming fellow, but some of the old buffers were not impressed.

The only celebrity that I have taken to the Commons who

literally stopped the traffic was Frank Bruno. We had become friends as we both supported the same charity in Harlow for mentally handicapped kids. He always came to the Christmas party and was fantastic with the children, who adored him.

I suggested lunch at the Commons.

I met him at Westminster station and walked him across the road. Cars, buses, lorries and vans ground to a halt and scores of people abandoned their vehicles just to shake him by the hand. And when we got to the Commons and word got round, he was surrounded by well-wishers. And he was charming to everyone. I have never seen anyone, not even Margaret Thatcher, have the same effect on so many people. He made everyone feel good about themselves.

Poor Frank has had a very rough time in the last few years and he has behaved with great dignity. He really is genuinely loved by the public. And rightly so.

When it was suggested that we take the *Whale Show* on the road, I thought that it might be quite good fun, so I agreed. And as the money was considerably more than the fifty quid that I was paid for each TV show it was a bonus. What could possibly go wrong? Sadly, just about everything. The venues were to be Butlins holiday camps in the winter, where punters could pay £25 for the weekend. They were not the most sophisticated of audiences and in those days Butlins wasn't the upmarket (ish) chain that it is now. The first venue was a nightmare, the last a catastrophe.

So we flew up to Ayr in Scotland. God, it was grim. The 3,000-strong audience were all out of their brains, as we were booked in at happy hour where trebles were sold for the price of singles. And the punters – you would have put straw

down in their bedrooms and given them their tea in a trough
garnished with a dead dog. It made the Glasgow Empire, that
graveyard for performers, seem like the Royal Opera House.
It wasn't helped by the fact that Bernard Manning had been
on a couple of hours before. All in the best possible taste, of
course.

'Reet. Are there any black lads in the audience?' And the
spotlight eventually rested some poor young man.

'Come on up here, son.' Which, rather nervously but fortified with a keg of lager, he did.

'Put the spotlight on him. Good, now I can see you. Right,
son, we are now going to have a public hanging.'

And who said that family entertainment was dead?

Well, Manning went down well but the next act was a gay
panto. This, of course, was as welcome as a cup of cold sick. I
was sharing a dressing room with the strippers and we could
hear the shouting and swearing of the angry mob as the cast
were hooked off the stage. Some sprog at the *News of the
World* later got wind of this and asked me, with a salacious
leer, what had happened. No doubt he expected me to say
that I made my excuses and left. My quote was that we spent
an enjoyable time discussing the tracts of Wittgenstein. And
he printed it.

The howling drunken mob at Ayr were not the sort who
would have enjoyed me and James having a bit of light-hearted
political banter.

'What should we do, mate?' I pleaded, consumed with terror.

'Aw, just go on and tell a few jokes,' he grinned.

This was not a recipe for success. I was an MP, I was a Tory
and I was in Scotland. The devil incarnate.

So, on I strode with a swagger in my step and water in my bowels.

'Are you having a good time?' I yelled, hoping for the usual 'Yeah!' followed by me saying, 'But I can't hear you.' Which would be followed by louder shouts of joy.

Well, it didn't quite work like that. The shouts were not of happiness but of 'No! Fuck off, you Tory bastard.' The ice had not quite been broken.

So I told a few jokes. Very badly. But at least they didn't lynch me. That time.

The last venue was Pwllheli, Wales. Here was the same number of drunks but without the sophistication of the Ayr crowd. These were Scousers on holiday. Now, I am very fond of Liverpool, but for this lot, straw in the bedroom would have been an unthinkable luxury and food in a trough could only be countenanced if both hands were tied behind their backs. You got the impression that their clothes were well past their steal-by date. They were in a very ugly mood.

First on was comedian Charlie Chuck, who had a very odd but very funny routine. He appeared in a tatty raincoat, hair in disarray and carrying a broken piece of wood. Every now and again, in a sort of Yorkshire display of Tourette's, he would shout 'donkey', then move over to a drum kit and smash it all over the stage. Usually, by this stage the audience would be in howls of laughter. In Pwllheli they sat in indifferent silence. I was on next, to be met by an angry Charlie staggering into the wings. 'Don't go out there, lad, they're all fucking pork.'

So again in utter terror I started my routine of off-colour jokes. What with the toilet rolls that were being thrown in my direction, coupled with a level of abuse that could have won a

Turner Prize for anatomical imagination, I ran for cover. James fared no better. So we despatched our agent, Phil, to go and get the car, a fantastically vulgar white stretch limo, so we could get the hell out of Dodge. In the meantime we had to improvise. How do we keep this feral mob from stringing us up?

Well, one of the acts was a very pretty magician. But her magic was exotic, which basically meant that she took her kit off and produced budgies and bunnies from unusual places. She had been kind enough to tone things down so I didn't get into trouble with the press. But now was the time to press the nuclear button.

'Luv, you're on, and don't spare the horses.' Although, being a tasteful act, there were no actual horses involved. But she got the message. On she went. Still no limo. The crowd was becoming hostile again.

'Luv, time to flash your tits.' She duly obliged. Still no car. Time for the nuclear option.

'Luv, time to flash the Hitler moustache.' I will leave that to your imagination.

Then the limo arrived. I bounded onto the stage with a sheet, wrapped the girl to protect her modesty and off we drove like bats out of hell.

We were tired, hungry and thirsty. Where could we relax? Then, out of the Welsh mists we saw a blue sign: 'Pwllheli Conservative Club'. With me as a sitting Tory MP there may not be petals, brass bands and vestal virgins, but there would be a warm welcome. So in we strode.

I suppose as we were still in full make-up and in showbiz attire we must have cut an odd picture to the dozen or so gnarled, interbred faces sitting supping their pints at the bar.

"'Allo,' said the barman, 'are you a member?'

And, puffing my chest in the best 'Don't you know who I am?' mode (uncharacteristic for me but I was traumatised), I announced that I was the Conservative Member of Parliament for Harlow.

'So you are not a member 'ere, then?'

'Well, no.'

'Then you and your fancy friends 'ad better bugger off, then.'

To this day if anyone mentions Butlins or Pwllheli I break into cold sweat and begin to twitch.

But I am very grateful to James Whale. He gave me a great opportunity which I grasped. Most important of all, after I was kicked out of Harlow he made me employable.

CHAPTER 19

THE END OF THE BEGINNING

The run-up to the 1997 election was nothing short of poisonous. In reality we were a minority government, which meant that the lunatics had taken over the asylum. In the land of the politically blind, the one-eyed loons were kings. And John Major's brave attempt to civilise the party was coming apart at the seams. Of course, the economy was booming, unemployment was on a downward spiral and all the indicators that would normally lead to a resounding election victory were in place. But the Euronutters had declared war. They were still mourning the political death of Thatcher and they genuinely believed that it would be in the party's interests to lose so that they could regroup with a right-wing agenda that would sweep us into office after five years of root-and-branch socialism under Tony Blair. Utterly mad. They had forgotten the lesson of the 1980s: voters do not vote for divided parties. And we weren't just divided; we were ungovernable, mutinous and deeply unpleasant. Worse, the electorate were fed up with cash-for-questions and had never forgiven us for Black Wednesday, when interest rates hit 15 per cent. For the very first time in years they were no longer afraid of Labour and had fallen in love with a youthful and vigorous Blair, who promised an end to the old politics. It was all motherhood and apple soufflé.

At home I still had a security detail. Fellows with sub-machine guns were in foxholes on the cricket pitch and we had a chap with a Beretta stationed outside our bedroom door. An extremely effective contraceptive.

It wasn't without its moments of humour. One evening, some poor devil ran over a cat outside our house. He screeched to a halt, which attracted the attention of the guys with guns. The driver's door was wrenched open and the driver found himself with a gun at his head and lots of little red dots on his torso. 'Sorry I killed the cat,' he wailed.

And then one evening I came home early. The village was taped off and the army was a significant presence. I tried to get through the barrier.

'Can't go through there, sir, there's some MP with a bomb outside his house.'

'But it's me!'

So I was allowed through to see that a car had been dumped outside my house, with a robot investigating. I walked through the door to find Alison baking cakes and the kids enjoying the spectacle. Suddenly, the order went out: 'Principal down.' Which meant that two burly men threw me to the floor while there was an almighty explosion outside. When the smoke and the dust had cleared we saw that the army had blown up the car. Excitement over. Until the lady who couldn't get a place at the station car park and dumped her car outside my house arrived, rather depressed to see a smoking wreck. Now, you will be asking the same question that everyone else asks whom I've told the story to:

'Who paid the bill?' The truth is that I haven't a clue. Except that it wasn't me.

And then one evening there was another shout of 'principal down' and again I was hurled to the floor as a man dressed in camouflage with a shotgun sauntered down our lane. He had the usual red-dot treatment and fell to his knees in terror. It was the local poacher. But at least he lived to tell the tale. Until relatively recently I was pathetically grateful for the protection until I discovered that Operation Centurion was not designed for that at all. The likes of me were mere bait for the men of terror. If I was plugged so would they be. It would have been nice if I had been asked.

I used to share the security detail of Southend East MP Teddy Taylor. As much as they liked the guy, they hated their turns there, as Taylor had a very yappy and very ferocious little terrier. Dear old Teddy wanted to have his own handgun, but the chief constable was of the view that he would be more of a danger to himself than the IRA.

So, election day approached. *The Sun* was supporting New Labour, as was the *Mail*. It was like being a turkey when the Christmas jingles are being played in the stores. To be fair, Major did an amazing job of trying to get the good news across. But when the punters have stopped listening, it is a waste of time. We fought hard, though. I even had a moment of self-delusion that I might just win. Mad.

The good voters of Harlow were charm itself. But that was the problem. They were just being nice. It was like taking an old and faithful Labrador to the vets to be put down after he has outlived his usefulness. I was a dead man walking. I remember walking down a street being followed by a Jehovah's Witness.

I gave him a hug and told him to savour the moment, as he was going to be welcomed with open arms.

The only highlight of the election was the arrival of my old mate, *Mirror* man and old leftie Paul Routledge. We had a three-bottler. 'You're fucked, Comrade!' Tell me about it. But he did write a lovely piece about me. You will hear a lot more about Routers in this book. He is one of the most talented journalists and decent human beings that I have ever met.

God, the election was awful. Someone even tried to kill me with a bag of flour. This may seemed far-fetched, but if one of those hit you from twenty-three storeys there wouldn't be much left of your head.

And then it was time for election night. We knew that the game was up. I got quietly pissed in a hotel, waiting for my good friend Dave Roberts, the chairman, to ring when the time of my execution had arrived. I spoke to the troops before I went in to the count. 'We are stuffed. But I don't want a single photographer to get a picture of a sad face. We go in with our heads held high with a smile.' And that's what we did.

When the time came for the announcement and the speeches, I thought back fourteen years to when I had won and made a speech thanking the man I beat, Stan Newens, for all his hard work in the constituency. And then in 1992 when I defeated Bill Rammell, I thanked him for being such a splendid candidate. So, in victory, what would he say about me? Nothing. He gave a political rant and I was airbrushed out of history. I would be lying if I said I didn't think that was pretty shitty behaviour.

After it was all over Dave Roberts came to the rescue and

brought his car outside the sports centre where the count had taken place. Sadly, he couldn't get the car up to the door, so it meant a bit of a walk with a media scrum in tow. There was one particularly unpleasant cameraman who wouldn't stop crowing that me and all my wicked Tory chums had been kicked out. He was running backwards at the time. I warned him about the fast-approaching steep bank. He just told me to piss off.

Oh well, I did try. And when I saw him hurtling down the slope in the process of breaking his arm, I couldn't suppress a small smile.

So that was it, fourteen fascinating years as an MP were over. What on earth was I going to do? I hadn't practised as a barrister for years. Thank heavens for the resettlement allowance. All those hair-shirted puritans who think that it should be abolished should experience what it's like to be deprived of your only means of earning a living. Without some form of financial cushion most ex-MPs would be signing on within a couple of months. And then the phone began to ring. The first call was from my old friend and head of chambers, Sir Desmond de Silva QC.

'Dear boy, you would be most welcome back in chambers.'

'But I don't know any law.'

'Dear boy, you never did, you are an advocate. Best you read the Police and Criminal Evidence Act.'

It was time to dust down my wig, if only I could find where I left it.

The next call came from Dominic Midgley, who worked at Mohamed Al Fayed's newly acquired *Punch* magazine. Did I fancy lunch? Of course.

I had already written bits and pieces for the magazine and rather fancied the idea of a column. Lunch was a great success from what I can remember as rather a lot was drunk. But I did make a pitch for a job. He said he would put in a good word with the editor, Paul Spike. And off I staggered, only to be chased by a waiter asking me to pay for a bottle of wine that I had forgotten about. Of course, it was all a set-up and appeared in the *Telegraph* diary the next day.

Two days later and I received another call from Dom.

'Sorry, mate, the editor says he can't stand you.' Strange, as I had never met him.

A week later I received another call from Dom.

'Spike's gone. We've got a new one called James Steen. He wants you on board. Are you interested?'

Does the Pope shit in the woods? Of course.

And thus began four of the happiest years of my working life. I suddenly found myself as a columnist for a magazine edited by a delightful genius, with a deputy who taught me how to make a story zing and an assortment of some of the most witty, charming, creative and generally bonkers people I have ever been privileged to work with.

James and Dom, his deputy, were fantastic guys to be around. The place was a powerhouse of creativity and fun. My job was to trawl Westminster for stories and put together a column of about 3,000 words. A serious 'think piece' in the middle and loads of gossip around the sides. Richard Brass, another legend, would then sort out either a cartoon or a witty Photoshopped mickey-take of whatever I had been writing about. And I would be asked to write the odd feature about whatever took my, James's or Dom's fancy.

When I think back I realise how blessed I have been. Many who had lost their seats were pining for a comeback. I even got a lovely handwritten note from the Chief Whip, Alastair Goodlad, offering help. That was very kind. But I had done fourteen years as an MP and the thought of coming back to a fractious and frothingly insane parliamentary party with the possibility of ending my days with a very junior and dull shadow portfolio didn't seem like a barrel-load of laughs.

For the past fourteen years I had been working hard for my constituents and propping up the bar with my mates in the press. Weekends were never my own, filled with speeches, surgeries and constituency events. Now I was a member of the parliamentary press gallery, gazing down on the very benches where I used to sit, and still propping up the press bar with my old mates. The nearest thing to heaven that I can imagine.

The transition from poacher to gamekeeper was almost seamless and my good friends in the press rallied round. Nigel Nelson, Paul Routledge and Ian Hernon helped me get on my feet with all sorts of helpful advice about how to get stories. It was basically that MPs love to talk, usually about themselves, their friends and – particularly – their enemies. James had given me an expense account so I could buy them drinks and the odd lunch, and the stories started to roll in. But the guys also gave me some very good advice about how to deal with the boss.

Editors are strange creatures who wield enormous power and sometimes they become very eccentric, power-crazed megalomaniacs. Get on the wrong side of them and you are dead. Make a list of their enemies and slag them off, and make another of their friends and say nice things about them. James was an exception. The fellow we had to keep sweet was our proprietor, Mohamed Al Fayed.

James is a creative genius, laid-back, with an amazing sense of fun: an all-round good guy. He now ghostwrites for world-famous chefs, makes a small fortune and never starves. He could edit any national newspaper with distinction, but I suspect he just can't be bothered with all the office politics.

Editorial meetings were rather different from those of the rest of Fleet Street. I would roll into the office at about eleven, have a chat with Richard Brass (Brasso) and the lovely Jenny, who used to sub my copy, then me, Dom and James would disappear for a few sharpeners before lunch. This meant about four large gins at one of the many watering holes not far from Harrods, the eyrie of our great proprietor, Mo. Then off to the Swag and Tails or Monza for lunch. All I can remember is drink, gossip and laughter. It was like being a student with money.

James had a particularly mischievous side. He was also a fantastic mimic who used to love to wind up the rich and pompous. One of his favourite targets was the *Daily Mail*'s gossip king, Nigel Dempster. Poor old Nigel had lost the plot by this stage and was hitting the bottle in a big way. His column had descended into a terrible 1950s confection about Princess Margaret, unheard-of aristo totty and fading Bond girls. And he was rude and pompous to everyone below the rank of a belted earl. He treated his staff abominably, once thumping the splendid Adam Helliker, who is now chief gossip column-ist on the *Sunday Express*. James decided to have some sport and rang Dempster, who had a running war against Mo. The conversation went something like this.

'Yes, what do you bloody want?'

'Nigel, it's Jonathan.'

'Jonathan bloody who?'

'You know! My father used to speak most highly of you.'

'And who the hell is your … was your bloody father, for God's sake?'

'Nigel, it's Jonathan Rothermere here.' He had just become the proprietor of the *Mail* group.

There was a deathly silence, then followed the most revoltingly obsequious conversation that I have ever heard. Then came the real sting.

'All this stuff about Al Fayed has run its course, don't you think?'

'Of course, of course. You are so right.'

'In fact, why not say some nice things about him?'

'What an excellent idea.'

'And while you're about it, why not give his magazine *Punch* a bit of a plug? I am quite a fan.'

'I will do it straight away. Always wonderful to speak to you, Jonathan.'

The remarkable thing is that Dempster did start writing some nice things about Mo and gave some great publicity to *Punch*, until Steen printed the transcript of the conversation. And why didn't Paul Dacre, the editor of the *Daily Mail*, smell a rat when Dempster started love bombing Mo? Because he thought that he had had a cosy chat with Rothermere too. I rather like Paul. I always used to tease him about how rotten the *Mail* was about Major. Sadly, it always tended to be when his rag had just won Newspaper of the Year. He really is a bit like a Wagnerian opera; not as bad as he sounds.

One of my favourite Steen stings was when he rang up *Sun* editor Kelvin MacKenzie pretending to the legendary actor and director Dickie Attenborough. After a while, Steen had persuaded a doubting MacKenzie that he really was Dickie, and even got him to be enthusiastic about his latest exciting project, a musical about the *Titanic*.

'But darling, there is a magnificent twist – she doesn't sink!'

It is hard to believe that Britain's best-known red-top editor had become another one of James Steen's victims.

Punch was going to be not just fun but one long, joyous party of lunches, pranks and Steenian mischief. And I was being paid.

CHAPTER 20

THE PRESS GALLERY

Ironically, my first difficulty on entering the press gallery was very similar to my problem in the first few months of being elected: where do I sit? Press accommodation in the Commons is very cramped. It is all open-plan, with rival newspapers sitting next to one another cheek by jowl. No newspaper has an office to itself. It is marginally better today, but not much. Getting a desk is very, very difficult. Journalists are separated by a corridor where there are offshoots. That corridor is known as the Burma Road and the offshoots, the Rampton Wing. So I was indebted to my old friend Ian Hernon for letting me squat at his desk in the best room, shared by Trevor Kavanagh and the *Sun* team, Joe Murphy of the *Mail on Sunday* and Patrick Hennessy of the *Evening Standard*. This place was a power-house of breaking news and a very good place to learn my new craft. And the hardened professionals showed me nothing but kindness and friendship. The atmosphere was great.

It's hard to believe, but the best diary stories often come from other journos. If I couldn't fit a story in one week, I'd give it to a mate and vice versa. Trade was great and the gossip awesome.

One guy who was really helpful was Piers Morgan. We

have been friends for years, although I haven't seen him since his television stardom. I first met him when he was a student of journalism at Harlow College and gave him a tour round the House. I can never really understand the bad press he gets. I always found him friendly and a good laugh. I suspect that when you are made editor of the *News of the World* at the tender age of twenty-eight it will arouse a great deal of jealousy. And many journalists despised him even more when he became editor of the *Mirror*. It was really quite sickening to see the collective glee of chippy, older and far less talented hacks crowing over his sacking. But Piers is having the last laugh. All the way to the bank.

One day I bumped into him at a party.

'Matey, I've got a great story which is a bit too gamey for a family newspaper; see what you can do with it.'

Gamey? It was beyond outrageous. The gist of it was that the chairman of a council had borrowed his next-door neighbour's video camera. Eventually, he gave it back. One evening the neighbour's family was sitting down to watch clips of a recent wedding. Excitedly, these pillars of respectability sat down with a sweet sherry or two as the camera was plugged into the television. The wedding was a great success, with oohs, aahs and tears. Suddenly, the picture began to fade and a new scene appeared. An enormous erect penis dominated the screen. And there was no doubt that it belonged to Mr Chairman.

But things got worse. The penis was then seen to penetrate the rear end of a dog. And after a bit of wobbly camera work, it became clear to this poor assembled family that it was *their* dog.

My editor, James Steen, thought that it was hilarious. But even *Punch* had a line in the sand.

James once sent me off to the Colony Room in Dean Street, Soho, to do a piece on an absinthe tasting evening. The Colony was a notorious hang-out for artists, reprobates and drunks. I had been a member for a few years. On Wednesday evenings a celeb would serve behind the bar. Mercifully, I missed the night when Damien Hirst did it – naked. But it was a fun place and I got some amazing stories. Sadly, it closed a few years ago.

To get into the place you had to press a button on a dingy green wall with the word 'CUNTY' on it. And when you went up to the bar you were greeted with amazing club memorabilia. Works by Hirst and many others. The ancient mechanical cash register also had 'CUNTY' emblazoned across it. This was because the legendary proprietor, a waspish old queen called Ian Board, long dead, used to call members 'cunty' as a term of endearment. Well, sort of.

Suggs from the group Madness was a regular, as was his fiery mum, Eddie. When we first met she nearly thumped me because I was a Tory. But after a while we became friends and still have the odd drink at the only place worth going to in Soho anymore, the French House.

The idea was that I was to write a louche piece about the Colony serving that badge of depravity, the blindness-inducing absinthe. It was all disappointingly tame. Nobody lost either their sight or their rag. I even moaned that the stuff had no effect on me whatsoever. Until I peeked into my notebook the next day to see a mass of unreadable gibberish. The danger with absinthe is not the high alcoholic content but its hallucinogenic effect. Well, I know now.

One of the most fascinating things about being in the

gallery after losing your seat is that one moment you are sitting on the green benches and the next you are sitting up in the gods with a bird's-eye view of the chamber. And you can see everything. Every snigger, every whispered comment and every grimace. Since cameras were introduced, the habit of doughnutting had become popular. The idea was if one of your chums was speaking you would gather round, look up admiringly at your hero, nod sagely and smile in the right places. All in shot.

And then some bright spark mischievously invented the poisoned doughnut. The idea was that if a certifiably bonkers colleague was about to make a certifiably bonkers speech, out of solidarity with sanity, some of the hounds would surround the poor devil and rather than nod their heads in agreement would shake them in despair, grin and make signs to the forehead indicating that this was not the sort of person that they would wish to stand next to when there was a full moon. Sadly, the mad and the bad have sussed this one and ensure that when they speak they are surrounded by a praetorian guard of the deranged.

One of the many good things about working for a national was that it is a great handle to crowbar your way into other money-making activities. The first Labour Party and Tory Party conferences of 1997 turned into a little gold mine. *Channel 4 News* asked me to make short film about the Tory one and Rebekah Wade (as she was then) gave me a daily column on *The Sun* at Labour's. I was so excited about the unlimited expenses that I texted my good chum Paul Routledge (Routers) of the *Mirror* that we could now get pissed courtesy of Rupert Murdoch. Unfortunately, he was addressing a conference on the ethics of journalism, and read it out, to the cheers of the hacks.

I used those expenses to very good effect. After a refreshing lunch I suggested to Routers that he wait outside the main conference hotel while I grabbed us a cab. When I returned I saw him slumped on the steps with his hat fallen to the ground in front of him. Passers-by, who thought that the great man had fallen on hard times, were filling it with pound coins.

The Labour conference was a fascinating one. I remember attending a reception with Tony Blair at a time when a senior Tory was about to announce his defection to New Labour. Tony got to his feet and spotted me in the room. He gave me a quizzical look, as if to say, 'You too?' I just smiled and shook my head.

One of the highlights was the great Tony Banks speech at the Tribune rally. Tony was a minister and hated Peter Mandelson. 'I don't want to hear a word against that man. I want the whole bloody library.' He was cheered to the rafters. This was the time when he rather innocuously referred to the new Tory leader, William Hague, as resembling a foetus. Mandelson leaked this to the press as a great insult, totally wiping out coverage of the real insult, which was to him.

Mandelson was a very shrewd operator and despised by the hacks. Except those lazy ones whom he used to drip-feed stories. *Punch* carried a piece (not written by me) about the rather gay parties he used to attend when he was in Rio. I was in the gallery at PMQs when Hague referred to him as Mandelson of Rio. Mandy was not amused.

And he was particularly unamused when the *Sunday Express* published details of his Brazilian boyfriend. Heads rolled and

Routers and I rolled up to the farewell do of the journalisti-
cally deceased at the Golf Club, then a hacks' drinking den just
off Fleet Street. Andrew Pierce, now a star at the *Daily Mail*,
made one of the funniest speeches I have ever heard, telling
us that Rosie Boycott, Amanda Platell's replacement as editor,
was well known for her scoops, 'mostly vanilla, chocolate and
strawberry'. All have done well but it showed the unhealthy
power that Mandelson had over the press. If the mood took
him he could and did destroy people's careers.

He could also be very subtle. Once, when I was a Member,
he sidled up to me and made a veiled threat.

'I understand that you have been in the Red Lion making
accusations against Gordon Brown's sexuality. Desist, or there
will be legal proceedings.' And off he went.

I hadn't a clue what he was talking about. But thinking
about it a few years later, I realised that he was planting a
seed about his old foe.

Brown, as is well known, is completely heterosexual. Once,
a pretty young journalist told me that she fancied him and
asked me to play Cupid. When I mentioned this to Gordon,
he just grinned and walked off.

I never bothered to enquire if anything came of it.

One guy who gets a very unfair press is the king of all spin
doctors, Alastair Campbell. We have always got on rather well,
as I first knew him as a hack on the *Mirror* and *Today*. Even
when I became a hack myself we would often have a laugh
and a chat. He could be very tough. But that was his job: to
instil ministerial discipline and try and get a grip on the media
agenda, which could always spiral out of control with journalists forever seeking an angle. He used to keep tabs on ministers'

diaries so that he could work out who had been leaking to whom. One left-wing senior minister who was always good for an anti-Blair story would put our lunches down as a visit to the dentist. But as Ali once thumped Michael White of *The Guardian*, he can't be all bad.

One day I was up in the gallery when I saw Ali in the PM's press box, waving at me. Then he started nudging, winking and grinning. Then the penny dropped. That week I had written that 'New Labour is nothing more than the politics of nudge, nudge, wink, wink. And the biggest winker of them all is Alastair Campbell.'

Thank God he found it funny. I would not have wanted to end up with the same fate as Michael White.

But once I did.

One day I was having lunch in the press dining room with some chums when the *Mail on Sunday*'s Simon Walters came up, frothing at the mouth. 'Where is that bastard Hayes?'

Well, he found me and started giving me a good thumping. He was dragged off by *The Sun*'s Trevor Kavanagh.

Evidently, *Punch* had run a piece about Walter's wife and I got the blame for it. In all honesty, I had nothing to do with it. But the *Telegraph*'s talented columnist Peter Oborne had wound him up in the bar about it. In truth, it was all a bit scary. Here was I having a quiet lunch with my chums in a room that was filled with the good and the great of Fleet Street and their distinguished guests to watch PMQs. Then my chum Simon waded in and pummelled me into a quivering wreck. A few days later I bumped into Michael White, who had witnessed it all. 'Blimey,' I said, 'I was amazed to be thumped by Walters.'

'You were not thumped at all. He beat the shit out of you.'

It wasn't all that long before Simon and I made up and became good friends again. Last year he led me to the very spot and insisted that someone take a photo of us with our fists up and looking fierce. He is a seriously good guy and one of the most talented journalists that I have ever encountered. The scariest words that any politician can hear when they answer the phone on a Saturday night are, 'Hello, this is Simon Walters.'

The 1997 Tory conference was a strange affair. People were obviously disappointed at being wiped off the political map but rather naively believed that this was just a blip. As soon as the party reverted to the true path of Thatcherism the voters would come flocking back and Blair would be unmasked as nothing more than a socialist fraud. *Channel 4 News* asked me to make a short satirical film of it all. It was the usual stuff, making mischief with an Ed Boyle-style voice-over accompanied by some appropriate music. I slow-moed a Tebbit speech played to the Queen track 'I'm Going Quietly Mad', with 'The Party's Over' as the general background music. And to really make friends with the insannati I played a clip of some old duffer saying that the Tories would win the next election with a landslide, cutting away to a mechanical clown laughing manically at the end of the pier. This led to a lot more filmmaking, mainly for Andrew Brown (Gordon's very civilised brother) for his Parliament programme. I slow-moed a Prescott rant to 'Eat the Rich' by Aerosmith and manipulated his mouth for the burp at the end of the song. It was also great fun to speed up William Hague's shadow Cabinet in *Teletubbies* style, with their introductory song with Hague's face superimposed on the sun. And when Humphrey the Downing Street cat mysteriously disappeared, I managed a shot of him prowling outside No. 10 in time with 'Another One Bites the Dust' by Queen. I loved all this stuff, but there no longer appears to be a market for three-minute shorts taking the piss out of politicians. It's a shame because they are incredibly cheap to make. And I am available.

At the Labour conference I was enjoying doing my daily *Sun* column. The trouble was that I couldn't get an online connection so I had to dictate my copy down the phone. I only had one disaster. I had thought up what I thought was a clever little line to illustrate a mess-up in a National Executive Committee election. My bons mots were 'the poll muddle martyrs', of which I was rather proud. But pride comes before a fall. The next day I opened *The Sun* to see my baby delivered. Somehow, some sub-editor had managed to mangle it to 'poll models'. I hit the roof and immediately got on to Routers.

'Bloody subs.'

'Welcome to journalism, son.'

Anyhow, Rebekah and Les Hinton, News International's chief executive, were very pleased with the columns. They led me into the main conference hotel bar, which was awash with journalists. 'Have you guys been reading Jerry's column?' boomed Les. 'It's brilliant.' That was the kiss of death. I never wrote for News International again.

All sorts of other offers came in. I was a regular contributor on Sky and the BBC, mostly reviewing the papers. And then all sorts of weird stuff. I used to appear on some Granada TV teen show with Sacha Baron Cohen and eventually did a pilot with him which included his Ali G character. Except he was called Wanker Boy instead and was white. He did a delightful send-up interview with Dr Madsen Pirie, who should be very thankful that it was never aired. I appeared in a game where I had to test my wits against a hamster in a wheel. It goes without saying that I lost. The only surviving part of the programme was Sacha's new creation. The rest is history.

But if you think that politics is a swamp of backstabbing chancers, it is infinitely worse in the media. You are always the last to know if you are about to be sacked, and if you are in the running for a presenter job, it will be months before anyone bothers to tell you that you haven't got it.

One day I was wandering back to the *Punch* office when my mate Simon Bates screeched his Beemer to a halt and wound down his window. 'Luv, we must meet, may be a programme in it for you. Terrible station, the manager's a complete tosser, but you'd be great presenting the breakfast show. I'll arrange a meeting with the tosser.' And, true to his word, he did.

The radio station was Liberty Radio, owned by Mo and two floors above the *Punch* office. To be fair, although hardly anyone listened to it, the product was rather good. Richard Arnold, now of *Daybreak* television stardom, and former children's TV presenter Toby Anstis presented excellent shows, while Bates, that great old pro, did drive time. His idea was to crowbar me into presenting the breakfast show. But Bates was right about the manager, a grade-A tosser who wore polyester suits and was a complete caricature of the Smashie and Nicey Harry Enfield creations, a combined confection of Fluff Freeman and Tony Blackburn. He tried me out presenting a night-time show consisting of off-the-wall interviews and music of the 1980s and '90s. He would let me know if I got the breakfast gig.

An old friend from the *Whale Show*, Victoria, was my brilliant producer. Once, with about thirty seconds' notice, her voice in my ear told me that there was a guy live from Miami whom I was to interview about tantric sex. To be honest, I wasn't quite sure what it was … only that I wasn't getting any. So off we went.

'So tell me, Chip, how do you achieve this great sexual marathon?'

'Well, Jerry, first you have a well-greased hand and carefully thrust it into a well-greased…'

Well, that's as far as I let it go as I turned up the fader for Sister Sledge's 'We Are Family' to drown out what I knew Mo would regard as a rant from a 'filthy pervert'.

I did quite a few of these programmes and Victoria was very pleased. She would recommend me for the breakfast job. But did I hear a word from Smashie and Nicey? Not a word, and not for the want of me trying. The ghastly little man gave me the runaround. Eventually, one afternoon I bumped into him on the stairs.

'Well, you know how to treat the boys in the big school, don't you?'

'What on earth are you talking about? We haven't spoken in weeks.'

'Don't you remember lurching into me yesterday, calling me a tosser and saying that you were going to rip out my eyeballs and piss in the sockets?'

'Actually, no. But I am happy to repeat it.'

In fact, I had no recollection of speaking to him at all. Then I had a vague flicker of memory. I had been lunching with Steen the day before and we had been rather thirsty. I must have been forcibly expressing my views about Mr Polyester and Steen must have gurgled, 'Well, go and tell him then.'

I never got the job. A few weeks later Mo sold Liberty to an evangelical Christian broadcaster. I don't think I would have fitted in very well. Bates went off to Classic FM.

But it stood me in good stead a few years later when I did a month's stint on a mid-morning programme at BBC Essex, playing music and doing phone-ins. I loved it. And my great producer Stuart schooled me in the art of driving a desk, which means twiddling all the knobs and faders. I can only recall one little mishap. To set the scene, let me explain how a desk operates. In the middle is a red fader for your voice. On the left are faders for news, weather and callers, with a screen saying who they are and what they are going to bang on about. In the middle is a screen setting out beds (background music to talk over), jingles and tracks to be played. To activate these you move a fader on the right, click the screen and press 'GO' on a machine called 'Radioman'.

One day we had a caller getting very uptight about paedophiles. The time came to wrap him up and play a track. Sadly, I was on autopilot.

'Well, thanks for your views, John,' I said as I cut him off. 'And enough of paedophiles. Let's play some Michael Jackson.'

Sadly, listeners just heard the beginnings of my hoots of laughter before 'Thriller' burst onto the Essex airwaves.

I learned to my advantage that it is not just MPs who go on fact-finding missions; journalists do too. So I was delighted to be invited on a trip to northern Cyprus to get the lay of the land and interview the President, Rauf Denktaş. It was all arranged by my mate Ian Hernon, who, apart from being a cracking journalist, is a very fine historical author. So, him, me, Eben Black, political editor of the *News of the World,* and Peter Willoughby, doyen of the Press Association, were feted by the Turkish Republic of Cyprus.

It really was an eye-opener. Of course, we were shown the usual sites of atrocities committed by the Greeks. Beautifully preserved spattered brains lovingly presented behind Perspex was a highlight. But I suspect that if we had been entertained by the Greeks we would have been shown exactly the same sort of thing.

I have always been a Turkophile and found Denktaş a personable and attractive fellow. Although it was a little disconcerting to see so many bits of blue circled pottery, to ward off the evil eye, in one room.

We only had one little mishap. While waiting in the VIP lounge in the early hours of the morning we thought that it would be a good idea to have a few swifties to ease the pain of the flight back home. This didn't agree with Willoughby, who made a mad dash to the bathroom. Ten minutes passed. Twenty and then thirty, without any sign of the old boy. Somehow he had locked himself in a cubicle and had been wailing for help. Our flight was being called by now and there was a very real possibility that we would miss it. So drastic measures had to be taken. We broke down the door and scuttled guiltily off to the plane.

However, I did learn a serious lesson on that trip. Although most journos and editors (the ones who haven't been dried out) drink like fishes, it cannot be admitted publicly, for reasons well beyond the comprehension of my little brain. So in all innocence I wrote a light-hearted piece mentioning that 'Eben Black was permanently plugged into a life-support machine known as Stella Artois'. He went ballistic, fearing that his editor would give him his marching orders. In retaliation he printed a less-than-flattering photo of me astride a very phallic cannon. I learned my lesson.

Then I organised a trip to Gibraltar. The then First Minister, Peter Caruana, was a friend, as was the Governor, Sir Richard Luce, a former Minister for the Arts. Ian Hernon, the splendid Jon Craig, then of the *Sunday Express* and now chief political correspondent for Sky News, and I set off for a great jolly on the rock.

Craig is the master of teasing out a story where there is none. He casually mentioned to a senior official that Prince Andrew would make rather a fine Governor when Richard's tour of duty was over. This translated into the headline 'Andrew tipped to be next Governor of Gibraltar shock'.

Then he learned that the fierce little Barbary apes which were a menace to tourists were breeding too fast. He managed to get a two-page spread plus pictures out of that one on the lines that they were going to be issued with contraceptives. The man is a genius.

CHAPTER 21

IF WE CATCH YOU AT IT, YOU'RE IN IT

'If we catch you at it you're in it' was the slogan we adopted at *Punch*. And one of the first was none other than Cabinet minister Peter Mandelson, when we uncovered his controversial mortgage 'loan'. He resigned. Through the sheer creative ingenuity of James Steen, Richard Brass and Dominic Midgley, *Punch* had become enormously popular with opinion-formers, though sales were not as good as any of us really wanted. The trouble is that under previous and short-lived editors like Peter McKay (now a columnist at the *Daily Mail*), the legendary Stewart Steven (former editor of the *Mail on Sunday* and the *Standard*) and Paul Spike (God knows where he is now, probably the seventh circle of hell) a gradual mountain of debt had built up. One reason: millions of pounds had been spent on a TV advertising campaign for the relaunch.

Under Steen's editorship, the advertising was restricted to billboard posters in Underground stations. These would never be seen by Steen because his view was that travel on the Tube was some sort of perverted torture. Our advertisers gave a very excitable pitch once they'd created the posters.

'James, let me take you round the Underground one morning

next week. We'll look at the new posters in the stations, and then we can do a lovely lunch.'

Steen drew on a fag while he considered the idea for about two seconds. 'Let's just do the lovely lunch,' he said.

But the people who mattered, editors, political editors and senior politicians, loved the magazine, even if the public were lukewarm. They just didn't get the fact that *Punch* had become fun, innovative, original and totally outrageous. We were stuffed by our old brand image, mild middle-class humour which would make the vicar and his wife contentedly smile over pre-bedtime cocoa, with a few safe cartoons thrown in. Worse, it was perceived as dentist waiting room fodder. This wasn't helped by the launch editors, who thought they were carrying on some quaint British tradition like incest or Morris dancing.

Spike was certainly anti-Establishment and brought in exciting new columnists, but the new *Punch* under Steen was cutting edge and sometimes downright dangerous. Even better, we were totally unpredictable. This seriously angered old-school humorists like former *Punch* editor Alan Coren, to whom humour post-1965 was no laughing matter. In truth, the circulation of *Punch* had been on a gradual slide decades before the title was acquired by Al Fayed.

Within about an hour of becoming editor, Steen tracked down the very first issue of *Punch* magazine. He wanted a proper look at the roots of this grand old-timer of the magazine world. Sitting quietly in his office, he chained his way through a pack of Benson & Hedges while reading the issue that was published on 17 July 1841. On page three there was a leader item entitled 'The Moral of *Punch*', which included the

founders' objective: '*Punch* hangs the devil.' Steen was capti-
vated by this mission. And so we set a course, '*Punch* hangs the
devil...' Or, as a young trainee in the advertising department
put it, '*Punch* gets the baddies.'

Steen instilled in us a totally different mindset. I mentioned
a few chapters back the time when John Prescott thumped
me, a story that I had dined out on for years, thinking that
it was rather funny. I did a few hundred words on it in the
magazine. Prezza, now Deputy Prime Minister, went ballistic
and instructed solicitors on an action for defamation.

This was, incidentally, a couple of years before Prescott
delivered a left jab to a man who'd thrown an egg at him.

As always in these matters, David Price, by far the best
in the business, was instructed as our solicitor advocate. He
arrived to discuss the matter, accompanied by his colleagues
Paul Fox and Rose Alexander. This formidable legal team was
in conference with Steen and, after an agonising wait outside
the editor's door, I was called in. They were ashen-faced.
James said, 'Jerry, can you take David and the team through
it, please? Tell them what happened on that day in the House
of Commons.'

It was as if I had been waiting stage left, and now I was
ready to deliver my lines. I went into full theatrical mode,
rolling on the floor, giving agonising groans and not a bad
Prescott impersonation of 'Ya little Tory cunt!' David's eyes
sparkled. Steen told me many years later that while I was
waiting outside, Price had given him a stern warning: 'Do you
realise,' Price had said, 'we're up against the Deputy Prime
Minister? This is serious.' Price, like me, had the capacity for
drama. However, when Price saw what I was saying was true,

his little eyes sparkled. Perhaps he could also see how it would look before a larger audience upon the right platform; namely in the Royal Courts of Justice, in front of a jury. This could be an enormous, glittery, high-profile case for him.

Prezza's grand solicitors assumed that we ghastly little Al Fayed oiks, spots on the bottom of Fleet Street, would be quivering in our shoes and would roll over. They did not bet on the total unpredictability of Steen. In the next issue, on the front page was a photo of Prezza in a judge's wig. A few pages in, readers were treated to a photocopy-style image of the pompous letter before action from his solicitors ('not for publication', it screamed). Turn the page and there, a *Sunday Times*-style graphic of what actually happened: the two protagonists illustrated before, during and after the punch. Fleet Street loved it. Prezza sensibly caved in. And the Thumper had been thumped. But it was all good clean fun. Well, ish.

I am often asked what Al Fayed was really like. The answer is simple: fun. There are so many myths surrounding him that it is difficult to know where to start. Myth One was that he bought *Punch* to counter *Private Eye*'s attacks on him. Myth Two was that as proprietor he exercised editorial control. Myth Three was that it was just a vehicle to trash his enemies and laud his friends. Myth Four was that it was all part of a clever campaign to improve his image so that he could be given the coveted British passport.

All of these are hopelessly wrong. He never once told James, or any of us, what to write. Or rather, if he did then James ignored him. He didn't interfere, other than to make suggestions and take an interest in the magazine as a business entity. Yes, he was keen for the magazine to succeed, of course. But he had a mile-wide mischievous streak, as did each member of the staff at *Punch*, and there was a mutual desire – almost a compelling need – to ridicule the Establishment. In other words, it was not that Steen needed to approve of Al Fayed's instincts; more that Al Fayed did approve of Steen's instincts.

The first he saw of what was going in the magazine was when he was handed the 'mocked-up pages' or the 'book' (printed-out pages of what had been despatched to the printers), and by that time the pages were rolling off the press. Al Fayed's problem was that, from time to time, he had to placate his friends who had been parodied or ridiculed. It was usually with a shrug and a roll of his eyes and an apologetic sigh of 'It is James. What can I do?' And as for getting his passport, we probably made the situation even worse. *Punch* was his toy, but the toymaker, unpredictable and sometimes totally off-the-wall, was James Steen whom he forgave everything, just revelling in the fun of it all.

You may recall the great cash-for-questions scandal, when MPs were said to be given brown envelopes by Fayed. These envelopes were stuffed with £50 notes in return for putting down parliamentary questions. It dominated the news for months and resonated throughout the country for years. One day, Steen thought of a wheeze. He rang up a friend in the travel business (a specialist in dives in the Red Sea) and memorised one sentence phonetically. He then rushed from our offices, crossed to the other side of Brompton Road, into Harrods, and up the escalators to Al Fayed's office. As usual, sitting in the chairman's chair was not Mo but the enormous white polar bear that always occupied his place. But he was there, as always. So Steen rattled out his words of Arabic, which stunned Mo, who was sitting at a meeting with the good and the great. They were rather perplexed. Who is this man and what has he just said to Al Fayed in his native tongue to make him roar with laughter? For their benefit he translated. 'Where is my brown paper envelope?' Nobody but Steen could get away with that.

One great scoop was 'Life with Rupert Murdoch', by Philip Townsend, who had been Murdoch's butler at his apartment overlooking St James's Park in London. It was a hilarious three-parter (run over three issues) and was so comical in content – heaps of behind-the-front-door stories about the 'media mogul' – that some readers even mistook it for a spoof. When the first instalment was heading to the printers, Steen took a copy of the butler's story to Al Fayed. He was giving the proprietor a sneak preview of what would be on the newsagents' shelves a day or two later. Al Fayed was a little anxious. He knew Murdoch and wondered how he would take it. 'Oh, it'll be fine,' said Steen. 'Rupert has a great sense of humour.'

On the evening of publication, at the local pub, Steen phoned the Harrods switchboard and, adopting a ridiculously strong Australian accent, he said, 'Can you put me through to Mohamed Al Fayed, please?'

'Who's calling?'

'Rupert Murdoch.'

Eventually, the call was transferred through the ranks of Al Fayed's regiment before reaching his personal assistant. The conversation went like this:

'Hello, Mr Murdoch?' she said.

'Can I speak to Mohamed?' said Steen-Murdoch, sounding a bit grumpy.

'Can you hang on a moment, please?'

Steen was put on hold. Followed by:

'I'm terribly sorry, Mr Murdoch, but Mr Al Fayed has gone travelling.'

It was a wheeze, but when Mohamed found out that he had been the victim of a practical joke he phoned Steen the following day and tried to play the same trick. Alas, it wasn't as successful because Mo used his personal assistant to make the call. She said, 'Hi James, I'm putting you through to the boss but you're not supposed to know it's him.'

Then Mo came on the line, with an Australian impersonation that was even worse than Steen's. He said, 'Hello, James Steen. This is Rupert Murdoch...' Then he burst into laughter.

This story illustrates the workings of *Punch* – a lot of miscreants causing a lot of mischief, and all at one man's expense.

There was an interesting spat with Ian Hislop, the editor of *Private Eye*. One day he rang up James about some story we had written. They had rather a serious conversation in which Hislop let slip that he didn't like animals and couldn't bear dogs. In the next issue there was a calendar involving mocked-up photos of Hislop posing with a different dog for every month of the year. It goes without saying that the taped conversation was available for all to hear on an 0800 number, these being the days before Twitter and YouTube. I don't think Ian found it very funny.

The atmosphere in the office was always quirky, creative and fun. We were like a bunch of kids thinking up new wheezes. It must have been what *Private Eye* was like when it started.

The first thing that anyone who came in noticed was an amazing work of modern art by Richard Brass's desk (Brasso was later to become a superb editor). Everyone admired the vivid colouring and avant-garde style. Nobody had the heart to tell them that this was the office betting plan. In those days there was a lot of betting in the office on gee-gees, football, investments and just about anything else, and this was his totally incomprehensible grid. It was there to say how much was being won and lost, though it was mostly a mass of red lines. He should have put it in for the Turner Prize.

The office was also a hub for some fascinating people. Bank-robber-turned-journalist John McVicar was a columnist, and always up for a laugh and a good lunch. Philip Townsend, aforementioned former butler to Rupert Murdoch and on the road as a photographer with the Rolling Stones, would also appear from time to time with a story. And don't let's forget George Best, who wrote for us on football. Cartoons still featured within the magazine, and Steve Way was the cartoons editor.

There was also Debbie Barham, the highly gifted gag-writer who died a few years later, her life cut short by anorexia. You couldn't call her a gag-writer to her face for fear of her delivering, at rapid speed, a dozen obscene gags about gagging. For her column, Debbie was asked to file 800 words. Instead, she filed five times the amount. One of Steen's delights was subbing the copy, laughing uncontrollably as he read while he trimmed.

There was George the genial security man, who was always on the look-out for solicitors posing as couriers – they'd be delivering writs. He'd phone up to Steen, 'I've got a courier down here. Says he must deliver something to you personally. Not so sure about this one...' Steen would traipse down to reception and return with another writ. Eventually, so many piled up that the magazine's front cover had a banner that read 'Putting on the Writs!' The legal battles were frequent but someone once calculated that we won 90 per cent of cases. Most people who sued did so because they wanted to prevent Fleet Street following up the stories, sharing them with a wider audience. We're talking bruised egos.

Then there was Benji the bin man (Benjamin Pell). Benji was delightfully eccentric and his passion was hunting through other people's dustbins to see what delights he could find. One day he stumbled upon an amazing story which we ran with for weeks. Outside a well-known NatWest bank in one of the poshest parts of London, bin bag after bin bag was filled with un-shredded bank statements and personal details. The headline was 'How Your Secrets are Left on the Streets'. It took months before they appreciated that this was not just plain wrong but was a serious breach of their duty of care to their customers, who were now open to identity fraud. We even published a helpline so that customers could come and collect their discarded details.

One day, George the security man rang to say that a judge was in reception and that he wanted to speak to the editor. Oh dear, this could be a problem. Not at all. Instead, he was a customer of the bank who just wanted to retrieve his accounts. Nobody dared have a peek. It could have been rather embarrassing to show up his regular payments to Madame du Pain or Miss Fellatia de Cock.

Two delightful guys appeared as if from nowhere one day.

Anil Bhoyrul and James Hipwell were the *Daily Mirror* share tipsters who had been sacked, quite wrongly, for allegations of rigging. This was nonsense, as all they wrote was that they would be buying certain shares. The poor lads thought they were never going to work again and were off to the pub to drown their sorrows. Until Steen rang them offering a job. And that's how the great Steen wheeze to reduce our mountain of debt was born. He persuaded Mo to let them have a pot of about £100,000 to invest. With these guys it would be a no-brainer. To be honest, it would have been better to have put it on a horse. We lost about £40,000 before the plug was pulled. And Mo? Tantrums? Sackings? Vile retribution? No. He just thought it was hilariously funny and dined out on it for years.

Steen liked me immensely, and he once said to me, 'The thing is, Jerry, you are not only a gifted writer who knows how to tell a great story, but you have what very few political writers possess – a wicked sense of humour that enables you to laugh not only at others but also at yourself.' Mind you, that was after a very good lunch.

Steen was, for once in his life, seriously fazed when he could not find his credit card. So he rang up the company. And they were very perturbed.

> Sir, we have been looking at the history of usage and it bears all the hallmarks of a fraud. This man, clearly an alcoholic, has been on a spree, in restaurants, pubs and off-licences. What provides even more cogent evidence of a copper-bottomed fraud is that all these transactions took place in just two days.

When they ran through the litany of very familiar pubs,

restaurants and off-licences, Steen realised that there had been no fraud at all. Just a regular couple of days in the life of the editor of *Punch*. We all went out for a drink to celebrate. Our usual watering hole – though water was rarely consumed – was the Swag and Tails, where Bernie Ecclestone would also go most lunchtimes.

Punch Christmas lunches were fairly wild. We were nearly thrown out of the Criterion when the lads from Graphics started pinging elastic bands into the heads of very irritated customers. But the strangest affair for me was when some-one thought it was rather amusing to put me on a table with a number of manic depressives and crackheads. Guests, not employees.

'Do you do crack, Jerry?'

'Er, no.'

And then a discussion with others about the highs and very lows of the practice.

'Ever contemplated suicide, Jerry?'

'Er, no.'

Well, not until then anyway. And then a long discussion about pulleys, pills and every conceivable and inconceivable way of topping yourself.

Well, all good things eventually have to come to an end. Mo realised that his wonderful toy was becoming rather too expensive, and new people were brought in. By far the best was Andrew Neil, who just let us get on with it. But then came Phil Hall, a former editor of the *News of the World*. Mercifully, I had no dealings with him, but he wanted to interfere. Mo, finally and reluctantly, accepted James's resignation (he'd tried twice before). James was a free and innovative spirit and to suddenly be involved in corporate political bollocks was never his style. Dom Midgley, the deputy editor, one of the most principled men that I know, resigned because he couldn't take any more. Both joined the *Mirror* and created a fantastic gossip column called 'The Scurra'. Piers Morgan called Steen 'the world's most mischievous journalist'. Too right. When he hired Steen, he did so on this condition: 'I want you to do to others what you did to me in *Punch*.'

Brasso took over the editorship. Considering the witch hunts (Hall would ask members of staff who they thought should be fired), he did a remarkable job of keeping up our spirits when our numbers were dying in the Hallian trenches, and keeping the flame of Steen alive. One day, Brasso rang me.

'Mate, it's the end.'

'Not to worry, keep the flag flying.'

'I can't. We're all fucked. *Punch* is to close.'

I have no doubt that if Steen had been the first editor of the relaunch, *Punch* would be making money hand over fist and would be a serious rival to *Private Eye*. And with a much more contemporary and original take on politics.

So that was the end of the most creative and fun time in my working life. I had travelled a very long way from the back benches. I had learned a craft. I had enjoyed a mad magic carpet ride into journalism. And my liver was wrecked.

It was time to go back to the law.

CHAPTER 22

BACK TO THE BAR

While I was thoroughly enjoying myself as a journalist, I was desperately trying to build up my practice at the Bar. The law had travelled a long way since 1983 and I had a lot of catching up to do. Fourteen years in Parliament meant that all my instructing solicitors had either moved on or forgotten me. The civil law procedure rules had totally changed, so I was not going to start all over again with personal injury or employment law. And although years previously, in a moment of madness, I had taught commercial law, the thought of practising it filled me with the dread of mind-numbing boredom. Anyhow, jury advocacy was what I really loved. So that is why I decided to specialise in crime.

My mate Gary Jacobs, from the *Whale Show*, was a solicitor, so he helped me out. He sent me down to Snaresbrook Crown Court to defend a guy for arson with intent to endanger life. Gary told me not to worry about it too much as the evidence was overwhelming, but if I could keep the sentence down to lower double figures he would be more than happy. To the amazement of the client, the judge and me, the lad was found not guilty. As a result, Gary began to regularly brief me on serious stuff and send me all over the country.

One evening I was in Sheffield representing a man accused of murdering his wife's lover in front of the children. It was a particularly gruesome case in which he cut the body up into eleven pieces and got the kids to help him bag it up. Then, as a thank you, he took them to Blackpool in mid-summer, with the body still in the back. Oh, and before that he had fed bits of it to his brother's goat, which died.

These sorts of cases can be a bit stressful so it was great to hear from Gary, who broke up the gloom. We set a date for lunch and he briefly mentioned that he was going into hospital for a routine operation the next day. I wished him well.

It was the last time that we spoke. He died unexpectedly on the operating table the next day. I really do miss him and will be forever grateful to him for putting me back on my legal feet.

❦

The one thing about fourteen years in Parliament is that it gives you a tremendous amount of confidence. If you can deal with the howling jackals in the chamber, have altercations with Margaret Thatcher and live to tell the tale, the judiciary will hold absolutely no terrors for you.

I first started in the courts in the late '70s: think of *Rumpole of the Bailey* as the most accurate depiction of what life was really like at the Bar back then. Many of the judges were mad and quite terrifying.

In those days, once the Lord Chancellor had appointed you to the bench you became a law unto yourself, an unelected dictator in your own court fiefdom. Nothing could be more depressing than appearing before a whisky-sodden judge reeking of last night's single malt, disappointment and the failed advances to a pupil young enough to be his granddaughter.

One of my first Crown Court trials was a shoplifting case at the Inner London Crown Court. The judge was an eccentric Irish peer named Paddy Dunboyne. Apart from being very dim and amazingly biased against any defendant, Paddy was very deaf. When it came to his summing-up he had a habit of making bits of evidence up if he thought it might help the prosecution case. So he waded in with his hobnailed boots.

> Members of the jury, you might think that as this was a cold November day the defendant was wearing a greatcoat, and within this garment was a poacher's pocket and it is within this pocket that he had hidden the goods that he had stolen.

The trouble is, the only accurate piece of evidence in that statement was that it was November; everything else was pure fantasy. So I protested. After the usual 'What, what? Speak up, boy' farce that took up so much of Paddy's court time, the penny dropped that I was politely asking him to just sum up the evidence that the jury had heard. He exploded.

'Outrageous ... impertinent ... you are misleading the jury ... I will report you to the Bar Council ... disgraceful behaviour.'

And then counsel for the prosecution jumped to his feet. 'Your Honour, I support my learned friend.'

That was the cherry on the cake. Paddy had a minor nuclear explosion. We were both being sent off to the Bar Council. A few weeks later, the prosecutor and I found ourselves appearing before Mr Justice Rougier for a disciplinary hearing.

In those days it was very informal. Now we are governed by a ghastly, self-serving hanging court called the Bar Standards Board. So desperate are they to appear independent that you might just as well plead guilty to any ridiculous charge that they might bring and perhaps one or two others for good measure.

But back to our hearing. Rougier peered at us over his half-moons.

Gentlemen, a very senior judge has accused you of misleading the court. This could have very serious repercussions for what could be glittering careers. However, I note that the judge was the Lord Dunboyne, who is both mad and deaf. Might I suggest that you retire to El Vino and forget about it all.

Paddy Pakenham (son of Lord Longford) was not quite so fortunate. He rolled back to court after a drunken lunch and was in no mood for Dunboyne's antics. His leg was in plaster after a skiing accident. He was due to make his closing speech to the jury for the defence. So he heaved his plastered (although not as plastered as him) leg onto the desk, sat back and lit a cigar.

'Members of the jury, I don't know why I bother. You are too dim to understand a word of the defence and the judge is deaf, biased and profoundly stupid.'

Of course, it was all true, but not a good idea to say so in open court, particularly when drunk. Paddy was sent off to rehab for a while and died a couple of years ago.

El Vino in Fleet Street is the legendary watering hole for judges, the Bar and the press. It is an alcoholic black hole where whole days can be lost. On most evenings you will find my chums Philip Shorrock, a judge sitting at Woolwich, Michael Latham, an old-fashioned criminal hack like me, and Gareth Jones, a whizz-kid tax lawyer, propping up the bar. As convivial a bunch as you could ever meet. I think all barristers and criminal judges are hefted to EV; it has a dangerous magnetic pull. It is also a home from home. In the old days before cash machines we used the place as a bank. Pommeroy's Wine Bar in the *Rumpole* stories was based on it.

Traditionally, women weren't allowed to stand at the bar. They could only be served seated. EV was taken to court over this and lost. I was drinking with an ancient Bailey hack called Crespi on the day of the judgment. Brilliant, witty and weighing in at about twenty-five stone, he was regaling me with his legal war stories when suddenly the door burst open and in marched a pretty young girl dressed in a fur coat, followed by a snapper from *The Sun*. Clearly, a red-top set-up. Christopher Mitchell, a co-owner of EV (and uncle to Plebgate MP Andrew), who was always impeccably dressed in pinstripe trousers and a black jacket, did his best to evict her. It led to them wrestling on the floor and her revealing that she was totally naked under the coat. It was not very dignified but delightfully entertaining. And great photos in *The Sun*.

Just off Blackfriars Bridge there is EV2. Not so much of a den of iniquity as the Fleet Street branch, but it has had its moments. When I was an MP I attended a hack's farewell. A few Cabinet ministers were in attendance and in particular the delightfully camp, but very straight, John Patten, who used to greet you in the lobby with a cheery 'hello, duckie'. I was in mischievous mood and went up to a young gay hack suggesting that he pop over and give Patten a kiss, as he might get a story out of it. About two minutes later I saw the lad in the arms of two burly men, who threw him out onto the pavement. This, after all, was the unenlightened 1980s.

Suddenly, a journo dripping with blood staggered up the stairs from the gents. 'I've just been attacked,' he wheezed. Fleet Street at its drunken best excitedly rushed down the stairs, expecting a brawl. There was nobody there. The boozed-up hack had just fallen down the stairs and the rest was nothing but a product of his addled imagination.

When I came back to the Bar it was rather a different place from when I left it. Judges were properly trained and accountable and most of the seriously deranged had taken early retirement. It wasn't long before I was leading high-profile murders for the defence. A few stick in my mind.

Fifteen years ago I was at the Bailey defending a man accused of strangling his wife. There was prosecution evidence that just before she died her uncle received a phone call from her and claimed that he could hear my client shouting in the background. This was tricky as our defence was that we were somewhere else at the time. And then I remembered Lulu. She was the defendant's parrot who did a very passable imitation of him. So I had a brainwave. Let's call Lulu!

The thought of an out-of-control parrot flying round the Old Bailey squawking expletives and 'Chelsea for the cup', and crapping indiscriminately, was potentially fantastic entertainment for the red tops, but would not be very popular with the judge. So I sent a solicitor not so much to get a statement from it, but to see how it behaved. Well, Lulu proved to be a little star and sounded remarkably like the defendant. The trouble was that every time a tape recorder was put in front of her, she clammed up. That sparkling line of defence had sadly bitten the dust.

I had a beautiful and brilliant junior called Grace Ong, who kept an almost word-perfect note of what was being said on her laptop. At one stage I suggested to the judge that he might care to refer to her note. After staring at the laptop he passed it back with a grunt and gave us both a very odd stare. Over lunch we had a look at the notes. Earlier, we had noticed that some old silk had been taking an unusual interest in the laptop.

'Just admiring the software, old boy,' he grinned.

What he didn't tell us is that he had just altered the default settings. So every time Grace typed in 'judge', it defaulted to 'boring old fart', and 'prosecution' became 'twat'.

Then I got a fascinating case which was dubbed the 'great postal ballot fraud'. I was parachuted into Birmingham for the first Election Commission in 100 years. I was representing two Labour councillors found in a factory unit surrounded by postal ballot papers, pens and Tipp-Ex. The commissioner was Richard Maury QC, sitting as a deputy High Court judge. And jolly good news he was too. A great sense of humour and impeccably fair. The hearing, which lasted for about a month, was held in a theatre. This was odd in itself as members of the public would walk in, eat their lunch and then saunter out. It was like care in the community. The petition was issued by John Hemming, now a Liberal Democrat MP. Sadly, I had to rough him up a bit in the witness box for a couple of days.

This case became notorious as it showed widespread abuse

of the totally inadequate postal voting rules, leading Maury to comment that our electoral system was like that of a 'banana republic'. The abuses were horrendous and the administration of the election dire. Bags of uncounted postal votes were found in council offices and one official was accused by Maury of 'throwing away the election rule book'. We went crashing down.

A week later I received a phone call from John Hemming, then a parliamentary candidate. I thought he was going to have a moan about my treatment of him in the witness box. Far from it. The starting gun for the 2005 election had been fired. Would I represent him in the High Court to try to halt the election until the postal ballot rules were made compatible with European law? Of course.

This was going to be a high-profile case in the administrative court, not somewhere that I was particularly familiar with, so I persuaded Simon Baker, a very able barrister in chambers with a brain the size of a melon (albeit a small one), to be my junior. He would do all the heavy lifting, while I would do the jazz hands. Neither of us would be paid, but the publicity would be enormous.

You may remember a few chapters back the story of my long refreshing lunch with the *News of the World* and a dash to the Oxford Union for a debate on Europe with Bill Cash? Well, Simon reminded me that he was the teller on the vote and that he had had to break me out of the gents' lavatory as I had somehow locked myself in. His skills would be particularly useful, then.

The court was packed with journalists, this being the middle of an election campaign. Presiding was Mr Justice Collins, a formidable intellectual presence, who certainly wasn't going to take any nonsense from me.

I did my best to persuade him that politicians could not be trusted to amend the law and that the only protection the public could have against unfair elections was judicial interference. After all, politicians are well known for breaking their promises.

'But you were a politician, weren't you, Mr Hayes?'

'Yes, my Lord.'

'How many promises did you break?'

'My Lord, the highways and byways are littered with them like used Yorkie wrappers. That is why the public need your protection.'

Well, it didn't wash. One red judge wasn't going to stop a general election. But for a parliamentary candidate like John Hemming, leading the national news that night was very pleasing indeed. So we went to celebrate in El Vino. A couple of weeks later John romped home with a very respectable majority. He is still in the House and is rather good news.

Next were the Birmingham riots. I was co-defending with a very old friend, Steven Hadley (Hadders). He is one of the great characters at the Bar, with a delightfully risqué past. He is also a seriously good brief. His last incarnation was as a vicar in the Church of Wales, where he was a delightfully naughty cleric who had a bit of a brush with the *News of the World*.

The Birmingham riots were very scary. I remember the jury being shown CCTV footage of a gang of black men rushing to the only Asian family in the road. The suggestion was that they were going to kill the poor woman and her children. They were cowering in fear. We saw CCTV of Asian taxi drivers being pulled from their cars and murdered with machetes. This was a very stressful trial.

Hadders and I were involved in what is described in the trade as a 'cut-throat'. This meant that both our clients were attacking each other. Soon the time came for our speeches. I was first on the indictment and therefore had first crack, so I had to give Hadders a bit of a kicking.

'Members of the jury, my learned friend is a serial philanderer [pause just to make him go pale] ... of juries. First will be the flirtation, then the walk upstairs. The last thing that you will remember will be the click of the bedroom door locking, the creak of the bed springs and the terrible guilt in the morning. This man would tap dance naked on the jury box with a rose between his teeth to get an acquittal. Turn around, take a good look into the eyes of his client and what do you see? Three words: guilty, guilty, guilty.'

In response Hadders laid into my client, and of course me, with a skilful and witty speech. We were both convicted, although it pains me to say that Hadders got a slightly better result than I did.

Although we worked very hard during that trial we also had a great deal of fun. My abiding memory of that time was cheering Hadders while singing 'Is This the Way to Amarillo' on stage at a tranny bar.

The convention at the criminal Bar is that after a long trial and after the jury has been sent out to deliberate, all of us take the judge out for dinner and let our hair down. Our judge was the delightful Trevor Faber, now retired. All of us, apart from Trevor, had hoovered up an awful lot of hooch. But Trevor suffered from low blood pressure and was beginning to sway. I yelled to the prosecuting silk to catch him, but sadly the poor chap could hardly walk nor talk. This called for immediate action, so I dived in to rescue our judge. Sadly, I mistimed it, knocked him to the floor and out cold. Killing a judge is not a particularly good thing to have on one's record. The ambulance arrived, Trevor revived and he was sped to hospital. My parting words to him as he was stretchered aboard were, 'For God's sake don't die on us; we don't want to do this bloody trial again.'

The next day he sent us a lovely letter thanking us for a great evening out, the medical check-up and the free ride home. A good man.

Then, after the war in Iraq, I was instructed to lead the team in the defence of a delightful young soldier, accused with others of drowning a fifteen-year-old Iraqi boy while on manoeuvres. He was just nineteen and had seen his friends blown apart and maimed during the war. I won't bore you with the details save to say that he was rightly acquitted.

There was obviously a lot of press attention with this case and my old mate *Mirror* legend Don Mackay was in permanent residence. We had some cracking dinners. One day he came up to me and said how much he'd enjoyed my closing speech.

'But, Don, I haven't made it yet!'

'Well, son, this is what I am going to write in the paper.'

And bloody good it was too. Needless to say I nicked his best one-liners. Although, strangely, the *Mirror* didn't print this bit about a very dodgy witness:

'Members of the board, this man is so dishonest and so corrupt I am amazed that he was not greeted personally on the steps of this court by Tony Blair, shaken warmly by the hand, given a peerage and shoved into the Cabinet.' After the defence cuts, they rather liked that.

A few years ago I was doing a fraud in Bradford. A juror became ill and we had a day off, so I rang up my old mate Paul Routledge of the *Mirror*, who lived in a remote farmhouse. 'Come for lunch, Comrade.'

I arrived at about midday and his lovely wife Lynne had put some food in the oven for us. We cracked open the gin, then a few bottles of red, and then out came the slivovitz. When Routers has had a few he tends to revert to speaking in pidgin Russian. Which is quite entertaining although mostly incomprehensible.

But it was getting late and I needed to get back to Bradford. So I asked Routers to call a cab. Off he staggered to the phone. He didn't return after about half an hour, so I thought it would be a good idea to go and find him. He had fallen asleep on the stairs. He gurgled where I could find the number for a taxi. I rang and got hold of a chap who spoke very little English, who asked where I was. By this time all I could I remember was that I was in a farmhouse somewhere in the wilds of Wharf Dale. I asked Routers the address, but all he was capable of was burbling, 'Tell him we are at home.' Which wasn't much use. So I decided to walk about a mile to a pub and ring from there. It was dark and beginning to snow. In the gloom behind me I could hear panting and then a crash. It was Routers, who had followed me out and fallen in a ditch. He was in his vest. So I escorted him back. And set off again. Only to have the same pantomime repeated another couple of times. I eventually locked him in and hoped Lynne would be home soon. Routers, apart from being a great columnist, is a seriously good guy.

Being a criminal barrister would probably be the best job in the world, were it not for knuckleheads like our present Lord Chancellor, Chris Grayling. Well, he was at the time of writing. Lord Chancellor that is. Sadly, knuckleheadism is incurable. Hopefully, by the time this book is published Cameron will have given him the heave-ho.

I can forgive politicians for a number of faults. But being dim, playing to the right-wing gallery and possessing no political judgement is a toxic combination. Sadly, Grayling has them all. And he wants to be leader of the Conservative Party. Spare us all from mad hysterical laughter.

The awful truth is that he has been sucked into the civil service plan to destroy the publicly funded Bar. Over the years our fees have been cut by over 40 per cent. And he wants more. Worse is his grand design to allow the likes of Serco, G4S and the Co-op (say it with Flowers) to take over our services. All of whom are under investigation. Cheap, inexperienced lawyers will take over the criminal justice system. The independent Bar will wither and die. And most high street solicitors will go to the wall. Justice for the most vulnerable would be non-existent and, the most pernicious proposal of all, lawyers will be given a financial incentive to persuade their clients to plead guilty.

It is a tragedy to see the profession I love so much being traduced, prostituted and destroyed by some dreadful little political chancer. The President of the Supreme Court, the Lord Chief Justice, and the judiciary are united with both solicitors and barristers to fight this threat to justice.

The criminal Bar is a remarkably friendly, convivial place to work. If I won the lottery tomorrow I would still roll up to court. Chambers, and in particular mine, Argent, are like families. We all look after each other. The friends I have made at the Bar, with solicitors and the judiciary, are lifelong. They are like my brothers and sisters. All of us feel blessed. And the shit quotient is fairly low.

To see this efficient, cost-effective, impartial, impeccably fair and internationally admired system of justice being broken up and handed on a plate to commercial bloodsuckers is a travesty as much as it is a tragedy.

CHAPTER 23

FROM THE WILDERNESS

The Labour win of 1997 was a pretty depressing time for middle-of-the-road Conservatives. I was delighted that William Hague won the leadership, as it was ludicrous to believe that the straitjacket wing of the party could possibly support someone as nationally popular as Ken Clarke. They would always vote for political purity as opposed to supporting someone who could actually win an election. The ideal scenario would have been a Ken win, severely rattling Blair and Brown and preparing the way for a Hague victory an election later.

Despite a harsh press, Hague was a good party leader. Effective and witty in the chamber and a miracle-maker in keeping a fractious and deranged mob reasonably together. He would have made a great Prime Minister. He was unlucky being in the right place at the wrong time.

And then came Iain Duncan Smith. Oh dear.

Personally charming, but a true representative of the Amish wing. The poor fellow lurched from crisis to crisis and was booted out before he had the chance to lead us into oblivion. I did not have a great deal of sympathy, as he was one of the Euro guerrillas doing his very best to undermine the Major government. So his desperate pleas for loyalty made it difficult for some of us to suppress a malicious snigger. To be fair to him, his time in the wilderness has made him an effective and caring Secretary of State at the DWP. He has changed the political weather over the public's attitude towards benefit reforms. Although whether he can pull off his reforms, with all the IT problems that will haunt them, remains to be seen.

And then there was Michael Howard. A delightful and talented man who never quite got over Ann Widdecombe's 'something of the night' jibe. It struck a chord, not helped by Rory Bremner's brilliant skit of him as a quasi-Dracula figure chillingly asking us to believe, 'Don't worry, I'm not going to hurt you...' After a perfectly respectable defeat he sensibly fell on his sword to spend more time with his directorships.

His departure led to an interesting leadership fight. David Davis was the clear favourite. A charmer, a bruiser and on the sentient right. Davis's problem is that he is not a charismatic speaker. And his conference speech was very 1980s and lacked sparkle. Compared to David Cameron's, which came across as fresh, exciting and a clear break with the past, it was the beginning of the end for Davis. It is not a state secret that they can't stand each other. I was having a drink with a senior member of the shadow Cabinet the night Davis called a by-election over Britain becoming a police state. I asked the simple question, 'Why?' The response was, 'I haven't got a clue.' Davis may not be a team player but he is a good-hearted guy and a friend. He really ought to be in the Cabinet.

Backbenchers are like meerkats: they can collectively sniff out potential winners and losers. They realised that Cameron had the hallmarks of a winner. What they didn't bargain for was that he *really* wanted to modernise the party. Gay friendly, woman friendly, environment friendly. Which basically means not lederhosen-backbencher nor Colonel-and-Mrs-Mad-from-the-shires friendly. He realised that the Tory brand had become toxic. As Theresa May said, we had become the 'nasty party'. She got a kicking for it, but she was right. There had to be root-and-branch change or we would be consigned to political purgatory. And we still have a long way to go. It is a waste of time trying to keep 25 per cent of the electorate happy and expect to form a government.

I am proud to be an unreconstructed Cameroon. I knew him as a boy at Central Office and saw him develop into a highly regarded special adviser. Starting off in a lowly position at Central Office, he impressed his boss Alistair Cooke and became an indispensable firefighter for ministers by devouring the newspapers at 5 a.m. and providing a 'line to take' by 8.30 a.m. He is also a genuinely nice guy without a side. Working for Norman Lamont during the terrible economic whirlwind which destroyed the party's economic credibility for a generation prepared him for crisis management and the relentless onslaught from the press that comes with the job of Prime Minister. He is remarkably unflappable. Within three years of Cameron doing his best for Lamont at the Treasury, his good friend George Osborne was guiding Minister of Agriculture Douglas Hogg through the burning pyres of BSE-infected cattle. Both men spent their formative youths being tempered and fired in the furnace of events and shaped on the anvil of backbench treachery. Things don't change an awful lot.

Cameron's critics say that he is a smooth PR man who

doesn't have a belief in his head. Nothing could be further from the truth. What makes him refreshingly different is that he approaches problems with an almost legal approach: 'What is the mischief and how can it be remedied?' Hardly brain surgery, but it sends the right into paroxysms of deep loathing. Theirs is a simple faith: that the country is crying out for the certainties of Thatcherism. They can't wait to leave the EU, want tax cuts yesterday, and all this stuff about global warming is just a left-wing fantasy.

Yet grown-up politics isn't about faith and certainty, it's about common sense and pragmatism. And the one certainty that you can have about the way Cameron operates is that he is utterly committed to 'doing the right thing', whether it is popular or not.

Effective government has to be about leadership, and not just running in front of the pitchforked mob. Three examples come to mind: the invasion of Libya, same-sex marriages and his plans for a surgical strike on Syria.

But Cameron has a number of deep-seated problems. The party is still grieving for Thatcher, is obsessed by UKIP, and many don't seem to appreciate that they didn't win the last election. And they despise the 'yellow bastards' as the tail wagging the Tory dog.

It is worth exploding the myth that the reason the Tories didn't win an outright majority was because our policies weren't right-wing enough. This flies in the face of polling data, which comes to precisely the opposite conclusion. But, like the American Republicans, they don't believe it and shout to the rooftops that the only way to win an election is to repeat those policies that exiled them to the wilderness for a generation. But though the Tories may have their share of deranged politicians, there are no Sarah Palins ... yet.

What some people don't seem to understand is that all governments are coalitions of one sort or another. Just look at the 'dries' and the 'wets' under Thatcher and the Brown–Blair empire massacres when whoever won a skirmish ran the country for the day. Compromises have to be made or else governments grind to a halt. Interestingly, Thatcher avoided compromise unless she was forced to, and Brown's obstinacy and almost psychotic greed to have the keys to No. 10 led civil servants and ministers to despair. In the land of the policy-blind, the one-eyed man ended up as king.

What has confused so many Tories is that they have to make compromises with the Lib Dems.

The remarkable thing about this coalition is not that it works but that it works so well. Policies are thrashed out with proper debate. The top table have grown-up discussions and compromise. And to be fair, the Lib Dems, who at grassroots level are the most dirty and dishonest of campaigners, have been a force for moderation. The Tories have been a brake on the woolly-headed left and the Lib Dems have kettled the howling full-mooners of the right.

In many ways, this has been the problem. Backbench Tories find it very difficult to work with those who have personally trashed them in their constituencies, while the Lib Dems feel uncomfortable working with those who they feel are in a different political solar system.

A good example of sensible cooperation was the Lansley NHS reforms. Only Andrew and a few civil servants under-stood them, so what hope was there of selling the policy to the voters? The brakes were put on and a more patient-friendly spin emerged.

This is where Health Secretary Jeremy Hunt has been surprisingly masterly. He doesn't bang on about 'outcomes' and other impenetrable jargon; instead, the new health speak is about compassion, care and professionalism. For once we have a Health Secretary who appears to be on the side of patients.

To be fair, he was lucky with the Francis Report, which grimly detailed the horrors at Mid Staffs. Even more fortunate for him is that it all happened on Labour's watch and in particular when Andy Burnham, his opposite number at Health, was in charge. For once, in the eyes of the public, the Tories have the moral high ground on the emotive issue of the NHS.

Whether it will translate into votes is another matter. Hunt is a man to be watched. He has rescued Cameron twice, first as a human shield over the Murdoch difficulties and now in humanising the Lansley reforms. Hunt will now start acquiring enemies.

Despite the collective moans from the usual Tory claque, YouGov polling data regularly shows that 57 per cent of Lib Dems and 67 per cent of Tory supporters think that the coalition is a good thing. Yet this is not represented in Parliament, as a significant minority of Tory backbenchers genuinely despise Cameron with a passion that borders on the bipolar. They keep hearing voices telling them to do unspeakable things. And it is always *her* voice.

But Tory armed insurrection is a mere skirmish compared to the civil war that Ed Miliband has unleashed on Labour. All things Blair have been airbrushed out of history and there is a genocidal war against his supporters. This should be a gift for the Tories. Miliband was put there by the unions and in particular Len McCluskey's Unite, who are manipulating the candidates lists to elbow in their own creatures. More horror stories will emerge from the scandal of Falkirk, Grangemouth and cronyism in the Cooperative movement.

Worse, he is saddled with Ed Balls as shadow Chancellor, whom he never wanted nor even likes. The two Eds still live in the dark and sinister shadow of Gordon Brown and the Labour sky is becoming black with Brownian chickens coming home to roost. And as for Balls, if there was a Dangerous Politicians Act he would have been put to sleep long ago for belonging to a dangerous breed.

Those who know him well tell me that Miliband is a really nice guy. I am sure that they are right. But he, Balls and Mad Dog McBride were Brown's attack dogs, smearing and destroying anyone who stood in his path. Their devotion was not to party or country but to Gordon Brown. It was a deeply unpleasant and poisonous time in Labour's history, particularly as they weren't the slightest bit interested in attacking the Tories, just their own. Maybe Miliband wasn't personally involved, but he must have known what was going on. Alastair Campbell didn't dub him the emissary from Planet Fuck for nothing.

And what about UKIP? What a deeply unpleasant raga-muffin army of racists, homophobes and the seriously flawed. You always have a sneaking suspicion that they are the sort of people who would watch *Roots* backwards so there is a happy ending. They are the flotsam and jetsam of the dispossessed and unelectable. The trouble is some of them do get elected, usually to waste-of-space jobs in the European Parliament. Apart from a sort of vague nod to Euro-democracy, being an MEP isn't worth a bucket of warm spit. Except financially. It is a licence to print money.

I remember a meeting with Thatcher when we first introduced elected MEPs; she just gave me the scary stare and growled, 'It's a gravy train.' Too right.

UKIP's difficulty is that they are a one-man party. And Farage, since his plane accident, is not a well man. What happens when he goes? Who will fill his boots? Will the party fall apart? They tried it once by replacing him with Lord Pearson, who did for policy presentation what King Herod did for babysitting. And then my old friend Robert Kilroy-Silk (a former Labour MP and daytime chat-show host) tried to civilise them. He failed.

UKIP's attraction (how those words stick in my throat) is that they are just the spittoon for the electorate's angst. Dog-and-duck politics; but only in the saloon bar and the golf club. Not so much a party of policy as of a deep and unpleasant snarl. They are the last refuge for the politically dispossessed. The snigger in the woodpile. It appears that the Conservative Party line is to be more cuddly towards them so as not to upset our grass roots. This is a mistake. They should be Febrezed out of British politics and the grass roots should be warned that a vote for them gives us Miliband by stealth. The trouble is that recent YouGov polling suggests that many UKIP supporters don't care too much about the consequences of their vote. This is a serious dilemma for the Tories. I don't pretend to know the answer except to expose UKIP for the ghastly bunch that they are.

Yet it is immigration rather than the EU that exercises their supporters most. The trouble for UKIP is that by the time the election comes both foxes will have been shot and hung outside the gamekeeper's lodge.

Theresa May has been a remarkably effective Home Secretary. Through sheer tenacity and force of will she has managed to get to grips with her dysfunctional and disloyal department. She is as tough as old boots and does more than just make guttural grunts; she takes action – which strikes a chord with the voters.

YouGov polling indicates that most people support the idea of the educated and skilled coming over to work but are totally opposed to those who come over just for the benefits. Intriguingly, 77 per cent support the right of the Romanians and the Bulgarians to come over here to work. The most interesting polling data shows that the public don't trust any party on immigration. Neither fact is particularly surprising.

The last fox to be shot is Europe. The latest YouGov material indicates that there is a very fine balance between those who think that the UK will benefit from leaving the EU and those who think it won't. The interesting statistic is that if Cameron does renegotiate our position with Brussels, 57 per cent would vote to stay in. It is too early to make any judgements, but this suggests that Cameron may have found a voice. There is also the startling statistic that 81 per cent are critical of the government for not speaking about the benefits of being a member of the EU. The trouble is that the Euronutters want Cameron to publish the list of his 'demands' for renegotiation. That is a trap that he would be unwise to fall into because they would want to highlight the failures rather than the successes.

The EU can be a perverse organisation. The Commission and their support staff don't live in ivory towers; rather, they hover on fluffy white clouds suspended way above us mere mortals. They are the Euro Volturi, utterly committed to enforcing the doctrine of political unity. There is the beginning of a groundswell among the northern nations suggesting that there will have to be revision of this thought process, as a lot has changed since the Treaty of Rome, particularly with mass migration from the poorer countries. The challenge for change is not just for Britain but for all member states. So let's have more openness, transparency and democracy. But this doesn't go anywhere near solving the awful truth that none of us want to publicly admit: the Commission's doctrine of political unity has a point. The reason the euro has been a catastrophic failure is because there is not a central fiscal policy, as the only way that that can be achieved is through some form of political unity. Member states have been able to get away with lying about their level of debt and the inevitable has happened. There is a respectable argument that Greece should leave the euro and go back to the drachma. There is only one question: who picks up the bill? Sadly, the European way of dealing with these crises is to brush them under the carpet and hope that they go away. This one won't. And if the Greeks, the Spanish, the Portuguese and particularly the Italians revert to their old ways, our perilous recovery will hit the skids.

But back home, politics is as poisonous as ever and politicians have never been more distrusted by the public. Historically, the Tory Party only seem to have three gears: complacency, panic and self-destruct. We've had the first two and have been teetering on the brink of the latter. I was genuinely shocked when backbenchers in the early part of 2013 were almost queuing up to tell me how much they wanted to get rid of Cameron at any price. Even if it meant annihilation at the election. Amazingly, before the economy began to pick up there was a genuine prospect of an Adam Afriyie (a wealthy Tory backbencher from Windsor) challenge and serious promises of a forced vote. At the moment this has been whittled down to a hard core of about fourteen. But the situation is still remarkably fragile. And Afriyie is still courting the disaffected. One minister, sacked in the most recent reshuffle, told me that he had been offered a place in an Afriyie Cabinet. This may be in the territory of Walter Mitty but there still remains a seething discontent. Quite what Cameron is meant to do to quell this, apart from agreeing to stop breathing, is a mystery. He has tried every weapon in the prime ministerial arsenal. Knighthoods are being showered like confetti, and backbenchers and their wives and partners are invited in for cosy chats, drinks and even lunches at Chequers. But rather than lap it up, many tell me they rather resent it. 'He's just patronising us,' they squeal. Leading the Conservative Party is a thankless, joyless grind.

What should encourage the party is that Labour has had only a consistent lead of about six points, which at this stage of the game borders on the disastrous for them. Cameron has a healthy lead personally on who would make the best Prime Minister, most able to take tough decisions and run the economy. Where he will be in danger is if there is another hung parliament. Backbenchers want more of a say in any negotiations, and if press reports are true (discuss) he has presented Graham Brady, the chairman of the 1922 Committee and a well-known Cameron hater, with a big red button with 'NO' engraved on it. But the irresistible temptation to press it would not only explode any prospect of another coalition but would detonate the explosive jacket that Cameron appears to have voluntarily donned.

And the consequence of this mutually assured destruction? Why, governing in partnership with the DUP and any other minority mad hatter's tea party, with the prospect of St Boris descending to earth to save us all.

To normal, sentient people who actually care about growth, employment and improving the standard of living for everyone, this borders on the criminally insane. But it provides more than just a greater frequency of night emissions for the Tory right; it gives them hope. Hope that Cameron will be sent packing and hope that the Lib Dems will be driven into the arms of Labour. But not as much hope as it gives to the man who sends shivers down the spines of Ed Miliband, Ed Balls and the Young Pretender, Chuka Umunna: Tristram Hunt. He is dismissed as just too good-looking, just too bright, just too inexperienced and just too good to be true. Maybe. I've seen the future and it has perfect white teeth. The question is: 'When?'

In 2013 I appeared on *Question Time* with Tristram. He had just been appointed as a spokesman on higher education. After the show we had a chat over a glass of wine.

'So, what are your policies?' I politely enquired, expecting the usual gushing, starry-eyed five-point plan delivering universal happiness that tends to be beloved of the newly appointed. Instead he just paused, scratched his head, smiled and said, 'I haven't got a fucking clue.' I tell that story in his favour as I found it rather refreshing.

I just wonder whether the country has had enough of the old party system. They are all dying on their feet, with a dwindling band of ancient retainers shuffling round their constituencies knocking on doors and raising money before their final death rattle, which usually means the end of another branch. And who funds them? The Tories seem to receive their cash from betting empires, cheap loan companies and wealthy eccentrics. Labour is funded by the Jurassic Park of the unions, while the poor Lib Dems accept anything from anyone willing to slip them a few bob.

This addiction to donors disfigures British democracy. That a party that loses a general election faces bankruptcy and is often driven into the financial arms of those it would not normally cuddle up to is clearly troubling. And forget about the public paying for their political games. It is a non-runner.

There are the beginnings of a solution. At the moment, the amount spent in each constituency at election time is strictly capped, with serious consequences if there is an overspend. Yet the amount spent by the parties nationally knows no bounds; 'Who Spends Wins' is not a bad rule of thumb. Why not have a ceiling on all election spending? This will be resisted by all the main parties, particularly those who are attracting the most money. But with 24-hour news, do we need glitzy party broadcasts? Apart from political anoraks and the press, who actually watches them? And is anyone really swayed by them? And what is the point of spending a small fortune on buying up poster sites before an election? Does it really make a difference? I very much doubt it.

One day someone is going to wrestle with the simple question of whether the public have outgrown two-party politics.

Both main parties are hopelessly split. What do the Tory modernisers have in common with the hard right? Nothing except for a large umbrella with the word *Conservative* written on it. And what do the Milibanders have in common with the Blairites? Nothing except for a large umbrella with the word *Labour* written on it. They have even excised the word *New*. And within the Lib Dems, what do the orange bookers have in common with the wild and woolly left? Nothing at all, not even an umbrella.

So, what binds all the main parties together apart from fear of the unknown and habit?

But there is the potential for a realignment based on reason, pragmatism and basic decency. At that I can hear the collective groan from political correspondents that I have finally taken leave of my senses. Yet Conservative modernisers, the Blairites, and the orange bookers could be a formidable force for good in British politics if they joined forces. They have more to unite than to divide them. David Cameron has far more in common with Alan Milburn and John Reid than with John Redwood and Iain Duncan Smith. And what does Nick Clegg have in common with Vince Cable and Tim Farron apart from mutual loathing?

When the next election campaign finally descends into a poisonous, vicious brawl, rough-and-tumbling into personal abuse and making the seventh circle of hell seem like a quiet night at the Rovers Return, the time might be right for a new politics. Oh dear, I can hear another groan from the political correspondents. Whether there would be enough good men and women with the courage to break free from a system that is hopelessly out of sync with the electorate and is on the cusp of moral questionability is probably an ask too far. I suspect that the resolution will be typically British. We will just muddle through. How mind-numbingly depressing.

EPILOGUE

This may just be me slipping into my anecdotage, but politics is not as dull as many people make it out to be. It is just different. There is still the same naked ambition, treachery, bitterness among MPs. And of course the same deluded flotsam and jetsam bobbing along in a sea of self-induced fantasy that one day they will lead their party. But, by and large, they are in the anguished minority. The majority of MPs don't spend every hour plotting and scheming, desperate to be invited to shine on a heavyweight radio or television show. They are hardworking, underpaid, stressed and spend their days working in the best interests of their constituents. They have to deal with a 24-hour instant-reaction media, Twitter, Facebook and flotillas of emails from constituents who want an immediate response, not just about personal problems but about policy. So the workload has increased. This can be a problem because policies can be a bit transient. Remember the wonderful vote-catching policy of selling off the forests? There would have been a CCHQ brief with a line to take and probably a draft letter to write or ping. So poor old Tory backbenchers would have had to send off another line to take while the smell of burning rubber was still searing their nostrils. All horribly embarrassing. And worse for Labour, whose idea of policy is a moveable feast. The humble pie is not a popular dish with MPs.

But social media is a serious nightmare. If MPs think that they have so many followers because of their personal popularity, they are in need of a prefrontal lobotomy. Journalists, opponents and all-round loons are just hoping for them to say something really daft. My heart went out to dear old Jack Dromey, whose computer went haywire and put down as a favourite 'Big Black Cock', not a website he would have even heard of. The biggest dangers to MPs are irony and sitting in front of their terminals after a stressful, frustrating day. And if they have been victims of a good dinner or a refreshing reception they can land themselves in serious trouble.

UKIP are the brand leaders in telling the world and his wife what they *really think* and sharing the dark teatime of their souls. As a party, they have double firsts in toss-pottery pure and applied. The run-up to the European and general elections is going to be a gold mine for the press and CCHQ.

The real difference in modern politics is that the boozy phallocracy is not so widespread. Much of this is due to tireless campaigners such as Harriet Harman. She unfairly gets a terrible press as a humourless harpy. Nothing could be further from the truth. I have always found her warm, witty and sincere. Many years ago I had her young children sat on my lap when I was dressed as Captain Hook at the press gallery Christmas party. Nowadays I would probably find myself on a register.

There is also a myth that MPs have all become worker drones and that the larger-than-life characters have all but disappeared. Not so. There are still dogged and tenacious campaigners who stick their heads above the parapets at great personal political risk. Rob Halfon, my successor in Harlow, is a name that springs to mind. He is doing a really great job. And Labour has the splendid Steve Pound, witty, charming, with the gift of being able to reduce the chamber to howls of laughter with a pithy one-liner. And you could hardly call the Lib Dems' Sir Bob Russell a shy and retiring flower.

So I am optimistic for the future. Being an MP should never be seen as a career, rather a vocation. Even the safest seats can evaporate at the stroke of a boundary review pen. But it would be far more sensible if we selected those with more experience of life, those who can relate to their constituents. Yet it is a wickedly traduced job. Never have they been more disbelieved and despised. And the expenses scandal still hangs in the air like a stale fart in a lift. It will take a generation to ventilate it. But if you really care about people and doing your very best for them, it is a noble occupation.

And as for me? I just don't know. Many people are trying to persuade me to stand again. It's tempting but it no longer offers the excitement that it once had. Although the red benches would be fun, I have got to be realistic. There is a mile-long queue of very well-qualified people who would bite their hand off for it.

So I content myself with blogging and a bit of media. I greatly enjoy clashing swords every Friday night with Mohammed Shafiq and Stephen Nolan on 5 Live. Stephen is a great broadcaster with heart and a smile. He is a name to watch. I just wish he wouldn't eat quite so many sweets. A few weeks ago I brought him in a bag of healthy snacks.

It was as if the devil had entered the room and offered him a vial of poison. His brow furrowed and in his most menacing Belfast accent he warned, 'Argh, I can't eat that. It will make me physically sick.' And I think that he meant it.

And Mohammed? Sometimes I could strangle him. But he is a lovely guy and one of the few Muslims who dare to speak out about extremism in their community, sometimes putting himself in physical danger.

Friday nights are great, great fun.

And to the young who are considering standing? Go for it. Expect disappointment, frustration and the lunacy of the system. But the rewards and satisfaction are incalculable. I wouldn't have missed it for the world.

ACKNOWLEDGEMENTS

One day in June of 2013 we were delayed at Gatwick Airport for an eternity. The people who kept us sane were a delightful young couple and I spent the time boring them to death with tales of fun and games in Westminster. 'Why don't you write a book?' they asked. So, a month or so later I contacted Iain Dale, who told me to knock out a couple of chapters and he'd let me know. So, Chris and Kath, this is all your fault!

A very big thank you to Biteback for trusting me to write it – and to Iain Dale for not rushing to therapy over any potential libels. I am told that at the commissioning meeting someone suggested that, as I was a barrister, I could do the libel reading. Dale nearly burst a blood vessel. 'Hayes doesn't know the concept of defamation!' he exploded. He had a point.

Thanks to Grant Tucker for being so loyal and encouraging, and Suzanne Sangster for her deft handling of the publicity. And Sam Carter for being such a fantastic and wise editor. I am indebted to you and the team for being so patient, with Hoby doing a great job on the illustrations.

Now for those who toiled away for no reward. Geoffrey Vevers for doing the first proofreading and keeping me entertained with his animal impersonations; he was brought up in the London Zoo, not in an enclosure but in a house. Joe Lewis, the *Express* whizz-kid libel lawyer, who performed the first libel read. And the multi-talented Will Timmins, who painstakingly sorted out the index. Thanks, guys.

A fantastic thank you to Nick Giles and Michael Hayman of Sevenhills, who sponsored the launch party. They had the courage to set up a campaigning (*the* campaigning) business start-up company at the height of the recession and have been tremendously successful. Many young entrepreneurs owe them one hell of a lot. And it's good to see that they now have a serious impact on government policy by working closely with my old chum Lord Young of Graffham.

I mustn't forget my friends at the Savile Club, who have been tolerant of my banging on about *the book* for the last four months and restrained themselves from assaulting me, no matter how great the temptation.

A big hug to my wonderful family, Alison, Francesca and Lawrence, who, as always, have been there for me.

Finally, to all of my friends, whose friendship and general lunacy kept me reasonably sane, and who allowed me to write about them without being too cross. I hope.

INDEX

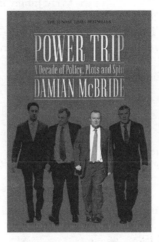